Ponder Anew What the Almighty Can Do

Ponder Anew What the Almighty Can Do

160 Years of Change in Worship Leader Training at The Southern Baptist Theological Seminary

MARCUS W. BROWN

Foreword by JOSEPH R. CRIDER

WIPF & STOCK · Eugene, Oregon

PONDER ANEW WHAT THE ALMIGHTY CAN DO
160 Years of Change in Worship Leader Training at The Southern Baptist Theological Seminary

Copyright © 2025 Marcus W. Brown. All rights reserved. Except for brief quotations in critical publications or reviews, no part of this book may be reproduced in any manner without prior written permission from the publisher. Write: Permissions, Wipf and Stock Publishers, 199 W. 8th Ave., Suite 3, Eugene, OR 97401.

Wipf & Stock
An Imprint of Wipf and Stock Publishers
199 W. 8th Ave., Suite 3
Eugene, OR 97401

www.wipfandstock.com

PAPERBACK ISBN: 979-8-3852-4171-2
HARDCOVER ISBN: 979-8-3852-4172-9
EBOOK ISBN: 979-8-3852-4173-6

In obedience to God's call and for His glory

Table of Contents

List of Tables and Figures | ix

Foreword by Joseph R. Crider | xi

Preface | xv

Acknowledgments | xvii

1. Introduction | 1
2. Church Music Education at Southern Seminary, 1890–1944 | 9
3. The Beginning of the School of Church Music, 1942–1952 | 28
4. The School of Church Music, 1952–2000 | 60
5. The School of Church Music and Worship, 2000–2009 | 107
6. The Division/Department of Biblical Worship, 2009–2019 | 135
7. Conclusion | 161

APPENDIX 1: Chronological Timeline of Faculty and Degree Offerings | 195

APPENDIX 2: Faculty Listing | 201

APPENDIX 3: Interview Participants | 215

APPENDIX 4: Enrollment Trends | 218

List of Tables and Figures

TABLES

1. Enrollment Trends in Worship Leader Degree Programs 1988–2019 | 159
2. Preferred Worship Leader Competencies in 1980 and 2019 | 178
A1. Faculty and Librarians for School of Church Music/Department of Biblical Worship | 201
A2. Interview Participants | 215
A3. Total Enrollment Trends in Worship Leadership Degrees (1988–89 through 2018–19) | 218

Figure

A1. Music and Worship Enrollment Trends 1988–2019 | 220

Foreword

CHURCHES ARE FACING A crisis across all denominations, and specifically in my own tribe, the Southern Baptist Convention. If not daily (certainly multiple times a week), the faculty in our School of Church Music and Worship at Southwestern Baptist Theological Seminary in Fort Worth, Texas, are contacted by pastors or search committees from every part of the country pleading for help in finding someone who can lead the music and worship ministries in their churches. And in my conversations with faculty members from other seminaries and Christian universities that facilitate worship programs, a common refrain is echoed among my colleagues with eerily similar words, "We can't train students fast enough to keep up with the demand for worship leaders." In a recent group text message to our music and worship faculty, the author of this volume—my friend and colleague, Dr. Marc Brown—wrote: "Please pray with me that God calls more students to train in music and worship who will come to the aid our struggling churches."

Due to a myriad of complex issues—from the fallout of the worship wars, to pragmatic approaches to the weekly gathering; from the influence of "simple church models," to churches jettisoning graded choir programs and adult choirs; from seminaries having little to no required courses in worship theology for those training for the pastorate, to churches hiring worship leaders with no musical training and even less theological training; from churches seemingly forgetting that young people were once-upon-a-time called to ministry in their churches, to a shrinking number of churches with active music ministries, we find ourselves with a massive deficiency in the sheer numbers of young men and women *called to* music and worship ministry leadership.

The book you hold in your hands by Marc Brown is not only incredibly helpful, but even more incredibly timely. The similarities of concern between Southern Seminary's president (Ellis Fuller) in 1944, and L. R. Scarborough at Southwestern in 1915 are striking. Fuller had a vision for the new music school in Louisville because he knew Southern Baptist churches needed and wanted higher quality music and intentionality in corporate worship. Scarborough had the very same concern for churches in the plains of Texas. Although separated by three decades from the point of their inception, the significant growth in the music schools of both SBC seminaries reflected not only viable avenues for training and curricular programming at the seminaries, but even more importantly, a significant need among SBC churches.

A century later, very similar struggles face SBC and evangelical churches—a need for better quality music and more intentional worship. Furthermore, there are documented and concerning trends among younger adults (especially men) as they leave evangelicalism in alarming numbers for faith fellowships with more formal liturgies, such as Eastern Orthodox, Anglican, and Catholic churches.

As Brown deftly recounts in this important work, there has always been a tension (sometimes healthy and sometimes not-so-healthy) between training musicians and ministry leaders. In most of our SBC seminaries, there seemed to be a time when leaders and faculty were convinced that developing curricula more akin to a conservatory of music was preferable to theologically-rooted ministry training. With the rise and ubiquitous saturation of modern music expressions in local churches, highly trained church musicians more comfortable with J. S. Bach than P. Baloche were left figuring out the newer musical vocabularies on their own. As Brown so clearly and concisely articulates, the Southern Seminary School of Music's "beautiful synchronization between culture, competencies, and curriculum fell apart."

The sad fact is that most of our schools lagged behind in relevant training paradigms, so much so that our constituent churches lost their trust *in* those training institutions. In other words, the constituent churches we (the educational institutions) were created to serve, lost confidence in our interest and ability to train ministry leaders for their churches. And now, five of the six seminaries in the SBC are playing catch up, scrambling to share the good news that we are actually training men and women who are musically adept in all styles *and* theologically deep.

The reason Brown's work is so important is that it not only focuses on the unique story that is specifically Southern Seminary's through an

Foreword

engaging, data-infused narrative, but he winsomely analyzes and synthesizes the external forces that also shaped Southern's story—the unrelenting realities of a changing cultural landscape and the unique complexities of the Southern Baptist Convention of churches. We need this study to help us navigate our future, a future that should be marked by our institutions doing more listening to our churches and less prescribing how they should sound; more focused on preparing students for ministry and less on protecting a particular artistic preference. That doesn't mean we shouldn't train well-informed musicians who are able and enlightened to sing John Rutter's *Requiem* one night and lead a new Shane and Shane hymn the next. It does mean, however, the students we train know *why* they sing what they sing and that they do so to God's honor—for beauty and glory (Exod. 28:2).

I believe the future is bright for our seminaries and Christian colleges that are carefully curating not just effective curricula to serve the church, but helping to shape and mold godly men and women who are passionately and convictionally committed to helping churches respond in praise to Jesus Christ, and to worship him in Spirit and truth.

Joseph R. Crider
Dean and James C. McKinney Chair of Church Music
Southwestern Baptist Theological Seminary
Fort Worth, Texas

Preface

MY FAMILY HAS A long Southern Baptist heritage. The pastors and ministers leading the local congregations where my family worshiped were always some of the most important and respected people in my life. As I became a teenager and began to realize God was calling me to a life of full-time Christian service, I investigated questions I had previously never considered. One of these questions involved how ministers came to serve the churches where we worshiped. I discovered that most came through one of the six Southern Baptist seminaries—usually Southwestern Baptist Theological Seminary in Fort Worth, Texas, New Orleans Baptist Theological Seminary in New Orleans, Louisiana, or The Southern Baptist Theological Seminary in Louisville, Kentucky. In 1993, the Lord led my wife, Cyndi, and I to Louisville for me to pursue my own masters-level training in church music in the School of Church Music at Southern Seminary.

The three years Cyndi and I spent at Southern Seminary were life-shaping, eventful, and not to be our last. After a long ministry post in metropolitan Washington DC, we were called back to Kentucky in 2015 to serve in a Louisville-area church. While there I reconnected with Southern and began to pursue a PhD while I served as an adjunct professor and a full-time worship pastor in our church. In 2022, after serving local churches in full-time music and worship ministry for 28 years, our family journeyed to Fort Worth, Texas, when I was appointed to serve on the faculty of the School of Church Music and Worship at Southwestern Seminary.

When I originally felt my calling to ministry as a teenager in 1986, church music and the Southern Baptist denominational landscape was quite different. The mid-1980s were the high point of enrollment for church music programs across the Southern Baptist seminaries. For someone like me, there existed a very clear path from calling to training and ultimately into a full-time ministry position in an SBC congregation. I am very grateful for

Preface

that system which trained me and prepared me for ministry service. I feel very privileged to now serve as part of that legacy as I help to train musically excellent, biblically knowledgeable, and pastorally sensitive leaders for today's churches in the ministry areas of music and worship. Over the course of my adult professional life however, I have witnessed the changing (some might say 'diminishing') of that old training system and its subsequent transition to what now exists. The numbers speak for themselves: in the 1988–89 academic year, enrollment in the School of Church Music at Southern Seminary was 539 masters and doctoral-level church music students, according to a special task force report. Just a few years later, when I started my program of study in the 1993-94 academic year, the enrollment had slipped to 309 students. By the time I graduated in 1996, the number of students had fallen further to 221. What was happening?

The decline in the numbers of students pursuing seminary training in music and worship reflected the significant changes occurring broadly in Western culture with regards to congregational values and preferences in music, worship, politics, and theology. The way those shifts impacted schools like the SCM at Southern Seminary must have seemed to faculty, students, and alumni as something quite apocalyptic. Within two decades, the SCM went from being a premiere institution for church music and worship training into a perceived dead-weight that might hinder growth in the SBC's flagship seminary. However, as things had been in earlier times of institutional transition such as the early 1900s, the Depression, the post-war 1950s, and the early 1980s, these changes occurring in the late 2000s would not be the end. I pray that through reading the story of Southern Seminary's School of Church Music (now Department of Biblical Worship), those invested in music and worship training within Christian colleges and universities as well as churches that are still trying to serve Christ in an ever-changing culture will be encouraged.

God's calling may necessitate adjustments but our response remains a fresh opportunity to "ponder anew what the Almighty can do."

Marcus Brown
Fort Worth, Texas
April 2025

Acknowledgments

Many people have encouraged me during my process of producing this book, but my first gratitude rightly looks to my Heavenly Father. God called me to follow him. Within that calling, over my life came several smaller callings. One of these smaller callings involved pursuing and finishing a PhD. Without God's good and sovereign work in my life through Christ Jesus and the power of the Holy Spirit, I most certainly would not have done the research and writing necessary to complete this project.

First among all people to thank is my wife, Cyndi, along with our daughter, Miriam, and my sister through grace, Patricia. Their emotional and spiritual support helped me continually persist in following God's will, and carried me through many days and nights of work.

I am also grateful to the community of God-called staff, administrators, and faculty of The Southern Baptist Theological Seminary. Beginning with my first master's degree from 1993 to 1996 and then through my terminal degree, this institution has continually invested in me. I am particularly grateful for my supervisor, Dr. Esther Crookshank. Her personal interest and enthusiasm for this work functioned as necessary fuel for my finishing. I am also very grateful for the wisdom offered by Dr. Thomas Nettles to a church musician attempting to write in the guise of a proper historian. Dr. Anthony Foster was also a constant guide and encourager. As a member of the church where I served through much of my research and writing, Dr. Foster not only served as a specialized mentor in the area of empirical research, he also sang in our choir. I must also acknowledge the encouragement of Dr. Matthew Westerholm, who patiently walked with me through many months of research and investigation that ultimately led me to the topic of this book.

Though not serving on my doctoral committee or as one of my instructors, Dr. Greg Brewton was one of the greatest sources of support,

Acknowledgments

encouragement, and friendship I received throughout the preparation and writing of this book. Dr. Brewton and I were cut from the same cloth, serving the local church for many years before accepting God's call to invest in the training of others called to his service.

Others have also helped me in crucial ways. Chief among these is Cheyenne Haste through her work as my editor. Cheyenne's expertise and positivity proved most necessary and without her I could not have completed this book. Three more Southern Seminary staff were particularly helpful to me as I gathered primary source documents necessary for the completion of this book: Registrar Norm Chung, Digital Archivist Chris Fenner, and retired Music Librarian Martha Powell were each crucial in my quest to obtain data essential in telling the story of worship leader training at Southern Seminary. Special thanks also go to Dr. Paul Akin, SBTS Provost, for granting permission for me to use seminary publication photos, helping the reader see some of the many people who contributed to the story.

Finally, I want to express my deep gratitude to those who helped me begin both my journey into PhD studies and full-time academy-level teaching: Dr. Joe Crider and Dr. Charles Lewis. These men taught me in the first stages of my coursework and have since become life-long friends as we serve together at Southwestern Seminary.

1

Introduction

"Ponder anew what the Almighty can do if with His love He befriend thee."[1]

HISTORICAL OVERVIEW

IN 1944, PRESIDENT ELLIS Fuller introduced a new school to the institutional landscape of The Southern Baptist Theological Seminary (SBTS): the school of church music (SCM). Fuller's pondering produced a vision for the new school after several years of Southern Baptist churches calling for higher quality music and intentionality in corporate worship.[2] Having become Southern's sixth president directly after his pastorate of the First Baptist Church in Atlanta, Fuller was well-acquainted with the job competencies necessary for a successful church music ministry. The key faculty he chose to fulfill his vision at Southern Seminary were Donald Winters and Frances Winters, graduates of Westminster Choir College who had served under Fuller in church music ministry, having designed and led the highly successful music ministry at First Baptist Atlanta. The Winters represented the type of pastoral musicians Fuller hoped would be produced by the new school. During the following decades, graduates of the school of church music trickled into Southern Baptist churches. As the SCM produced more graduates for service in local churches, those graduates inevitably brought with them a love for Christ and a passion for excellence in church music

---

1. Neander/German Hymn, "Praise to the Lord, the Almighty" (1).
2. Carle, "History of School of Church Music of SBTS 1944–1959," 5.

defined by the classical standards they had been taught at Southern Seminary. Their training and the programs they implemented in the churches, especially choral programs, lifted the quality of music and expectations for corporate worship within the churches of the Southern Baptist Convention (SBC). The synergy between Southern Baptist worship culture, necessary job competencies for ministers of music, and the curricula required to train properly such individuals swelled during the late 1970s and early 1980s when the SCM averaged over three hundred full-time, residential students for several consecutive years.[3]

This period would come to be described in retrospect by some faculty and students as the "Camelot" years of the SCM.[4] However, these perceived halcyon days began to diminish as early as the mid-1980s and then passed from the scene as tensions escalated between warring styles of music and worship towards the end of the 1990s and into the early 2000s.[5] The SCM's beautiful synchronization between culture, competencies, and curriculum fell apart. Expected norms for worship style, job competencies, administration vision for the training of worship leaders, and the general culture of the SBC all appeared to become increasingly disjunct. With this disconnect came a steady decline in student enrollment in the SCM that lasted for nearly a decade. When enrollment reached a crisis level, the seminary responded with a major institutional reorganization in August 2009. The SCMW was terminated and its programs absorbed into the school of church ministries with the newly formed department of biblical worship.[6] Subsequently, in August 2013, the school of church ministries, still housing the department of biblical worship, merged with the Billy Graham school of missions and evangelism to create the Billy Graham school of missions, evangelism, and ministry.[7] These institutional transitions were each accompanied by changes in philosophy, faculty, and curricula.

The culture of the SBC had changed since the 1980s and worship in churches had changed dramatically during that period as well. The job competencies and job titles for ministers of music, creative arts pastors, and worship pastors had also changed.[8] The faculty and administrators at

---

3. SBTS, "Special Task Force."
4. Sharp, interview, September 1, 2021.
5. SBTS, "Special Task Force."
6. See SBTS, *Academic Catalog (2009–10)*.
7. SBTS, *Academic Catalog (2013–14)*.
8. Randlett, "Training Worship Leaders," 238–39.

INTRODUCTION

Southern Seminary called to train leaders for church music and worship leadership found themselves compelled to rethink their mission and the kind of graduate they were producing in light of worship revolution that was underway—to "ponder anew what the Almighty [could] do" in their context.[9] In the same way as in 1944, a new generation of leaders in church music and worship had to prove they were up to the task of continuing to help shape and train worship leading pastor/musicians for the worship ministries of constituent Southern Baptist churches.

THESIS

The purpose of this study is to trace the development of the degree programs in church music and worship leadership degree offered at SBTS during the period circa 1980 through 2019, with particular attention to the master of church music and master of arts in worship leadership. The end goal is to trace and document from primary sources the changes in key degree programs of the school of church music and department of biblical worship at SBTS from 1980 to 2019, in the context of cultural mega shifts and shifts in educational philosophy that precipitated those changes.

This book examines the effects of four large trajectories (each embracing multiple variables) that impacted the changes in degree programs during this time:

1. Cultural and musical trends (mega shifts in U.S. culture and society), impacting church music during the period.
2. Musical and stylistic influences on Southern Baptist worship during the period.
3. Denominational changes within the Southern Baptist Convention.
4. Institutional change and restructuring during the study period.

The first three of these factors impacted the job competencies necessary for leading a successful music and worship ministry in a Southern Baptist church. Significant changes in these job competencies in turn required major modifications in curricula at Southern Seminary—curricula designed to train individuals to fulfill the competencies and to lead local church music and worship ministries in their SBC contexts. By examining the effects of these four variables, this project delves into the life of the

9. Neander, "Praise to the Lord, the Almighty" (1).

institution during a critical era—an era that has not yet received a thorough study.

RESEARCH QUESTIONS

The following research questions guided the study:

1. What were the cultural and musical trends at work in the United States between the years 1980 and 2019?
2. What were the musical and stylistic influences acting on worship in Southern Baptist churches in the examined time period?
3. What were the key changes occurring within the Southern Baptist Convention during the years of this study and how did these changes help to shape the worship culture of Southern Baptist churches?
4. What changes in educational philosophy (both broadly and specific to the training of church musicians and worship leaders) occurred at SBTS between 1980 and 2019 and how did these changes impact the requirements for pastoral and musical competencies in the church music and worship leadership training programs at the institution?
5. What institutional changes took place in SBTS's administrative leadership during these years, and how did those changes serve as a catalyst for administrative changes within the school of church music and department of biblical worship?

RESEARCH METHODOLOGY

The primary methodological model used in this dissertation is a hybrid based on frameworks of John Creswell and Teresa Volk. This hybrid also closely parallels that employed by Paul H. Randlett in his 2019 dissertation, a study of Liberty University's undergraduate Music and Worship Leadership degree programs during roughly the same period, from 1971 to 2018.[10] In crafting his methodology, Randlett borrowed significantly from the qualitative case study model exemplified by music education historian

---

10. See Randlett, "Training Worship Leaders."

Introduction

Teresa M. Volk, in her 2003 seminal article on conducting historical research in music education.[11]

Case study research can focus on an object of study or on the product of an inquiry. Educational psychologist and author John W. Creswell, defining this type of investigation, lists several salient features of qualitative studies. First, according to Creswell, qualitative research normally collects data at the site where participants "experience the issue or problem under study."[12] In my application of the qualitative case study model, I focus my examination on the institution, key faculty, and administrative personnel involved in the historical timeline.

Second, Creswell points out that in qualitative research, researchers themselves gather the information—as opposed to relying on research instruments such as questionnaires.[13] Third, according to Creswell, qualitative data is normally obtained from a variety of sources such as interviews, first person observations, and other documents.[14] Although Creswell observes that qualitative research can be built through an inductive process "from the bottom up," he notes that "deductive thinking also plays an important role as the analysis moves forward."[15] My research, based on this model, relies on both of these types of reasoned analysis.

I earned a master of church music from the SCM from 1993 to 1996. From 2016 until 2022, I was a doctoral student and an adjunct faculty member in the department of biblical worship. In writing the present project, I identified as a participant researcher. As such, my research is not free from my own perceptions, but I did strive to keep Creswell's directive; while participants bring their own meaning to the problem and/or issue, this meaning can provide key insights that may not be found in the written literature.[16] In the oral and written interviews, my research reflects Creswell's premise that information gathered from participants in qualitative research can sometimes change or be modified based on the reported perceptions and experiences and of participants. This caveat required that I faithfully learn about the issues from participants beyond any preliminary expectations I might possess. Creswell's list of qualitative research elements

---

11. Volk, "Looking Back in Time," 49–59.
12. Creswell, *Research Design*, 185.
13. Creswell, *Research Design*, 185.
14. Creswell, *Research Design*, 185.
15. Creswell, *Research Design*, 186.
16. Creswell, *Research Design*, 186.

also served to heighten awareness of my own internal bias and how my personal values may possibly influence my understanding of the data and even the direction of the study itself.[17]

Finally, in keeping with Creswell guidelines, my research attempted to develop and present the broad complexities of the story at hand.[18] Creswell identifies several types of case studies. For all case studies, he considers five procedures, or steps, necessary:

1. Determine if a case study approach is appropriate.
2. Identify the intent of the study and select the case or cases.
3. Develop procedures for conducting the extensive data collection drawing on multiple data sources.
4. Specify the type of analysis that will be employed when case descriptions integrate themes with contextual information.
5. Report the case study and lessons by using in written form.[19]

Within the parameters of case-study-based qualitative research, the following study functions as an intrinsic study that occurs within a bounded system pertaining to both time and place.[20] I collected information from several diverse sources during the course of my research. Based on procedures established by Volk, this process facilitated immersion in the subject.[21] A major factor of all qualitative research is its emphasis on interpretation. Interpretation in qualitative research, as opposed to that in a statistical study, occurs most frequently when the researcher "simultaneously examines . . . meaning and redirects observation to refine or substantiate those meanings."[22]

My research, for the data-infused narrative, was conducted in four stages, each with appropriate source types: (1) Institutional history, researched (from secondary sources and primary-source archival materials) into the cultural, musical, denominational, and institutional context of the school of church music at Southern Seminary from 1944 to 2019, in order

---

17. Creswell, *Research Design*, 186.
18. Creswell, *Research Design*, 186.
19. Creswell, *Qualitative Inquiry*, 98, 100. Creswell defines case assertions as the conclusions formed by the researcher about the overall meaning of the case.
20. Creswell, *Qualitative Inquiry and Research Design*, 97.
21. Volk, "Looking Back in Time," 49–59.
22. Stake, *The Art of Case Study Research*, 8–9.

to establish the starting point from which the paradigm shifts in church music and worship leadership training at the institution occurred. (2) Shifts in church music education: philosophy and curriculum, surveying the history of training leaders for church music in Protestant and evangelical churches in the United States, including commonly accepted competency standards. I obtained this history and these standards through a review of related literature, particularly recent dissertations on theological and musical education of pastoral and musical education of pastoral musicians. This stage included research in educational philosophies in music higher education and theological education. (3) Curriculum study, consulting primary and secondary sources in order to present a full representation of the history of worship leadership training degrees at SBTS. Primary sources include academic catalogs, course syllabi, accreditation program reviews, oral history audio recordings and transcripts, chapel, recital, concert programs, and official seminary publications. (4) Oral and written interviews of faculty and graduates, conducted by oral history interviews of all available current or former faculty and administration who had a significant role in or direct oversight of the development of church music and worship studies degree programs during the period studied. Subsequently, I synthesized and interpreted the data, drawing conclusions concerning the result of decisions and actions made by case study participants, with the goal of making recommendations to similar institutions based on the data.

SIGNIFICANCE OF THESIS FOR THE FIELD OF STUDY

The specific focus of this study is development of the degree programs offered by the school of church music, school of church music and worship, and the department of biblical worship at SBTS between 1980 and 2019. My study may have limited application to other schools of church music or institutions training worship pastors for other evangelical traditions. Even so, the story of the SCM at SBTS remains a compelling one. Because the cultural, musical, denominational, and institutional changes that exerted an impact on the Southern Seminary SCM were the same forces impacting other North American evangelical churches and educational institutions, this study provides a useful case study for how churches and confessional institutions can remain true to their purpose despite cultural changes that might threaten their mission or existence. Through examining how the SBTS school of church music navigated tumultuous years of change, other colleges and seminaries may find it instructive to consider the model of the department of biblical worship when examining or renewing their own curricula and degrees for church music and worship leadership.

OUTLINE OF THE ARGUMENT

The Southern Baptist Theological Seminary's school of church music was founded in 1944, with the express purpose of responding to the need to train church musicians and worship leaders for Southern Baptist churches. First, the cultural and musical changes that occurred in the final decades of the twentieth century, particularly the rapid spread of the church growth and megachurch movements, significantly impacted worship leader training for Southern Baptist and other evangelical churches.[23] Second, although church music training curricula may have met their perceived constituent needs at the time they were first designed, the school's initial reluctance to revise these curricula early in the period of study resulted in a perceived lack of relevance in SBC churches nationwide and ultimately a drop in enrollment. Third, although the SCM struggled through a period of declining enrollment, they hired a key new faculty, and adopted a renewed vision involving extensive curriculum revision. Gradually, subsequent to the curriculum revision, came an increase in enrollment and a successful transition to a new era.

The chapter presenting interpretation of the data and narrative addresses two large-scale questions: (1) In what specific ways did the curricular changes ensure the new department of biblical worship's ability to continue fulfilling the original mission of the SCM of training church musicians and worship leaders for the churches of the SBC? (2) What other factors may have contributed to the rebound in student enrollment? Finally, an ultimate goal for the project is that other institutions training church musicians and worship leaders will be able to apply the research and interpretation of this study of the SCM and DBW programs and the issues that influenced these curricular revisions at Southern Seminary.

---

23. Hong and Ruth, *Lovin' on Jesus*, 59–86.

2

Church Music Education at Southern Seminary, 1890–1944

EARLY CHURCH MUSIC EDUCATION AT SOUTHERN SEMINARY

ONE OF THE MOST beautiful worship spaces on the campus of Southern Seminary is Broadus Chapel, located on the western end of the Norton Hall complex. Named for one of the seminary's founding faculty, John A. Broadus, this space has served several roles throughout its history. From the beginning of its use in 1926, it served as the seminary library until the James P. Boyce Library was completed in 1959. The space was then left relatively unused for several years, serving mostly as a student lounge area before its renovation was finished in 1999. Broadus Chapel's interior replicates the original sanctuary of the first Baptist church in America, the First Baptist Church of Providence, Rhode Island.[1] The chapel is most appropriately named because Broadus's ministry encompassed training Baptist ministers for all aspects of corporate worship. Broadus not only instructed his students in preaching, but also served as Southern Seminary's first teacher of hymnology. As such, Broadus represents the origins of worship leader training (apart from preaching) at SBTS.[2]

---

1. Mohler, "Dedication of John A. Broadus Memorial Chapel."
2. Crookshank, "The Minister and His Hymnbook."

John Broadus and Hymnology

John Albert Broadus was born in Culpeper County, Virginia, in 1827. His pursuit of formal education brought him to the University of Virginia in Charlottesville where he graduated as valedictorian of his class. In partnership with James P. Boyce, Basil Manly Jr., and William Williams, Broadus later helped found Southern Seminary in 1859. During the Civil War, when classes were suspended, Broadus continued following Boyce's lead, serving as chaplain to Confederate troops under the command of Robert E. Lee.[3] After the seminary re-opened in Louisville following the Civil War, Broadus's first preaching class had only one student, who was blind (the entire seminary had only eight students).[4] Broadus's lectures for this class became the basis for his well-known book *A Treatise on the Preparation and Delivery of Sermons* (1870). Published through twenty-five editions, Broadus's book on sermon preparation and delivery is widely considered his most important scholarly contribution, but Broadus also made five significant contributions to hymnology and the training of those who lead in other aspects of worship[5]: (1) a seminary address in fall 1884 on "English Hymns of the Nineteenth Century" for which no extant copy remains; (2) his aforementioned textbook on preaching containing the chapter "Conduct of Public Worship"; (3) "The Minister and His Hymn Book," a lecture delivered for the Lyman Beecher lecture series at Yale University in January 1889; (4) his *Syllabus as to Hymnology* (1892); and (5) three bound but undated copybooks of handwritten lecture notes with loose handwritten pages inserted.[6]

Broadus's hymnological scholarship and instruction began during the seminary's first year (1859) as a unit on hymns and hymn writers within his course on homiletics.[7] The next year's course description for homiletics included the explanation, "Exercises in reading the Scripture and Hymns, with an account of the metrical structure of English Hymns."[8] After *A Treatise on the Preparation and Delivery of Sermons* was published in 1870,

---

3. Crookshank, "The Minister and His Hymnbook," 133–34.

4. Crookshank, "The Minister and His Hymnbook," 134.

5. Crookshank, "The Minister and His Hymnbook," 134.

6. Crookshank, "The Minister and His Hymnbook," 134.

7. Crookshank, "The Minister and His Hymnbook," 134; see also SBTS, *Academic Catalog (1859–60)*.

8. Crookshank, "The Minister and His Hymnbook," 134; see also SBTS, *Academic Catalog (1859–60)*.

Broadus added his text to the required reading list and wrote in the course description that "this class is freely exercised in reading the Scriptures, and reading Hymns, and much stress is laid upon the proper conduct of Public Worship."[9]

Within Broadus's *Treatise*, chapter 6 ("Conduct of Public Worship") represents a unique document in the Southern Baptist understanding of worship. Even as the book clearly means to direct the preaching portion of corporate worship, Broadus delivers an elevated view of the other elements making up a corporate worship gathering. The topics covered in this chapter provide Broadus a platform to describe and instruct pastors in the theological and pastoral value for crafting their public reading of Scripture,[10] hymn selection,[11] public prayer,[12] length of services,[13] and pulpit decorum.[14] By including this chapter within a book meant for preachers, Broadus made a positive statement toward the future of Baptist worship leadership long before most Southern Baptists were concerned with such things.

By the year 1879, the course catalog indicated that there was even a special series of lectures given on hymnology.[15] Broadus's value for hymnology as a needed component for the training of pastors leading worship eventually developed into a special study course offered on "Foreign Hymnology."[16] The course description tells of a class including "Latin Hymns, some Greek Hymns, and either German or French Hymns. Lectures are given on the history of hymns in several languages. Besides oral translations, the class make [sic] some written translation, in prose and in verse."[17] This special study was expanded in 1887–88 and in 1891–92, with the catalog stating that the course's "Books [were] furnished."[18] Broadus,

---

9. Crookshank, "The Minister and His Hymnbook," 134; see also SBTS, *Academic Catalog (1872–73)*.

10. Broadus, *On Preparation and Delivery of Sermons*, 359.

11. Broadus, *On Preparation and Delivery of Sermons*, 363.

12. Broadus, *On Preparation and Delivery of Sermons*, 368.

13. Broadus, *On Preparation and Delivery of Sermons*, 373.

14. Broadus, *On Preparation and Delivery of Sermons*, 375.

15. Crookshank, "The Minister and His Hymnbook," 134; see also SBTS, *Academic Catalog (1872–73)*.

16. Crookshank, "The Minister and His Hymnbook," 134; see also SBTS, *Academic Catalog (1885–86)*.

17. Crookshank, "The Minister and His Hymnbook," 134; see also SBTS, *Academic Catalog (1885–86)*.

18. Crookshank, "The Minister and His Hymnbook," 134; see also SBTS, *Academic Catalog (1887–88)*.

one of the seminary's founding faculty and the institution's second president, adamantly believed pastors needed knowledge of and practice in singing hymns. For Broadus, this facet of learning helped build a meaningful and necessary foundation for future pastors graduating from Southern Seminary. Broadus's legacy in this realm also set an important precedent for the future training of those who lead the reading, praying, and singing of Scripture in corporate worship.

John Broadus, founding faculty, second SBTS President, 1859–1895

Broadus's Hymnology Syllabus

Broadus's *Syllabus as to Hymnology* hardly resembles the average course syllabus that a student may receive in modern times. To a modern reader, Broadus's *Syllabus* may better resemble a short textbook or larger scholarly article within a Bible dictionary or other reference volume, as it contains eight "chapters" within two large sections addressing "Didactic" and "Historical" hymnology.[19] Within the "Didactic" section Broadus addresses the regulative and normative principles of Christian worship, though he does not use the same nomenclature. In his first chapter, Broadus indicates that the Bible contains "much poetry," including plays on words "marked with prose-rhythm."[20] Broadus also states that the Bible "enjoins *singing*."[21] In chapter 2, Broadus addresses how art should be used in corporate worship—that only poetry and music are indicated in both the Old and New Testaments as proper vehicles for the gathered congregation's response to God's Word. By this, Broadus reveals his belief that Scripture alone provides the authority to govern worship.[22]

Broadus goes further, attempting to answer the question, "What place may Art have in Worship?"[23] Sacred space, architecture, performance arts (including music), and visual art are all addressed within the first section of Broadus's *Syllabus*.[24] Also within this section, Broadus defines and describes the purpose and goals of hymnology, the material of hymns as tools of worship, and the literary style and form of hymns.[25]

The second large section, an historical overview of hymnology, includes a bibliography before Broadus launches into sections addressing "Scripture Hymns," hymns from the second and third centuries, hymns from the fourth century through the Middle Ages (which included Greek and Latin hymnody), and hymns in various modern languages, such as German, French, and English; the English hymns include works from famous collections such as Sternhold and Hopkins (1549 and 1550), and

---

19. Broadus, *Syllabus as to Hymnology*, 1, 4.
20. Broadus, *Syllabus as to Hymnology*, 1.
21. Broadus, *Syllabus as to Hymnology*, 1.
22. Broadus, *Syllabus as to Hymnology*, 2.
23. Broadus, *Syllabus as to Hymnology*, 1.
24. Broadus, *Syllabus as to Hymnology*, 1–3.
25. Broadus, *Syllabus as to Hymnology*, 1–3.

the "Bay Psalm Book," the first English book printed in North America.[26] Broadus devoted large sections to providing sufficient background on the hymnological contributions of Isaac Watts, the Wesleys, the Oxford Movement, Missionary Movement, Sunday School Movement, the YMCA, and the Salvation Army.[27] Baptist hymn writers such as Benjamin Keach, Anne Steele, John Rippon, John Leland, Basil Manly Jr., and William Doane were also included in Broadus's survey of important contributors to Baptist worship.[28] Finally, a section on hymnal resources was provided, including hymnals published specifically for and by Baptists.[29] At the time Broadus published his *Syllabus*, there were not very many hymnic resources in existence. Crediting John Broadus with some of the hymn-writing work accomplished by the next generation of Baptists appears to be a fair conclusion when considering every graduate from The Southern Baptist Theological Seminary between 1892 and 1901 were exposed to this significant training for local church worship leadership.

MUSIC AND WORSHIP TRAINING FOLLOWING BROADUS

During the 1892–93 academic year, Broadus's age may have begun to slow him down as professor, and Edwin Charles Dargan began to assist him in teaching the homiletics course. Broadus's homiletics course was still where the bulk of hymnology was being taught to Southern Seminary students.[30] This arrangement appears to have been wisely made, because when Broadus died in March of 1895, Dargan was prepared to complete the academic year in Broadus's place. For the duration of his homiletics instruction, Dargan continued to use Broadus's hymnology syllabus as one of the course texts.[31] Dargan also continued teaching Broadus's special study course on foreign hymnology until 1899, when the course was discontinued.[32] Dargan con-

---

26. Broadus, *Syllabus as to Hymnology*, 1–3.
27. Broadus, *Syllabus as to Hymnology*, 12–18.
28. Broadus, *Syllabus as to Hymnology*, 19–21.
29. Broadus, *Syllabus as to Hymnology*, 21–23.
30. SBTS, *Academic Catalog (1892–93)*.
31. Crookshank, "The Minister and His Hymnbook," 135.
32. SBTS, *Academic Catalog (1898–99)*.

tinued using Broadus's *Syllabus as to Hymnology* as a homiletics textbook as long as he taught the course—through the 1900–1901 school year.[33]

Although no special hymnology or music courses were taught at Southern Seminary between 1901 and 1913, the foundation for worship leader training laid by John Broadus continued to gestate.[34] In 1913, music courses reappeared in the course schedule as a weekly class in the Wednesday afternoon schedule, however no instructor was named.[35] Weekly music classes continued to be offered over the next six years, with no course name or description offered until the 1915–16 catalog. In 1915–16, the catalog also began listing students enrolled in this music class along with those enrolled in the other required courses.[36] Concerning the music course, the 1915–16 Catalog states,

> This course is designed to give such musical instruction as will fit pastors for effective leadership of the music of their churches. With this in mind no effort has been made to study instrumental music, to give instruction in vocal culture, or to teach the rules of composition, harmony, etc., but only to teach sight reading and the conducting of congregational singing.
>
> No text-books have been used, instruction being given from the desk and put in practice during the class hour. Such lectures are given from time to time as seem necessary for the best interests of the class.[37]

During the remaining years preceding 1920, music classes were offered and taught adjunctively by seminary students or graduate instructors. As the United States was being drawn into World War I, the seminary's efforts to continue offering music courses may reflect a desire to direct the hearts and minds of students past the worries of war in order to keep their eyes, ears, minds, and hearts aimed at Jesus Christ. The first of these student music directors was William Ernest Denham,[38] followed by Frank William Carnett.[39] The Wednesday afternoon music courses were held in addition to musical ensembles, which rehearsed at different times. Because

33. SBTS, *Academic Catalog (1900–1901)*.
34. SBTS, *Academic Catalog (1901–12)*.
35. SBTS, *Academic Catalog (1913–14)*.
36. SBTS, *Academic Catalog (1915–16)*.
37. SBTS, *Academic Catalog (1915–16)*.
38. Denham, "The Gospel Song Movement."
39. SBTS, *Academic Catalog (1914–19)*.

the names of students taking part in musical ensembles were not printed in the catalogs as were the students enrolled in other courses, it appears that the musical ensembles were meant to serve chapel services and the community, rather than for academic credit. Southern Seminary's training of those who lead worship was a seed that had been planted and was now beginning to sprout. The next academic year (1920–21) would soon see the appearance of one of the most significant professors of church music from the early days of Southern Seminary's worship leader training, Robert Inman "Prof" Johnson.

Robert Inman "Prof" Johnson

"Prof" Johnson as his students referred to him, referenced Exodus 1:8 when he wrote in his book *Of Parsons and Profs* (1959),

> "One generation goeth, and another generation cometh." How True! There arise those who "knew not Joseph!" It is not given to many men to influence humanity beyond their own generation. However, those who found an institution or spend their lives in its service will influence future generations as long as the institution survives, even though their names be forgotten.[40]

Though Johnson applies his words to founding professors of the seminary like John Broadus, the same may also be said of Johnson himself. Johnson was the son of a Southern Baptist preacher, the grandson of a Southern Baptist preacher, and the great-grandson of a Southern Baptist preacher.[41] Johnson claimed that his first exposure to "sacred music" came from hearing his grandfather loudly sing "When the roll is called up yonder, I'll be there," while riding in the family's horse-drawn buggy on the way to church.[42] Johnson's acquaintance with Southern Seminary came early, when his family moved to Louisville in 1893 for his father to begin pastoral studies. During his time in seminary, Johnson's father served as the pastor of Cox's Creek Baptist Church in Nelson County, Kentucky, and graduated from Southern in 1902. Inman Johnson himself, later graduated from Southern in the spring of 1920. "Prof" Johnson recounted that by the

---

40. Johnson, *Of Parsons and Profs*, 34.
41. Johnson, *Of Parsons and Profs*, 1.
42. Johnson, *Of Parsons and Profs*, 2.

seminary's centennial anniversary in 1959, he had personally been connected to the seminary for forty-five of those one hundred years.[43]

Presenting his life story in abbreviated form during a May 3, 1985, chapel address in Alumni Chapel, Johnson shared how Southern Seminary President E. Y. Mullins approached him not long after returning from service during World War I. After Johnson completed his ThM in the spring of 1920, Mullins asked him to serve in the coming fall as professor of music and elocution. President Mullins promised Johnson an annual income of eight-hundred dollars along with the benefit of sending him to Boston each summer for additional musical training.[44] Johnson's faculty tenure at Southern was prolific and diverse. In his time at Southern, Johnson conducted the music at five Southern Baptist Convention (SBC) meetings, served as a charter faculty member of Ridgecrest Music Week, served as a member of the Music Committee of the National Council of Churches, served as a member of the SBC Committee on Church Music (greater description to follow), led music in over two hundred fifty revivals, served as alumni director for nine years, and directed the male chorus on WHAS radio broadcasts for twenty years. He recounted that he "learned to help the evangelist into the front seat of the car, put myself in the back seat, and learn to keep my mouth shut."[45] Johnson's whimsical rural style remained a hallmark of his personality and a quality to which many accredited his success.

Under Johnson's leadership, the 1920s and 1930s saw a growth in church music and worship training at Southern. As previously stated, in the 1920–21 school year, Johnson was listed as professor of music and elocution. During that year all seminary students, in their first through third years, were required to take music classes on Wednesday afternoons and the course content appears to be similar to that which was listed in the aforementioned 1915–16 catalog.[46] In the 1924–25 school year, as the music hour on Wednesday afternoons continued, the course title of "Elocution" was changed to "Public Speaking."[47] During the 1926–27 school year, chorus rehearsal received some measure of recognition through its inclusion

---

43. Johnson, *Of Parsons and Profs*, 2.
44. Johnson, "Prof Johnson Reminisces," 25:10.
45. Johnson, "Prof Johnson Reminisces," 33:10.
46. SBTS, *Academic Catalog (1920–21)*.
47. SBTS, *Academic Catalog (1924–25)*.

in the official schedule of classes, meeting Thursday afternoons at 2 pm.[48] However in the 1929–30 school year, it returned to an after-school hours rehearsal time.[49] These arrangements remained in place until the coming of President Ellis A. Fuller (1942–50) and the formation of the SCM in 1944.

Though Southern Seminary offered no degree programs prior to 1944 that focused on the training of worship leaders, musical experiences and training were by no means non-existent. From the earliest inclusion of hymnology taught by seminary founder John Broadus, to the required music classes and choirs lead by student instructors and "Prof" Johnson, a precedent had been established for all students at Southern Seminary to receive instruction and training in all portions of corporate worship—especially church music. The building of this foundation at Southern Seminary paralleled a movement happening within the churches and denominational entities of the SBC.

Inman "Prof" Johnson, faculty 1938–1965

---

48. SBTS, *Academic Catalog (1926–27)*.
49. SBTS, *Academic Catalog (1929–30)*.

A GRASSROOTS MOVEMENT—FROM THE TOP DOWN

According to an official SBC report written in 1939, Professor I. E. Reynolds of Southwestern Baptist Theological Seminary (SWBTS) formally requested that the Sunday school board prepare "a real survey of the musical program in the Southern Baptist churches."[50] Though Reynolds had informally begun his requests as early as 1930, his earlier requests were denied. The reason given for the rejection explained that the Sunday school board "had neither the time nor the money."[51] Though their response may seem terse, it was accurate. The total debt faced by the executive committee of the SBC in 1930 was "several million dollars."[52] 1930 being the year after the great stock market crash, saw Reynold's seminary cut their salaries in half.[53] The Great Depression was just beginning, and finding five thousand dollars of unallocated money along with rallying workers to survey 24,500 (mostly rural) churches was no small undertaking for the Sunday school board. Despite the challenges, Reynold's formal request was granted, though it took a few more years to materialize. On May 16, 1937, the Sunday school board appointed a committee to "study the conditions of church music."[54] Reynolds, the director of the department of sacred music at SWBTS, was part of an informal group of Southern Baptist musicians who had been concerned for some time with the poor quality of music and worship they observed in the majority of Southern Baptist churches. A completed survey would give this group a clearer perspective as to the true quality of worship in SBC churches and a platform upon which to make positive changes.

The Committee on Church Music

The Committee on Church Music appointed by the Sunday school board in 1937 included five "outstanding pastors" along with "master musicians." Among the musical representatives were some of the more important people in the history of Southern Baptist worship leader training: from Louisville, Kentucky, Mr. E. A. Converse Jr. and Professor Inman Johnson, professor

---

50. *Annual of SBC*, 1939, quoted in Carle, "History of School of Church Music of SBTS."
51. Carle, "History of School of Church Music of SBTS," 5.
52. Reynolds, *The Cross and the Lyre*, 35.
53. Reynolds, *The Cross and the Lyre*, 35.
54. Carle, "History of School of Church Music of SBTS," 5.

of music and voice culture at Southern Seminary; from New Orleans, Louisiana, Professor E. O. Sellers, director of department of music in the Baptist Bible Institute (now New Orleans Baptist Theological Seminary [NOBTS]); from Nashville, Tennessee, Professor B. B. McKinney, music editor of the Baptist Sunday school board; and from Fort Worth, Texas, Professor I. E. Reynolds, director of the department of sacred music at SWBTS.[55] When the SBC next convened the following year on May 12, 1938, the committee's previous report was accepted and unanimously adopted. The points of the report are outlined as follows:

1. Your committee in its study and deliberations has discovered a widespread need for the promotion of higher standards of worship in our churches and recommends that this Committee be asked to continue its study and report at the next annual Convention.

2. In view of the fact that the Sunday School Board has rendered such valuable service in promoting the work of organization and instruction in our Sunday schools and other phases of denominational life, we recommend that it be requested to render a similar service in the development of the ideals of worship, particularly as they relate to the ministry of music.

3. We suggest that the Sunday School Board be requested to project a survey of church music in the churches of the Southern Baptist Convention and that it be along the following lines:

    a. The amount of money spent annually for—
        i. Paid leaders
        ii. Books and music
        iii. Organists—orchestras

    b. To ascertain the value of church musical instruments (organs–pianos)

    c. To learn the type of music being used—hymnals, song books, and anthems.

4. We recommend that the Committee seek to secure in our various educational institutions, summer assemblies, training schools, institutes, and the like, an emphasis on the importance of higher standards of worship in all of our churches.

55. Carle, "History of School of Church Music of SBTS," 5.

5. We believe that the Sunday School Board will render valuable service if it will provide tracts and books dealing with the matters of music and public worship.

6. We recommend that the Sunday School Board be requested to incorporate where possible, in its various programs of worship, hymns selected from the New Baptist Hymnal by number and title.[56]

7. We request the Sunday School Board through its literature and through its Book Stores to seek to induce our churches, Sunday Schools and other organizations to use the song books which are published by the Sunday School Board.

8. We endorse the revised edition of the New Baptist Hymnal with all its improvements and recommend it to the churches of this Convention.

9. We urge that our churches lay the same emphasis upon the quality and character of their music that they do upon the other departments of their work.[57]

In the following year's Convention (1939), the committee's report indicates progress and an increasing clarification in their blueprints for enhancing the worship of Southern Baptist churches. The committee urged churches to realize the necessity for higher standards "of music and verse in the worship of our God."[58] The committee further qualified their statement: "With the increased emphasis being placed on better music by radio and in all our public and private schools, our young people must not find their churches either ignoring this vital subject or lagging behind the upward trend so favorably known to them during the week."[59] Though the church growth movement may receive blame for creating tension between culture and the church with styles of worship music, it appears that the committee on church music demonstrated a Southern Baptist contribution to this tension—even before Donald McGavran published his theories of church growth.

---

56. *New Baptist Hymnal* (1926).
57. Alldredge, *Southern Baptist Handbook*, 9–11.
58. Carle, "History of School of Church Music of SBTS," 6.
59. Carle, "History of School of Church Music of SBTS," 6.

The results of the SBC church music survey were published in the Southern Baptist Handbook that year (1939). In his history of the first fifteen years of the SCM at Southern Seminary, David Carle notes that two things were most notable in the survey's findings.[60] First was the need and desire for the development of leadership to build comprehensives church music programs in local churches. The second was the great need for better quality music.[61] The committee worked tirelessly to convince Southern Baptists that these two needs held the very spiritual health of every Southern Baptist church and the SBC in the balance. The committee's second point, the need for better music, may strike a chord familiar to modern readers.

Although twenty-first century churches may tend to prefer popular musical styles, that was not the case in 1939. Carle notes the use of gospel songs in rural churches. These gospel songs bore a musical similarity to the popular country and folk songs of the time and proved to be one of the committee's most prominent targets of criticism.[62] The 1939 committee report states, "Most of the churches however, particularly the rural churches, prefer gospel songs over the hymns; for the simple reason —that they have a very limited acquaintance with or appreciation for the hymns, especially the older, classic hymns."[63] The report continues,

> But since no one but a master musician is capable, in many cases, of really differentiating between gospel songs and hymns, it really does not matter much what the churches prefer. *What is of the greatest importance, however, is that some effective movement should be launched to steer the country churches in particular away from the cheap, clap-trap, so-called gospel songs which in fact have little or no gospel in them and which in many cases are loaded with heresies of the worst sort.*[64]

Although the need for better worship music had been clearly identified, the best way to address the deficiency was not easy. As a denomination of mostly small and rural congregations, the path to change would likely not come through a grassroots movement. Changing the music that churches used in Sunday worship needed a strong denominational push

---

60. Carle, "History of School of Church Music of SBTS."
61. Carle, "History of School of Church Music of SBTS," 7–8.
62. Carle, "History of School of Church Music of SBTS," 8.
63. Carle, "History of School of Church Music of SBTS," 8.
64. Carle, "History of School of Church Music of SBTS," 8; emphasis added.

from the opposite direction. In 1940, the SBC commended the report and its author, E. P. Alldredge. Ideas were recommended for the enhancement and elevation of musical and worship standards in SBC churches that might be promoted on state and association levels.[65]

THE COMMITTEE ON CHURCH MUSIC REPORTS TO THE SOUTHERN BAPTIST CONVENTION

At the 1941 convention, the committee's report repeated the same earlier concerns for worship in SBC churches, but shared some hope for the future through anecdotal evidence of progress:

> We come now to the musical part of our worship, a matter which has been the subject of report before this convention for the past several years. It is heartening to observe that here we have much to record in the way of progress and good ground for hope of improvement. Music occupies from a third to a half of all our church exercises, including the preaching, teaching, training, prayer, missionary and evangelistic services. It is being no longer regarded as a stepchild of worship. Instead of begrudging time to musical performance, instead of tolerating secular-minded choristers who may have professional training but little understanding of true worship, or else allowing a type of trashy songs which often sadden or anger the thoughtful worshiper, Southern Baptists are awakening to an appreciation of noble, worshipful music....
>
> Another evidence of progress is the growing revolt against nondescript songbooks which specialize in the sort of swing tunes that find the feet and not the heart and utilize words which are neither literary nor Scriptural, such song books as are peddled by commercial publishers who for profit victimize many congregations. Our churches are requiring hymnbooks which have been competently edited for supplying the needs of real worship. Still another evidence of this progress is the growing ability of our children to sing the great hymns of the ages, those tried and proven, because they have been taught in the public schools to sing them. Joined with the public school systems in the effort to correct low musical ideals have been our Baptist Training Unions which have incorporated training in religious music in their weekly programs ....[66]

---

65. *Annual of SBC*, 1940, 100–101.
66. "Report of Committee on Church Music and Worship (1941)," 120–22.

The 1941 "Convention Report of the Committee on Church Music" also included calls for worship renewal and two recommendations:

> Helpful as the enumeration and elaboration of different causes for this deplorable decline in support of church worship might be, we must center our investigation in this report upon one, that of worship itself. Does our worship fail to attract and hold our people because of fatal defects in it? Are the materials used too poor? Does it lack . . . vitality? Is it deficient in unity, coherence, beauty? Are its shortcomings chiefly musical? Or is the congregational participation short? Or is the whole order understudied, that is, either a copy of dead traditions or a hodgepodge of prayers, hymns and preachments unrelated to each other or to life as it pulses today? These and other pertinent questions press for intelligent answer.[67]
>
> More gratifying evidence of progress in respect to church music is noted in the correlation of instruction in our denominational schools with that of our churches, in the training of musical leaders and of religious choirs. . . . Much, however, remains to be undertaken. Your committee rejoicing in what has been accomplished, would urge that we press on toward other highly desirable improvements in our worship and music. Two recommendations seem to us to be advisable:
>
> First, that this convention, welcoming the response of our denominational schools to the suggestion of correlating their musical instruction with the training undertaken in our churches, call upon them to extend in whatever ways may seem wise this instruction-correlation to the end that our denomination may be furnished with better standards, higher appreciation of good religious music, more general training in rendition, and that it may be equipped with more good musical leaders in the churches.
>
> Second, finding no authorized, strictly Southern Baptist hymnal in existence and believing there would be large advantage in providing our churches with one suited to the needs of our people, wherever they may choose to use it, we recommend that the Sunday School Board through its appointment of a competent, representative committee, take under advisement the creation of the proposed hymnal and report its finding a year hence.[68]

After several years of seemingly redundant calls for and points of action which had begun in the 1930s, the 1942 report to the Convention from the committee on church music related that the committee no longer

---

67. "Report of Committee on Church Music and Worship (1941)," 120–22.
68. "Report of Committee on Church Music and Worship (1941)," 120–22.

believed discussion on the worthiness of church music would be helpful. Action, not words, were now needed. The committee presented four action points they believed must be completed in order to solve problematic issues in Southern Baptist church music. First, the committee believed pastors needed to foster "a great religious and spiritual attitude, that which will love truth and the doctrines of Christianity as taught by the Bible."[69] Second, the committee called on Southern Baptists to provide a type of church music "that will express this religious and spiritual condition."[70] The committee believed that much of the music used in worship was not of great worth, either musically or biblically. The committee proposed that Southern Baptists needed to produce their own new "practical hymn writers."[71] Third, the committee proposed that the convention sponsor the development of a training system "that will increase the appreciation of our laity along good, wholesome singable and expressive church music."[72] And finally, the committee urged churches give special attention to a period in the services for congregational singing so that the congregations would simply learn more music with which to reinforce the preaching and teaching they received in worship.[73] The committee suggested churches diversify their musical styles and mediums so that all people would find music to help them worship, no matter their disposition. The committee used this point to push for the creation and use of graded choirs for young children through adults so that everyone in church may be evangelized and musically trained. The committee urged pastors to encourage their families to also sing hymns at home and not only in church. These points were presented as a result of the committee's conviction:

> All church music should have as its ultimate goal, not just the artistic for art sake, but to strengthen those who are saved, draw the drifting ones back to Him and cause the lost to feel their need of a Savior and Lord, and to come to Christ. May God help us in our churches to have in preaching, music and order of program that which tends to elevate those who come to our services.[74]

---

69. "Report of Committee on Church Music and Worship (1941)," 114–15.
70. "Report of Committee on Church Music and Worship (1941)," 114–15.
71. "Report of Committee on Church Music and Worship (1941)," 114–15.
72. "Report of Committee on Church Music and Worship (1941)," 114–15.
73. "Report of Committee on Church Music and Worship (1941)," 114–15.
74. "Report of Committee on Church Music and Worship (1942)," 114–15.

The committee believed that music and singing were as fundamental to the Christian life and to corporate Christian worship as were the other elements of congregational worship such as praying, reading Scripture, or preaching. Many agreed with their assertions.

In the committee's 1943 report, their recommendations turned almost exclusively towards the need for leader training and called for denominational schools and seminaries to take the lead.

> We have always been and still are, of the opinion that many of our problems in regard to worship will be solved when we have better Church Music, and certainly we can't have better Church Music until we train our people along better Church Music lines.
>
> We urge our Baptist Colleges, Universities and Seminaries to place in their curriculum a Department of Church Music and that certain, definite, courses be required of all ministerial students.
>
> Our small town and rural churches are at the mercy of a cheap, non-worshipful type of music promoted principally, by those who care nothing for the welfare of the Church and people, just so they are able to gain something in a material way. The conditions cannot be remedied, we feel, unless we as a denomination go into these places (and the pastors in these places are urging us to do so), and by teaching and demonstration help the people to have what they need. We did that very thing in Sunday School and Training Union and the results speak for themselves. Music is of such importance and is used so much in every service that it demands promotion not as a side-line but as a major.[75]

Finally, here is one of the last recommendations from the committee—a call that yielded very clear and immediate results:

> We feel that Southern Baptists are justified in asking that a considerable amount of the profits received from the sale of song books and other music be expended in a worthy Church Music Education Program. Therefore, realizing the dire need of, and the Macedonian call for, a better Church Music Program for Southern Baptists, we recommend that the Sunday School Board be instructed to increase the personnel of the Department of Church Music sufficiently to prepare and set going a constructive, educational program of Church Music among Southern Baptists.[76]

---

75. "Report of Committee on Church Music and Worship (1943)," 51–52.
76. "Report of Committee on Church Music and Worship (1943)," 51–52.

The committee on church music and worship was disbanded the following year. In its place, the church music department of the Sunday school board of the SBC was created. Part of responsibilities of the new church music department addressed one of the committee's calls—an annual music emphasis week to be held at Ridgecrest.[77]

During its six-year existence from 1937 to 1943, the committee on church music and worship functioned as the conscience and prophetic voice for corporate worship within the churches of the SBC. During its life, the committee succeeded in bringing to light Southern Baptists' collectively poor understanding of and vision for music and worship. Through the impact of commercial radio, American culture had become greatly impacted by broadcast media, and SBC churches understood the need to raise musical and theological standards within their corporate worship. SWBTS in Fort Worth, Texas, instituted the department of gospel music in 1915 under the leadership of I. E. Reynolds.[78] The Baptist Bible Institute of New Orleans (now NOBTS), led by E. O. Sellers, had begun its own department of music in 1919.[79] Although training in music and worship had been in existence at Southern Seminary since the time of John A. Broadus, SBTS had not yet taken the significant step of creating a department responsible for curriculum and instruction to train leaders for music and worship in the churches. This step would be taken with the coming election of Southern Seminary President Ellis Adams Fuller.

---

77. "Report of the Committee on Church Music and Worship (1944)," 147.
78. Reynolds, *The Cross and the Lyre*, 5–13.
79. NOBTS, "A Brief History."

3

The Beginning of the School of Church Music, 1942–52

ELLIS FULLER'S VISION

THE SIXTH PRESIDENT OF Southern Seminary (1942–50), Ellis Adams Fuller Sr., was born and raised in rural South Carolina, and was known during his life as an evangelist, pastor, and denominational leader. In addition to these accolades, one of Fuller's most significant legacies comes through his contribution as the determined visionary who founded the school of church music at Southern Seminary.[1] Fuller's love for music appeared during his college days—singing in the glee club and barbershop quartet at Presbyterian College in Clinton, South Carolina. After graduating with his bachelor's degree in 1912, Fuller went on to earn a master of theology degree in New Testament at SBTS under the teaching of A. T. Robertson. Before Fuller graduated, he accepted the call to pastor and consequently never completed his doctoral thesis.[2] Although Fuller never completed his dissertation, he nonetheless did receive "several honorary doctorates," including one from his undergraduate alma mater in 1924.[3] After serving two short pastorates from 1922 to 1924 and 1924–25, Fuller gained a reputation

---

1. Winters and Winters, interview by Carle, April 7–8, 1984, 26.
2. Carle, "History of School of Church Music of SBTS," 18–19.
3. Carle, "History of School of Church Music of SBTS," 19.

as a "dynamic speaker and a highly skilled evangelist."[4] Through his many evangelistic engagements, Fuller began to realize how difficult it was to find an evangelistic singer/musician who could sing solos, lead congregational singing, and prepare revival choirs that would represent each age group in the church.[5] Discovering an individual with this unique combination of skills was difficult, but Fuller thought such people should be readily available in every location he preached. When Fuller became pastor of the First Baptist Church of Atlanta, he found that even in large and prominent churches, church music programs had only one adult choir with a handful of paid soloists. In the late 1920s, musical leadership of this style and scope was common. Fuller's dissatisfaction with the state of church music leadership grew. Fuller was not only unsatisfied with the music produced by these types of church musicians, but he was also disappointed with the character he observed in those leading the music. Fuller's feelings became so intense that he even shared his thoughts from the pulpit:

> Those who lead us in music face the same terrific dangers. If they scramble for the spotlight, would have all eyes focused upon them, and selfishly seek to be heard of men, they are in the same class with the Pharisees who stood on the street corners to pray. One individual in the choir may seek the soloist's part because of the attention it would attract. If so, he needs to pray the prayer of the publican, "Lord, be merciful to me a sinner!"[6]

Fuller's sentiments on this matter were so frequently expressed, that they were remembered in the context of a colleague's interview:

> The large percentage of churches that had any music leadership had paid quartets . . . but Dr. Fuller had had unfortunate experiences with them. [He] called them "the war department of the church." Many times the singers would leave after the solos and not stay for the sermon. That would disrupt things. He felt that they were temperamental and difficult to work with."[7]

---

4. Carle, "History of School of Church Music of SBTS," 19.

5. Bates, unfinished biography of Fuller, quoted in Carle, "History of School of Church Music of SBTS," 4; note written in margin quoted in Carle, 18n3.

6. Bates, biography of Fuller; see Carle, "History of School of Church Music of SBTS," 20.

7. Winters and Winters, "Launching of School of Church Music," 1.

Fuller's desire for spiritually mature and musically qualified worship leadership helped cultivate a vision for something greater:

> As early as 1928, Dr. Ellis Adams Fuller had a dream.... As a pastor, as Southwide Secretary for Evangelism, as a person, he again and again had been aware of the power of music in the service of religion.
>
> Yet there was almost no leadership training in the Southern Baptist Convention for one who could come to a local church as a permanent, full-time staff member to carry on a music program for all age groups in the church. Even as late as 1939, approximately 79% of the existing music leaders throughout the Convention had no leadership training in music of any kind whatsoever.
>
> For years Dr. Fuller sought for and even tried himself to inculcate in the musicians serving his church a viewpoint of church music that would parallel the teaching ministries afforded Baptist churches in Sunday School and Church Training. This church viewpoint for the music leadership and total music program of the local church he pastored became almost a "magnificent obsession" as, through more than a decade, he continued to try to bring it to realization.[8]

John Finley Williamson and Fuller's Solution

Finally, in 1940, Fuller believed he may have found the answer to his problem. Fuller visited Westminster Choir College in Princeton, New Jersey, and heard the choir led by John Finley Williamson. Williamson originally founded the Dayton Westminster choir as a volunteer choir in Ohio in the 1920s. As the group began touring and singing outside their home area of south-central Ohio, they gained a strong reputation that led to "what is believed to be the nation's first coast-to-coast radio broadcast, with the Cincinnati Orchestra conducted by Fritz Reiner from Ohio station WLW."[9] Williamson's choir became the Westminster Choir School in 1926 after Williamson recruited a faculty of ten, selected sixty of his best singers, and moved to Princeton, New Jersey.[10]

---

8. Winters and Winters, "Launching of School of Church Music," 1.
9. Beck, "Westminster Choir College at Ninety," 156.
10. Beck, "Westminster Choir College at Ninety," 156.

The Beginning of the School of Church Music, 1942–52

The training method for Williamson's new school was different from existing musical conservatories at that time. No matter what area of music a student chose to study—piano, organ, conducting, composition, or vocal performance, all students were required to sing in a choral ensemble which rehearsed daily.[11] Another unique aspect to Williamson's choir was their readily identifiable choral sound. One of Williamson's most significant sources of choral inspiration came from renowned composer and choral director, F. Melius Christiansen, who founded the choir at St. Olaf College in Minnesota. Although Williamson greatly admired Christiansen, he disagreed with Christiansen's philosophy of vocal pedagogy which produced a particular type of sound in his choirs. As opposed to the pure, straight-toned singing of Christiansen's choirs, Williamson preferred a full-voiced, full-vibrato sound.[12] Williamson wanted to embrace the unique timbre of his singers' voices and allow free and open singing without the forced blending he observed in European-inspired choirs like Christiansen's choir at St. Olaf College. For Ellis Fuller, Williamson's singing philosophy and choral sound must have seemed a better match for the singing culture found in many Southern Baptist churches. In another interesting coincidence, Williamson called his choristers "ministers of music" and is widely credited with creating the job title held by many Southern Baptist church music leaders since that time.[13] For Fuller, Williamson's "Westminster Plan" looked like the answer to his problem of finding trained church musicians to serve Southern Baptist churches. In Donald Winters and Frances Winters, Fuller would find the right couple to bring the Westminster Plan to Southern Seminary.

---

11. Beck, "Westminster Choir College at Ninety," 156–57.
12. Beck, "Westminster Choir College at Ninety," 157.
13. Beck, "Westminster Choir College at Ninety," 155.

Ellis Fuller, SBTS President 1942–1950

Donald Winters and Frances Winters

Donald Winters was born in Greenville, Ohio, on December 2, 1910. At the age of eight years old, Winters had his first experience singing Handel's *Messiah* in Greenville's community chorus. The next year, at age eleven, Winters began playing piano for his Sunday school. The next year, at the age of twelve, Winters accepted Jesus Christ as his Savior and Lord.[14] In a possible foreshadowing of his role in Southern Baptist church music, Winters insisted that he be baptized by immersion at the First Baptist Church even though his conversion occurred at the First Christian Church of Greenville, Ohio.[15] Though Winters gives no account of encountering Williamson's

14. King, *Then Sings My Soul*, 1–3.
15. King, *Then Sings My Soul*, 3.

chorale, the overlapping years and locations make it likely Winters had some awareness of Williamson's choir and this early awareness may have played a part in his moving to Princeton, New Jersey, where he became a student at Williamson's school in 1935.[16]

Over the next five years, Donald Winters completed his bachelor's degree in sacred music and came within one course of completing his master of sacred music degree. It was during these impactful five years that Winters married fellow student, Frances Weaver.[17] With his graduation quickly approaching, Winters began looking ahead for what might come next. Tommy King records what followed:

> In the fall of 1940, Donald and Frances both submitted their resumes to the placement office at Westminster Choir College, hoping to find work to begin right away. Among the questions asked was, 'Where and in what denomination do you wish to work?' Donald answered, 'Any church except a Baptist.'" After a year with no leads, they withdrew their conditions and "within a week were contacted by Dr. Ellis A. Fuller of the First Baptist Church of Atlanta, who wanted to discuss a full church-wide music program. ... The couple began their work in Atlanta in June 1941, beginning with Vacation Bible School.[18]

It appears that Winters's childhood preference for his baptism to occur within a Baptist church may have indeed foreshadowed where his life would have its greatest impact, in the music and worship of Baptist churches.

Fuller appeared very excited to have the Winters join him at First Baptist Church Atlanta. Fuller shared this enthusiasm and his vision for the Winters's ministry in this newsletter article:

> Every church leader feels very keenly the responsibility to enlist the young people for active participation in the work of the church. Music offers a glorious opportunity for the realization of this worthy purpose. Everybody loves music. Nearly everyone has some musical talent. Music has been, through the ages, a voice of praise to God. It is a peculiar language for the utterance of emotions that the tongue cannot possibly describe. For that reason, every church should make the maximum use of music in a church-wide effort

---

16. King, *Then Sings My Soul*, 4.
17. King, *Then Sings My Soul*, 8.
18. King, *Then Sings My Soul*, 8–9.

to deepen the spirituality of the people and to inspire church-wide participation in worship.

The Westminster Plan of Music, which we have adopted for this church and which we are today inaugurating, was conceived and developed with exactly this end in view. If the plan is worked successfully, it will accomplish two ends without fail, namely, it will develop a consciousness and use of music which no other plan can achieve, and it will enlist the greatest number of people to a vital interest in the church and to an actual participation in its program.

The purpose of this program is to discover the musical talent in the church, to enlist it, to train it, and to use it. In this way we can make it glorify God and at the same time lead our people to new heights of spirituality.[19]

"The Westminster Plan," as Fuller had called it, appeared to display its success for the first time on the Sunday after Labor Day in 1941 when the choir of First Baptist Church Atlanta performed their first anthem from memory. Many critics in the church believed that the only means to beautiful, high quality church music came through hiring professional singers, and now Fuller, with the help of Donald and Frances Winters, had proven them wrong.[20]

In 1942, Fuller was elected president of Southern Seminary. Perhaps influenced by his experiences as a traveling evangelist, Fuller's goals for Southern Seminary sought to enlarge the seminary's aspirations. Similar to the path taken by other universities like Yale or Oxford, Fuller believed that Southern Seminary could grow beyond its original concept as a theological school to becoming a "great Christian university."[21] These plans were adjusted into more moderate and attainable goals as indicated by Donald Winters:

> Not long after assuming the duties of the Presidency, Dr. Fuller shared with some of the seminary trustees a dream he had cherished for some time of seeing developed at Southern Seminary a great Baptist Educational Center for the training of all church workers; – not pastors alone but with them missionaries and ministers of many kinds: those serving through education, music, visitation and social service ministers, church administration,

---

19. Winters and Winters, endnotes to "Launching of School of Church Music," xii.
20. Winters and Winters, interview, 23.
21. McCall, interview by Carle, June 6, 1985, in "History," 26.

The Beginning of the School of Church Music, 1942–52

church recreation, church secretarial work, – in short, training for the entire staff of a local church or mission. He envisioned that this training would be offered in such a way that all could study together, each getting a broader and deeper insight into the tasks and problems of the total church program and of each other; and in an academic atmosphere with the highest scholastic standards.[22]

Fuller's vision was embraced by the trustees, including one significant financial supporter. With the support of these key people, the SCM at Southern Seminary was about to take shape.

Donald Winters, faculty 1946–1952

22. Winters and Winters, interview, 26.

Frances Winters, faculty 1944–1952

Donald and Frances Winters, founding faculty
of the SCM at Southern Seminary

The Beginning of the School of Church Music, 1942–52

V. V. Cooke Sr. Supports Fuller

Perhaps the SBTS trustee who exhibited the greatest buy-in to Fuller's vision was Louisville businessman V. V. Cooke Sr.; he loved church music and had quickly become one of Fuller's best friends and staunchest supporters. The two frequently went horseback riding and their casual conversations led to Cooke's becoming interested in the type of music program Fuller had established at First Baptist Atlanta. As a businessman, Cooke realized that the two most significant challenges to be solved in establishing a training school for church musicians were the school's location and faculty.

The first of Cooke's issues was solved in 1943 when the Callahan family decided to sell their property that was located directly across Lexington Road from the women's missionary training union building (what is now the Carver and Rankin Hall complex). The process of purchasing this property for a future SCM was described in an article from the *Southern Seminary News* in 1943:

> When it became known that the property was available, President Fuller laid the matter on the hearts of members of the faculty, the Executive Committee, and the Financial Board. Authorized to proceed with the purchase, President Fuller virtually closed the deal early in June.
>
> A local Trustee said, "Go ahead and buy it; if you find that you don't want it, I'll take it off your hands." Dr. Fuller replied, "I want you to own it, but not possess it." The remark bore its fruit, for some days later Mr. V. V. Cooke, successful businessman and faithful deacon and Sunday School teacher in the Walnut Street Church, quietly announced to Dr. Fuller that he proposed to make a gift of the property to the Seminary. In the meantime, Dr. Fuller had discovered a Pilcher organ exactly suited for installation as a practice instrument. Mr. C. E. Gheens, member of the Seminary Financial Board and loyal deacon of Broadway Baptist Church, volunteered the gift of the organ.[23]

Ellis had already approached the Winters, asking them to follow him to Louisville and to help start a training program like their education at Westminster—but they had refused, citing their short time in Atlanta (one and a half years), their youth, and their lack of classroom experience.[24] When Cooke presented Ellis the deed to the Callahan property and said,

23. Fuller, "Magnifying the Ministry of Music," 1–2.
24. Winters and Winters, "Launching of School of Church Music," 8.

"Ellis, here's your School of Music," Ellis increased his efforts to persuade the Winters to join him at Southern.[25] When Ellis asked the Winters what Baptists they knew who had similar training and who might take on such a project, they recollect that "almost no names came to mind."[26] After several more pressing contacts from Fuller, the situation for the Winters changed:

> Mr. Winters was drafted and was to be inducted into the army in July. They were expecting their first child in September. It was thus apparent that regardless of their loyalties to their first call, they would not be able to continue the work at the Atlanta church, as the program by that time had grown to the extent that Mrs. Winters could not carry it alone.
>
> So, Mr. and Mrs. Winters resigned their positions in Atlanta, and she agreed to come to Louisville early in November in time for the official opening of the new Cooke Hall. Dr. Fuller had told her that he wanted her to draw up the curriculum, write the bulletin, help him in his search for suitable faculty and student personnel and take care of student correspondence and records, preparatory to the teaching that he wanted her to do also.[27]

Despite their laudable desires to continue serving First Baptist Atlanta, Fuller was getting what he wanted. Though Frances Winters had Fuller's full support, there were others in the Southern Seminary community who were not so supportive. Now, alone and pregnant, she had to move to Louisville and begin fulfilling the herculean list of jobs laid out for her by President Fuller.

Discouragement and Support

Fuller's greatest challenges in establishing the SCM revealed themselves to be not the logistical challenges of finances, facilities, and faculty. Rather, Fuller faced his greatest resistance from the seminary faculty. Some of the faculty believed the potential drain on the seminary's already precarious budget made starting the SCM an unwise decision. Some faculty did not believe that music was a legitimate academic subject. Some faculty believed that expanding the seminary to include a school of music represented too significant of a departure from the original vision of the school and

---

25. Winters and Winters, "Launching of School of Church Music," 5.
26. Winters and Winters, "Launching of School of Church Music," 8.
27. Winters and Winters, "Launching of School of Church Music," 9.

therefore an irrational one. Fuller tried to address these fears with an article published in the *Southern Seminary News*:

> President Fuller and the Faculty wish to make it perfectly clear that the establishment of the School of Music will in no wise lessen emphasis on the great main purpose of the seminary – the education of men to be effective preachers and good pastors. Indeed, the training of men and women as ministers of music and directors of education is intended to free the pastor from burdensome details, so that he can give himself more completely to his incomparably important work of preaching and pastoral care. For these fellow workers in a common enterprise to receive their education in the same school, and then to go out with full appreciation of each other in their common tasks, will be great gain for the churches whom they serve.
>
> Lovers of sacred music should be found who will especially endow the School of Music so that its conduct will never be a drain on the seminary's resources.[28]

Fuller's pastoral powers of persuasion were functioning at maximum capacity. Changing the critical minds and wills within the faculty, however, remained a daunting task.

The Winters's task was also made more difficult through the criticism that came from several faculty members and their families. The Winters related that "one of the most vitriolic critics of the entire effort and of Mrs. Winters in particular was Ella Broadus Robertson, daughter of second seminary president, John Broadus, and widow of A. T. Robertson."[29] Donald Winters describes, "On several occasions she took it upon herself to castigate Mrs. Winters for what she was doing, each time she said that she spoke for the entire Seminary community."[30]

The Winters also received support from some in the seminary community. The Winters reportedly "felt friendship and support from W. Hersey Davis and former president Sampey."[31] Francis Winters related that she was only able to endure the hard work and persecution because she was convinced of her calling to help form the SCM. Although President Fuller was on her side, it would be many years before the seminary faculty

---

28. Fuller, "Magnifying the Ministry of Music," 2.
29. Winters and Winters, interview, 31.
30. Winters and Winters, interview, 31.
31. Winters and Winters, interview, 31.

and community at large would truly accept the school of church music, its faculty, and its students as part of the SBTS family.

In addition to battling the heavy work load and personal attacks, Fuller and Winters also struggled with limited resources with which to begin the SCM. In order to start the school, Fuller and Winters needed a qualified faculty, proper facilities, and of course, students. For the initial faculty, Fuller had as his disposal Frances Winters (Donald would not return until after the end of WWII), R. Inman Johnson (teacher of music fundamentals, elementary hymnology, and elocution), and Claudia Edwards from the W. M. U. Training School (teacher of piano and supervised field work). These three were the only faculty who were already serving on the Lexington Road campus who were also qualified to begin teaching in the new music school.[32] The original Cooke Hall, the property that has since served as the president's residence, had been purchased for use of the school, but had not yet been renovated for class use.[33] Despite the lack of resources, the school was dedicated in a special service on November 5, 1943:

> The dedication was held on November 5, 1943. A Pilcher organ, a gift of Mr. and Mrs. Edwin Gheens, had been installed in one of the front parlors, and was formally dedicated on that same day by a recital shared by Dr. Stephen Morrisett, a graduate of the Seminary and former faculty member of Westminster Choir College; and Private Donald Winters, U. S. Army, who somehow had been granted an unheard-of three-day pass from Camp Campbell for the occasion.[34]

With no students, three faculty, and a facility improperly outfitted for its intended use, the school of church music at Southern Seminary was formally introduced.

CREATING THE FIRST CURRICULUM

Fuller may have been drawn to the musical excellence of the Westminster method of musical training, but Fuller was not interested in the school of church music becoming another musical conservatory that simply placed the moniker "sacred" in front of the names of degrees and courses offered.[35]

32. Carle, "History of School of Church Music of SBTS," 29.
33. Carle, "History of School of Church Music of SBTS," 29.
34. Winters and Winters, interview, 29.
35. Winters and Winters, "Launching of School of Church Music," 7.

The Beginning of the School of Church Music, 1942–52

Fuller wanted the school of church music to prepare students to lead Baptist churches in worship through music, lead the seminary community in worship, train each music student to personally "worship God more fully, not only with the mechanics of a church service, but in all of life."[36] For the remainder of the 1943–44 academic year, Frances Winters taught some voice lessons to the wives of seminary students but spent the majority of her time developing the curriculum.[37] Fuller asked her to develop a three-year degree plan that would culminate in a bachelor of sacred music degree. This undergraduate degree would be available to students after they had completed two years in an accredited college as a music major.[38] Fuller also asked her to develop a three-year curriculum that would earn a master of sacred music degree. This master's degree would be available to students who had completed a bachelor of music or bachelor of arts in music from an accredited college or university.[39] The development of these curricula proved neither quick nor easy.

Years later the Winters would recount that from the time they resigned their ministry positions at FBC Atlanta until they arrived in Louisville in November of 1943, practically the only thing they talked about together was the seminary music program.[40] This conversation would not last long, because on the day after the original Cooke Hall was dedicated, Donald Winters was assigned to be the chaplain's assistant at Schoffield Barracks near Honolulu, Hawaii. This meant that along with her teaching, Frances Winters would be spending all her time creating the curriculum . . . alone.

In 1943, the only real means of print communication came through the US Postal Service and this method was slowed even more due to the war. Mrs. Winters wrote to every college and seminary in the United States where she was aware of a church music degree or program emphasis, requesting degree curriculum information. Frances Winters also drew on her notes from many discussions she had with working church musicians, including her husband, concerning church music curriculum. Despite being stationed thousands of miles away, Donald Winters also spent his unallocated time in similar pursuit. In addition to their own experiences, Frances

---

36. Winters and Winters, interview, 29.
37. Winters and Winters, interview, 29.
38. Winters and Winters, "Launching of School of Church Music," 11–14.
39. Winters and Winters, "Launching of School of Church Music," 11–14.
40. The account is found in Winters and Winters, "Launching of School of Church Music," 11–14.

Winters drew upon Southern Baptist training materials from the Sunday school board including quarterlies and articles that addressed the subject of church music. Included with the information gathered, the Winters closely considered the recommendations of Dr. Fuller.

The core of a curriculum began to unfold and eventually developed into subject areas they felt were needed to develop solid musicianship. These subjects included music theory, composition, and music history. Also included were performing areas in conducting, ensemble leadership, and personal music study in organ, piano, or voice. Due to Fuller's requests, a strong emphasis on choral work was included in the curriculum. Finally, the Winters believed that church music students should have the same intensive introductory courses in biblical studies afforded all seminary students, including Old Testament, New Testament, and Baptist doctrine, along with courses in worship and religious education.

In late December 1943, Fuller asked for a finished copy of the curriculum to be in his hands by the first of January 1944. Despite all of the hard work that had been put into the project, and although Frances Winters reported to have begun and ended each of her planning sessions with prayer, she confessed to feeling helpless and inadequate to meet Fuller's deadline. This fear drove her to three days of almost constant prayer during the Christmas break of 1943, described as follows:

> During this time, along with everything else, Mrs. Winters had been keeping an infant on his daily four-hour schedule, and she reported that their son had expected that schedule to be quite promptly carried out. However, on the morning of December 26th, 1943, after his 6:00 am feeding, she put him back to bed, and for the first time in his four months of life he did not stir until 12:30. As soon as he was in bed she went immediately to her desk, and after another period of intensive prayer she began to write. She testified that for the next six hours, in the quiet of the large house, she wrote steadily, without a single interruption, and it was as though everything she wrote were being dictated. She had almost a feeling of detachment, as she simply wrote down what came to her, without hesitation and without fatigue. When she put down her pen at the end of that period, she had on paper an outline of both required and elective courses for three years of study for a Bachelor's degree and a three year course for a Master's degree in Church Music, different from those of any other known school. Completed also were the full catalogue-type course description setting forth the overall content and credit hours of each

course, and the order in which these courses would be taken. In the minds of the Winters there was no way to explain this except the Lord's hand was in the work. Temporary drafts of admission and graduation requirements were completed the next day and a temporary schedule of classes was drawn up to be sure the music classes would fit in with the Seminary schedule without conflict. Style and format followed the Seminary catalogue, and the whole was in the hands of the president before the deadline.[41]

Despite Mrs. Winters's miraculous work, the faculty of the seminary found issues to address which continued to be discussed for the next four months.[42] Some of the largest issues identified by the faculty to sort out included the "inevitable" presence of more women in the classes, the fear that music students (of both sexes) might lower the seminary's scholastic standing, the hesitancy on the part of some faculty to open their classes to music students, and the pre-existence of a one-hour hymnology course taught by Inman Johnson. The Winters asked for a two-hour course required for three terms and that the pre-existing class change its title due to the inclusion of other material.[43] Eventually, all of these issues were addressed to the satisfaction of the faculty and the trustees.

ESTABLISHMENT OF THE "DEPARTMENT OF MUSIC"

In the May 1944 issue of *The Tie*, an announcement was released by President Fuller, informing the seminary community of the upcoming school. In this announcement he refers to the SCM as the "Department of Music":

> The many letters which come daily to the seminary from pastors throughout the southland, asking for directors of church music, furnish positive proof of the urgent need for the training of young men and women to serve our Baptist churches in this capacity.
>
> At the last annual meeting of the Board of Trustees, the seminary was authorized to expand its present Department of Church Music to offer degrees to those young men and women who wish to give their lives in Christian service in the field of music.
>
> A curriculum for a three-year course leading to the degree of Bachelor of Sacred Music has been carefully prepared, including courses in: the theory and composition of music; the history of

---

41. Winters and Winters, "Launching of School of Church Music," 14.
42. Winters and Winters, "Launching of School of Church Music," 14.
43. Winters and Winters, "Launching of School of Church Music," 14.

church music; hymn appreciation, choir repertoire and methods; conducting; instruction in organ, piano, voice and so forth. In order that the minister of church music may become well acquainted with the work of the pastor and be familiar with the whole church organization, the course leading to a degree in music will include the Old Testament in English, the New Testament in English, Theology, Church History, and Religious Education.

The new Department of Music will open at the beginning of the next session, September 12, 1944, under the direction of Professor Inman Johnson. A limited number of students will be enrolled for the first session. Applicants for admission must have completed a junior college degree, or its equivalent, in a standard college, and must meet certain requirements in the field of theoretical and practical music. For obvious reasons the seminary cannot at this time provide elementary training in the general field of music. The purpose of the department at present is strictly to afford training in church music. Quarters for the women students will probably be provided in the new music building. Men students in the Department of Music will be housed at present in Mullins Hall. As in the case of theological students in the seminary, students in the Department of Music will not be charged tuition.

Since the number of students will of necessity be limited this year, we are especially anxious to enroll a group of young men and women who are particularly qualified for this field of service. We are asking our alumni to recommend to the seminary young men and women from their congregations who have felt the call to the ministry of music and who show special aptitudes for such a ministry.

It is anticipated that curriculum arrangements will soon be completed and that catalogues carrying a full description of the course to be offered will be available around the first of July. Requests for catalogues and other inquiries should be addressed to The Southern Baptist Theological Seminary, Department of Church Music, 2825 Lexington Road, Louisville, Kentucky.[44]

Fuller sent another message to alumni in the following month asking for recommendations of prospective students. Unfortunately, from three thousand posted requests, only one reply was received.[45] Similar requests were sent to the various state convention papers by the seminary publicity office in July, far too late to generate any response from prospective students.

---

44. Fuller, "President's Paragraphs," 1.
45. Winters and Winters, "Launching of School of Church Music," 22.

The Beginning of the School of Church Music, 1942–52

The first significant group of interested students came via personal contacts from Fuller and a handful of interested seminary students who networked through their friends and through personal contacts at the 1944 Ridgecrest summer meetings.[46]

Assembling the First Faculty

The SCM was not only President Fuller's passion, but also required much of his attention because he functioned as the director and head of the school. Therefore, in addition to finding facilities, curriculum, and approval from the trustees, Fuller was also responsible to assemble the school's faculty. While Frances Winters could teach voice and church music courses like hymnology, Fuller wanted to hold the instruction of organ and choral music for her husband, Donald. Therefore, Fuller needed to find someone qualified to handle these areas until Donald Winters's return from the war. Fuller also needed to find an appropriate instructor for music theory, music history, and piano.[47]

Though not for lack of trying, finding faculty did not follow the same path as it would have for the rest of the seminary. At this point in its history, Southern Seminary had never had a female faculty. Because of the SCM's status as a separate entity from the seminary, Mrs. Winters, being both female and a musician, was not allowed to come before the faculty, even as a consultant concerning the music curriculum.[48] Despite this negative aspect of the seminary's culture, the war situation and the need for qualified musicians eventually opened consideration to female candidates.[49] Despite the challenges facing Fuller as he completed the SCM's faculty, Providence smiled on his efforts. On May 25, 1944, Inman Johnson gave Fuller the name of someone he had met at Ridgecrest—Dr. Claude Almand. Fuller contacted him, set up an interview and Almand proved to be the missing puzzle piece,[50] according to the Winters:

> Thus May 31st, 1944 was a red-letter day, bringing two occurrences which Dr. Fuller considered to be the "dew on the wool,"

---

46. Winters and Winters, endnotes to "Launching of School of Church Music."
47. Winters and Winters, "Launching of School of Church Music," 16–17.
48. Carle, "History of School of Church Music of SBTS," 41.
49. Carle, "History of School of Church Music of SBTS," 42.
50. Carle, "History of School of Church Music of SBTS," 42.

indicating that in spite of discouragements he was supposed to go ahead.

One was the coming of Dr. Almand. Claude Marion Almand was a man who seemed to have all the right credentials. He had a Ph.D. degree in Theory and Composition with a minor in Musicology from the Eastman School of Music of the University of Rochester, one of the best in the country. He was a pianist who had teaching experience. He was a composer whose first symphony even then was being rehearsed for performance by the Cincinnati Symphony Orchestra under the direction of Eugene Goosens. He was a Southern Baptist, having joined that church in his youth in Louisiana. He was a man, and there had been much skepticism over the presence of a woman in the Music School. Dr. Almand had four years of college teaching experience in the very areas in which the seminary school needed help. He was director of music in a prestigious church in Nashville, Tennessee, very well liked by all who knew him. He would be coming from a southern institution of good reputation. A regular attendant at Ridgecrest Music Week from its beginnings, he was strongly interested in Southern Baptist church music; and once presented with the possibilities of Southern Seminary's new school, he felt a sense of mission connected with it which prompted him to be willing to give up a more secure and lucrative position for this one. Indeed, in every way, he seemed to be God's choice for the position, and almost at once everyone concerned in any way with the school was satisfied.[51]

Dr. Almand signed his contract and Fuller received it on June 6, 1944.[52]

Unresolved Issues

In September 1944, the school of church music at SBTS opened its doors. Although President Fuller had overcome all obstacles for opening the school, there remained several issues that would need to be addressed. Fuller, himself, represented the first obstacle. Although he had no formal training in music, Fuller was both the seminary president and acting head of the school of church music, serving as the SCM's only connection to the seminary. Although Fuller's role provided a sustaining strength to the

---

51. Winters and Winters, "Launching of School of Church Music," 17–19.
52. Carle, "History of School of Church Music of SBTS," 43.

The Beginning of the School of Church Music, 1942–52

SCM in its foundation, ultimately this condition opened the door to more resentment—and sometimes open hostility—from the seminary faculty.[53]

The second problematic issue came in Inman Johnson. On paper, Johnson served as the head of an expansion of the seminary's department of church music, but he had no actual connection to the SCM other than teaching some voice lessons. Johnson wanted to continue teaching ministerial students and had no desire to become a music faculty.[54]

Frances Winters had been placed in a very difficult situation. Although she had free access to Fuller's counsel, Frances Winters, herself, functioned as the administrator of the SCM.[55] The seventh president of Southern Seminary, Duke McCall, later stated, "The blunt truth is that she ran the music school, and essentially ran it after [her husband] came back."[56] Frances served as a direct extension of Fuller's authority, but she had no actual status as a faculty. She also had no terminal degree. Her musical skills were of little use in a culture where music was not considered an academic subject. Finally, and perhaps most significantly, she was a woman.[57]

The most significant unresolved issue was that the SCM "was not a structural part of the seminary."[58] This meant that the music faculty were not members of the seminary faculty. The SCM's lack of connectivity to the seminary also meant that there was no financial provision in the seminary's budget.[59] President Fuller was responsible to raise all of the money required to run the school of church music, including the faculty salaries. This final issue of official seminary connection and budget would not become resolved until the next seminary administration.

THE BACHELOR OF SACRED MUSIC DEGREE, 1944–47

The original bulletin from the school of church music described the bachelor of sacred music degree in this way:

---

53. Winters and Winters, "Launching of School of Church Music," 20.
54. Winters and Winters, "Launching of School of Church Music," 20.
55. Winters and Winters, interview, 44.
56. McCall, interview, 44.
57. Winters and Winters, interview, 44.
58. Carle, "History of School of Church Music of SBTS," 45.
59. Carle, "History of School of Church Music of SBTS," 45.

The seminary realizes the value of music in the life of the individual Christian and the church. It is also conscious of a rapidly developing standard of general musical culture among our people, which is resulting in a sensitiveness in taste toward church music and an awareness of the latent possibilities of music for spiritual growth.

This awakening is creating a demand not only for pastors who have some knowledge and appreciation of church music, but also for ministers of music who are equipped to give their full time to the musical ministries of the church.

The ministry of music is the office in which the trained musician serves as full time director of the churchwide program of music for the purpose of correlating music activities of the highest order with the worship and work of the church. The Minister of music administers the program of music participation, enlistment and training for all age groups, works with the pastor in presenting a unified program, and ministers through music to the spiritual needs of the congregation.

These ministers of music must have a technical knowledge of music, a sufficient background of church music and a well-developed interest in and understanding of the entire church program.[60]

The purpose of the School of Church Music is therefore to give training in the field of church music for the specific purpose of providing our churches and other denominational fields with competent ministers of music, and to give that training side by side with the ministerial student in order that each may fully understand the office, the viewpoint, and the needs of the other.[61]

If the purposes and goals for the new school and degree offerings sounded lofty, the entrance requirements were equally significant. After the application, each student was required to submit three recommendation letters plus a recommendation from their church, a personal essay-styled statement articulating their own purpose in pursuing the degree, and a certificate of good health.[62]

After these documents were provided, the applicants needed to show proof of a certificate of graduation from a standard junior college or to have completed two years' satisfactory work in an accredited college or university. Applicants were also to "demonstrate, by examination, skills

---

60. SBTS, School of Church Music Bulletin (1946–47); see Carle, "History of School of Church Music of SBTS," 47–50.

61. SBTS, School of Church Music Bulletin (1946–47), 4.

62. SBTS, School of Church Music Bulletin (1946–47), 5–6.

The Beginning of the School of Church Music, 1942–52

and capacities in the following fields: Theory (written, aural, and keyboard) and proficiency in sight singing and in melodic, harmonic, and rhythmic dictation."[63] The applicant's demonstration of competence in applied music was equally significant:

> In piano to the extent that the student is able to play Bach two and three-part inventions, easier Haydn and Mozart sonatas, easy accompaniments, hymns and chorales. If the student plans to begin organ as part of his first year's work he should have additional piano background to the extent that he is able to play preludes and fugues from the Bach "Well-Tempered Clavier," Beethoven sonatas, Brahms and representative works from the Romantic school.
>
> In voice to the extent that he is able to sing one or more standard songs from memory and to sing parts at sight at the corresponding level of Bach chorales.[64]

For those students who could not demonstrate the required proficiency, the requirements could be satisfied through taking pre-requisite courses that would be offered by the school of church music. Beyond the prerequisites, the requirements for graduation with the bachelor of sacred music degree included "the satisfactory completion in not less than three years of a minimum of 48 units of class credit preferably as specified in the recommended order of studies."[65] At least ten units had to be taken in other departments of the theological curriculum, and students were required "presentation of a recital in the student's applied field of major emphasis: organ, piano, or voice."[66] The school of church music printed a suggested curriculum map of a potential student's three-year program, as noted below:

First Year

	Session Hours
Music Foundations I	5
Conducting I	2
History of Sacred Music	2
Youth Choir Methods	2
Old Testament	2

---

63. SBTS, School of Church Music Bulletin (1946–47), 6.
64. SBTS, School of Church Music Bulletin (1946–47), 8.
65. SBTS, School of Church Music Bulletin (1946–47), 8.
66. SBTS, School of Church Music Bulletin (1946–47), 8.

Speech	2
Choir	1
Voice and Instrument	1 ½

Second Year

	Session Hours
Music Foundations II	5
Conducting II	2
Hymnology	2
Vocal Methods I	2
New Testament	3
Religious Education	2

Third Year

	Session Hours
Music Foundations III	5
Conducting III	2
Choral Repertoire	1
Vocal Methods II	2
Musical Ministries (Third Term)	2/3
Worship Music (Second Term)	2/3
Service Playing (organ majors)	1
Elective Hours	2
Choir	1
Voice and Instrument	1 ½
Major Recital	

In addition to the above curriculum of studies, the student must attend recital hours as scheduled, and physical education or exercise as specified.[67]

President Fuller asked for a curriculum strong on choral work. Frances Winters's course map included three years of conducting along with courses focusing on youth choir, choral repertoire, and vocal methods (vocal pedagogy) that also focused on choirs and choral singing. The other

---

67. SBTS, School of Church Music Bulletin (1946–47), 10.

courses such as the "History of Sacred Music" were also very choral-centric in their approach.[68] Finally, similar to the Westminster method, students in the school of church music were also required to participate in choir and choir rehearsals Monday through Friday.

Students of the First Class

On September 11, 1944, the members of the first class of the school of church music came to campus for placement exams. In an interview, Frances Winters later provided a wonderful account of what happened on this historic day:

> Auditions and placement examinations in music were held on the first day, and the music faculty was very much pleased with the musicianship and aptitude of the class as a whole. The goal for the year was met with twenty students matriculating. Four Louisville applicants were rejected after auditions. One of the latter was an older Louisville woman about whom and to whom some doubt had been expressed previously. The other three were wives of seminary students, all of whom had very little music background. All four were late applicants. It did not seem fair to these students to allow them to begin a course of study they did not give evidence of ability to complete satisfactorily. Other courses of study were worked out for the three student wives. They seemed to understand, and this evidence of attempting to meet a standard from the beginning was pleasing to the seminary faculty.
> Of the twenty entering students, seventeen were music majors, seven of them concentrating in organ. Three of the total number were men, and three majors were from the Training School. These students came from nine states.
> One of the problems in beginning this type of venture, was that there was really no nucleus from which to build. The school started from an idea, a need and property rather than people. There seemed to be nothing too tangible, from the students' point of view, to build on. New people of varying ages and experiences, coming in from all around the south, knew little if anything about Dr. Fuller's ideal, nor had they in most cases any real concept of what a ministry of music in its best sense was all about. How to inspire them and get the ideal over to them in such a way as to give them a true vision of what could be done was a big challenge to all

---

68. McElrath, interview by Carle, August 8, 1985, in "History," 51.

concerned. Credit must certainly be given to those first students. They were a stout-hearted group, interested in pioneering and very responsive to ideas new to them, and they formed the needed nucleus even sooner than expected.[69]

Another poignant reflection came from one of the first male students of that first class, Hugh T. McElrath. McElrath later became one of the school's faculty and one of the seminary's longest tenured and most loved professors. He recalls,

> As I look back to that first year, the thing that stands out in my memory was the sense of "togetherness"—the "esprit de corps" that prevailed in our small school. We were like one big family. In fact, we lived together for all practical purposes, because Cooke Hall was not only studio and classroom building, but second floor served as dormitory space for the girl students. There was a sort of undertone of excitement—a spirit of adventure among us students, because we felt that we were in on a new undertaking, a new experiment, if you please. We were pioneering, insofar as this institution was concerned, in a new area of instruction. We had found a new place of training that seemed to answer the unspoken needs of our lives as we faced the call of Christ. And so, in this little group, there grew up quickly a spirit which anywhere outside the fold of Christ's cause would have been amazing and totally unexplainable for such a brand new venture.[70]

McElrath's memories were shared as part of an address given at the 1952 yule log service. This Christmas time service within the school of church music was a fellowship rallying point for the students and faculty that was instituted by the Winters and that continued in unbroken tradition for many decades.

---

69. Winters and Winters, "Launching of School of Church Music," 23.
70. McElrath, "Ninth Observance of Yule Log Service," 53.

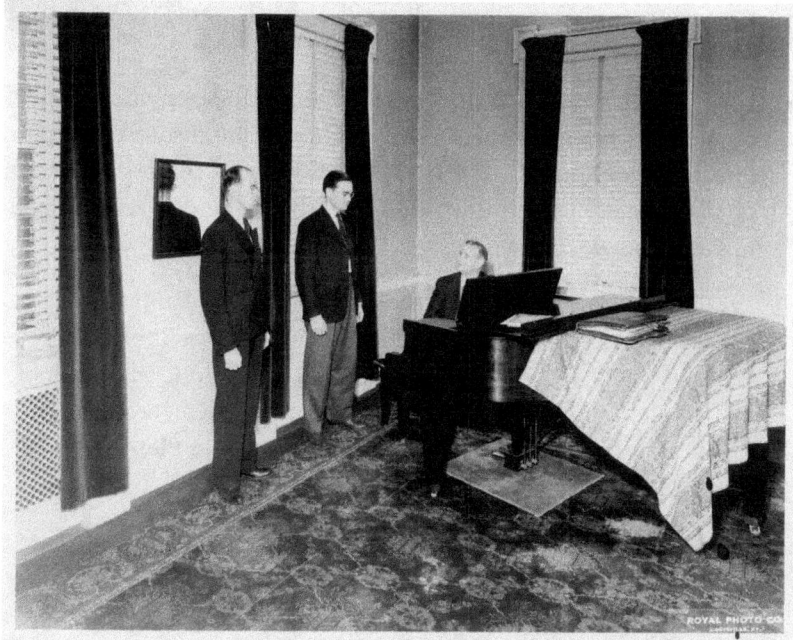

Inman Johnson (piano), Hugh T. McElrath (middle), and Howard Cates (left)

THE MASTER OF SACRED MUSIC DEGREE, 1947–50

The bulletin of the school of church music presented the master of sacred music degree in the 1946–47 publication. This graduate degree was intended to fulfill the goals of seminary President Fuller for the training of musicians in service of Southern Baptist churches. Applicants were required to demonstrate a higher standard of skill and knowledge in order to gain admission to this graduate degree program. The bulletin indicated the requirements in this way:

To qualify for full graduate standing, each applicant for admission to the master's course is required:

- To have a B.A. or B.S. degree with a major in music or a B. Mus. Degree from an accredited college or conservatory.
- For major emphasis in composition: To have an undergraduate major in theory.

- For major emphasis in musicology: To have an average of 85 in college work.
- For major emphasis in organ: To have an undergraduate major in organ. To have ability in transposition at sight, score reading, and improvisation. To have a balanced repertory of the organ literature of all schools, classic, romantic, modern, of the degree of difficulty indicated by the following:
  » Bach: (Widor-Schweitzer Edition) Book IV – Fantasy and Fugue in G Minor, Passacaglia and Fugue in C Minor; Book II – Prelude and Fugue in D Major, Toccata and Fugue in C Major; Book V, Sonata I, Sonata VI; The Liturgical Year (Riemenschneider Edition) – In Thee Is Gladness, Once He Came in Blessing.
  » Franck: Chorales, Piece Heroique.
  » Vierne: Symphony No. I.
  » Widor: Symphony No. V.
  » Reger: Passacaglia and Fugue, Benedictus.
  » Compositions of the same grade of difficulty for modern organ by representative American and foreign composers.
- To demonstrate by examination, skills and capacities in the following fields:
  » Harmony – written, aural, and keyboard
  » Proficiency in sight singing, and melodic, harmonic, and rhythmic dictation.
  » Counterpoint
  » The history and literature of music and the study of musical forms, analytic or applied.
- To demonstrate ability in applied music as follows:
  » In organ (see above)
  » In piano to the extent that he is able to play Bach two and three part inventions, easier Haydn and Mozart Sonatas, easy accompaniments, hymns and chorales. If the student plans to begin organ as part of his first year's work, he should have additional

» piano background to the extent that he is able to play preludes and fugues from the Bach "Well-Tempered Clavier," Beethoven sonatas, Brahms and representative works from the Romantic School.

» In voice by demonstrating a knowledge of recitative and ability to sing one of more of the less exacting arias of opera or oratorio and several standard songs from memory.[71]

Similar to the bachelor of sacred music degree, those students who could not demonstrate the required proficiency, requirements could be satisfied through taking pre-requisite courses that would be offered by the school of church music. The requirements for graduation with the master of sacred music degree were as stated:

The degree of Master of Sacred Music is awarded upon the following conditions:

- The completion of prerequisites as listed under the heading of Requirements.
- Satisfactory completion in not less than two years of a minimum residence (except for SBTS graduates) of minimum of 15 units of work (45 quarter hours). Of these at least 3 units credit must be taken in other departments of the theological curriculum.
- Presentation of a thesis or recital in the student's field of major emphasis as follows:

  » Composition: The composition and arranging of anthems and motets in both homophonic and polyphonic styles to be conducted in recital by the composer.

  » Musicology: The presentation and defense of an acceptable thesis on a faculty-approved subject.

  » Organ: Demonstration of playing ability, either in the form of a public recital or a performance before the faculty or a designated committee, such recital to be submitted in lieu of a thesis. It should be the student's objective to study an extensive and well-rounded

---

71. SBTS, School of Church Music Bulletin (1946–47); see Carle, "History of School of Church Music of SBTS," 67–68.

repertory considerably more comprehensive than that required or achieved during under-graduate study.⁷²

The required classwork for the master of sacred music was listed in the bulletin without a suggested order:⁷³

	Session Hours
Advanced Theory	2
Advanced Conducting	2
Advanced History	2
Seminar and Supervised Field Work	2
Thesis or Recital	1
Applied Music (Private Lessons)	1 ½–3
Choir (required, but with no credit)	
New Testament	3
Religious Education	2
Church Administration and Music Ministries	2
Worship and Worship Music	2
Service Playing (for organ majors only)	1
Hymnology	2
Choral Repertoire	1
Youth Choir Methods	2
Vocal Methods I and II (Vocal Pedagogy)	4

Compared to the curriculum of the bachelor of sacred music, the master of sacred music only required four further courses and a recital. Therefore, if a graduate of the school of church music's bachelor of sacred music entered the master's program, they could complete the requirements within one academic year. One of these four courses which was not an extension of the undergraduate curriculum was the seminar and supervised field work course. This course followed president Fuller's desire that the church music degrees remain significantly related to ministry in the local church. The bulletin described the course this way: "Practical demonstration in an actual church field of the student's ability to handle the organizational, administrative and musical problems of church choirs. A seminar for the

72. SBTS, School of Church Music Bulletin (1946–47), 7–9; see Carle, "History of School of Church Music of SBTS," 68.

73. SBTS, School of Church Music Bulletin (1946–47), 11; see Carle, "History of School of Church Music of SBTS," 68–69.

discussion of practical problems of the choir director and their analysis and suggested solutions accompanies the field work project."[74]

The Winters remained in the school of church music through the 1950–51 school year. The curricula for these two degrees remained basically the same throughout the Winters's time in the SCM. If not for Fuller's untimely death, the Winters, along with the degrees Frances created, would have remained longer as Baptist reflections of Fuller's "Westminster Plan."

THE UNEXPECTED PASSING OF ELLIS FULLER

In the summer of 1950, Fuller experienced a painful medical episode with kidney stones. Because his recovery was not progressing as quickly as had been hoped, Fuller canceled his plans to speak at the annual meeting of the Baptist World Alliance that summer in Cleveland. Still not sufficiently recovered, Fuller cancelled his autumn trips to both Japan and Nigeria. The family physician recommended a trip for rest and relaxation, so he planned a trip to the west coast. His trip proved anything but restful.[75] On his west coast trip, Fuller made stops in Texas, New Mexico, and Arizona. Due to Fuller's reputation as an evangelist, he was asked to preach at every stop, and he did.[76]

When Fuller and his wife reached San Diego, California, on Friday, October 27, he had already spoken fifteen times in the two weeks they had been away from Louisville, and he agreed to preach that night at the First Southern Baptist Church. He was in the best of spirits, and the congregation responded heartily to his witty opening remarks. He presented a part of the first chapter of Acts from memory and began to speak on "His Parting Prophecy." Fuller preached,

> From heaven to earth the Savior had come. Into the grave and out he had gone. To man and for man he had appeared through the space of forty days, showing himself alive after many indisputable proofs. He had shed his grave clothes and was arrayed in his resurrection garments. Now he was standing on the border line of two worlds, earth and heaven; on the line of demarcation between two great dispensations, law and grace.

---

74. SBTS, School of Church Music Bulletin (1946–47), 15; see Carle, "History of School of Church Music of SBTS," 70.
75. Shands, "Fuller – Man of God," 83.
76. "Dr. Fuller Goes to His Reward," 83–84.

> Never again will human ears hear audible words from those lips that had cried, "It is finished." He is about to depart this life. He turns back as it were, to make a final statement, which statement I am pleased to call his parting prophecy. Will you hear it? "But ye shall receive power after that the Holy Spirit is come upon you; and ye shall be my witnesses . . . ."[77]

At this point in his address, Fuller's speech foundered. He had completed his final sermon.

> He paused, stumbled slightly, and said, "I'm sorry, I can't go on." Men from the congregation reached Dr. Fuller before he fell. A doctor who was summoned took Dr. Fuller to the Quintard Hospital. After almost 24 hours, during which he was conscious most of the time, he slipped away quietly at 4:45 pm on Saturday, October 28.[78]

Fuller's funeral occurred on November 2 in Alumni Chapel. In fact, Fuller's funeral was the very first service to take place in Alumni Chapel. This location was most fitting, because Fuller had built Alumni Chapel to be the focal point of the seminary community's worship and a point of service for the SCM—his school of church music.[79]

With the inevitable selection of a new president, changes were coming to the SCM. In August 1951, *The Tie* reported that the trustees had elected Duke K. McCall as the seventh president of Southern Seminary. If the Winters believed they had already experienced criticism and abuse from the seminary community, they soon learned that things would grow worse.[80] Two weeks after the funeral of the Winters's infant daughter, a meeting to criticize their chapel leadership devolved into harsh verbal abuse, causing Frances to leave in tears followed by Donald. Frances had already blamed her daughter's death on the pre-natal pressures of running the SCM. After this meeting, "they felt the 'handwriting [was] on the wall,' if not for the SCM, at least for them as members of the faculty of the school."[81]

McCall did want to keep the school of church music, but he believed that the Westminster choir program that the Winters taught was

---

77. Shands, "Fuller – Man of God," 83.
78. Shands, "Fuller – Man of God," 84.
79. "Dr. Fuller Goes to His Reward," 6.
80. Carle, "History of School of Church Music of SBTS," 87.
81. Winters and Winters, interview, 88.

too restrictive for many Southern Baptist churches.[82] Harold Graves, who later became the president of Golden Gate Baptist Theological Seminary (now Gateway Baptist Theological Seminary), headed a search committee to find a dean for the SCM. According to an interview with McCall, the search criteria included someone with "an earned doctorate, administrative experience, and a commitment to church music, especially as a Southern Baptist."[83] He continued, "The man that the committee found was Forrest Heeren."[84]

---

82. McCall, interview, 88.
83. McCall, interview, 88.
84. McCall, interview, 88.

4

The School of Church Music, 1952–2000

FORREST HEEREN

IF THE WINTERS HAD struggled for academic credentials, Forrest Heeren excelled. Heeren was born in 1915 in Moline, Illinois. He earned his undergraduate degree from Augustana College in Rock Island, Illinois, and an MS from the University of Illinois. During his study at the University of Illinois, Heeren worked for two years on the staff of the department of music. During the two years Heeren worked on his MS, Heeren served as the conductor of the Illinois state chorus where he directed over three thousand singers. He later taught for a year as the head of the voice and choral departments of the University of Minnesota, Duluth Branch.[1] Heeren ceased working for the University of Minnesota when he was called into service with the Army during World War II. In 1942, Heeren began serving in a musical capacity as a chaplain's assistant and also as part of the Army's public relations divisions—again giving special attention to musical tasks.[2]

After serving in World War II, Heeren earned an MA from Columbia University in New York City, and subsequently began a doctor of education degree at Columbia, majoring in music. Like many music students in New York, Heeren sang whenever and wherever he could. While studying in New York, Heeren was selected by Arturo Toscanini to sing in the NBC choir.[3] After finishing his required residency at Columbia, Heeren became the head of the voice department at the Texas college that would later

---

1. "Heeren Chosen to Direct Music School."
2. "Heeren Chosen to Direct Music School."
3. Carle, "History of School of Church Music of SBTS," 91.

become North Texas State University in Denton, Texas. Through this opportunity, God led him away from his Methodist roots and into service as the minister of music at First Baptist Church, Denton. By anyone's criteria, Forrest Heeren could be deemed successful, especially considering that all of these achievements came by the age of twenty-nine.[4]

Heeren Comes to Southern

Heeren became convinced that, by training singers for careers in opera, his school in north Texas was doing its students a great injustice by preparing them for jobs that were nearly unattainable. Heeren's dissatisfaction with North Texas along with his positive experiences at First Baptist Denton led him to accept an offer to join the faculty of the School of Sacred Music at SWBTS in Fort Worth.[5] Harold Graves, serving as the chairman of President McCall's search committee for a dean of the school of church music, learned of Heeren and soon after brought him to Louisville for conversations with McCall in March of 1952. Not long afterwards, the seminary newspaper, *The Tie*, printed this article concerning Heeren's election as the New Dean of the SCM:

> Dr. Forrest Heeren of Fort Worth, Texas, was named Director of the Seminary's School of Church Music by the Board of Trustees meeting in annual session on March 11–12, 1952. Dr. Heeren is the school's first director since its founding in 1944. Prior to the late President Fuller's death in October, 1950, Dr. Fuller served as the director of the Music School.

Although there were still opponents to the SCM on Southern's campus, McCall wanted the SCM to continue—however, he absolutely did not want to continue Fuller's role as music school director.[6] McCall asked the Board to name a director in hopes that the SCM might continue to grow the quality and number of its faculty and student body.[7]

The most significant challenge for Graves as he searched for a director had been finding a man who was not only a qualified musician and administrator but also someone who knew the needs of Southern Baptist churches in the field of church music. In announcing Heeren's hiring, *The*

---

4. Heeren, interview by Carle, July 6, 1984, in Carle, "History," 91.
5. Heeren, interview, 92.
6. Heeren, interview, 92.
7. Heeren, interview, 92.

Tie mentioned Heeren's musical and ecclesial qualifications. The article recounts how "at the close of World War II, Dr. Heeren became professor of music and resident tenor at the North Texas State College, Denton, Texas, the fourth largest music school in the United States," and continues, "for the past two and a half years he has been Head of the Voice Department of the School of Sacred Music, Southwestern Baptist Theological Seminary, Fort Worth, Texas."[8] The article continued by describing his church music experiences: "He has served as Choir Director and Minister of Music for the following churches: Illinois Wesleyan Foundation, University of Illinois; First Methodist Church, Duluth, Minnesota; First Baptist Church, Denton, Texas; and College Avenue Baptist Church, Fort Worth, Texas. At the College Avenue Church, Dr. Heeren has conducted a fully graded choir program."[9] Finally, the article provided some personal information concerning Heeren's spiritual journey and family: "Reared in a Methodist home, Dr. Heeren became a Baptist 'for theological reasons,' he says. Mrs. Heeren is of Swedish Baptist extraction. She also is a musician, holding a B. S. in music, and serving as organist and soloist. The Heerens have two children, adopted, ages five and three. The family expects to come to Louisville June 1."[10]

Heeren's Philosophy, McCall's Support, and Changes to the SCM

Administratively, Heeren entered the school at the start of a cycle of growth. Heeren's strategy for growth began with good facilities, which then attracted strong faculty that ultimately drew strong students. This three-part cycle continued to repeat itself, generating a continual need for greater resources.[11] Heeren reported that at one point, McCall asked him why he did not choose to limit enrollment rather than continually ask for more instructional space, equipment, and faculty. Heeren replied, "[In order] for the cream to rise to the top, there has to be milk."[12] Heeren's desire for more room, equipment, and faculty required significant support from McCall. Gratefully for Heeren, McCall responded positively. In the October 1952 issue of *The Tie*, President McCall took his entire presidential column to lay

---

8. "Heeren Chosen to Direct Music School."
9. "Heeren Chosen to Direct Music School."
10. "Heeren Chosen to Direct Music School."
11. Heeren, interview, 102.
12. Heeren, interview, 102.

out his understanding of the seminary's need to train musicians for worship leadership in Southern Baptist churches.[13]

McCall began his article by astutely identifying that "the problem of music is much larger than the picking of hymns to fit the sermon and the personal relations of the choir members."[14] McCall went on to describe how the level of music appreciation held by church members had been raised through the increasing impact of music education in the public schools and broadcast media. McCall used this point to forecast an increasing demand for trained musicians and musical leadership in churches.[15] McCall described the growing difficulty for churches to find instrumentalists and directors to train their choirs and lead the music in their worship services. Though McCall was cognizant of the continual need for volunteers to serve in music and other church ministries, his article revealed a clear understanding of the need churches had for professional church musicians who would plan and rehearse and lead multiple choirs, ensembles, and high-quality musical worship services.[16]

The center of McCall's article first pointed to what had been recent successes in the SBC, as many SBC colleges had recently enlarged their music departments and how four of the SBC's seminaries had schools of church music.[17] However, McCall made the point that all SBC colleges and seminary music schools combined were not producing even "one-tenth of the trained musicians needed."[18] McCall did not mince words as he placed the majority of the blame for this lack of trained church musicians squarely on the shoulders of pastors and denominational leaders who "have failed to lay the challenge of a career in church music on the hearts of talented young men and women."[19] McCall pointed to the SBC's continual challenge to young men and women to take up the call to missionary service or to young men to pastor, but that there had been no such zeal pointing young believers towards service through church music and worship.[20] McCall, writing in pastoral tone, proclaimed that "the churches need such laborers

13. Carle, "History of School of Church Music of SBTS," 106; McCall, "Thinking Aloud," 2–3.
14. McCall, "Thinking Aloud," 2–3.
15. McCall, "Thinking Aloud," 2–3.
16. McCall, "Thinking Aloud," 2–3.
17. McCall, "Thinking Aloud," 2–3.
18. McCall, "Thinking Aloud," 2–3.
19. McCall, "Thinking Aloud," 2–3.
20. McCall, "Thinking Aloud," 2–3.

and I believe that the God of the harvest has provided them if we will take the trouble to seek them."[21]

McCall went on to describe the training for church musicians and worship leaders. As he did, McCall pointed to the similarities in quality between training a musician for the stage and training for leadership in the church, but pointed out the difference in content. McCall wrote of how he believed that young men and women who chose church music as a vocation should receive at least part of their training in an institution where the music and worship found in Southern Baptist churches was a primary concern.[22]

Concluding his manifesto for church music and worship training at Southern Seminary, McCall delivered his most clear and provocative admonition for SBC pastors:

> Personally, I am thinking about refusing to recommend a music director to the pastor of any church until that pastor has preached at least one sermon containing a reference to the opportunities of life commitment to church music. The only reason I have not adopted that requirement is that, in the face of the shortage of trained church musicians, I simply do not know of anyone whom I can recommend anyway. Instead, therefore, I will content myself with the plea that all Southern Baptists endeavor to send their talented young men and women to a school where their talents can be developed for investment in the service of God.[23]

McCall's feelings were clear on the need for church music and worship leader training. This firm conviction and his relationship with Forrest Heeren would provide a solid foundation upon which the SCM could flourish for the next several decades.

Heeren's philosophy of church music education was founded on ministry in the Southern Baptist context rather than the Westminster choir system. As Heeren developed his curriculum, he moved away from the Westminster focus on choirs to one that emphasized the individual training of students in their studio lessons along with a strong priority on music education applied to church ministry.[24] These goals were shaped by Heeren's experience; he had observed how many musicians who focused

21. McCall, "Thinking Aloud," 2–3.
22. McCall, "Thinking Aloud," 2–3.
23. McCall, "Thinking Aloud," 2–3.
24. Heeren, interview, 100–102.

on conducting did not have well-developed personal musical performance skills—skills that he observed were a great necessity in church music.[25]

Heeren believed in and advocated a three-sided approach that included musicianship, performance, and ministry.[26] Part of his method for achieving the first two sides of his triangle came through the hiring of academically credentialed faculty. In addition to their teaching responsibilities, Heeren expected new faculty to contribute as performers and scholars.[27] Heeren's first new hires came in 1953 with violinist Walter Odell Dahlin and tenor Farrold Stephens (both served 1953–57). Dahlin and Stephens were key in helping Heeren pull off his first major musical concert, a full performance of Handel's *Messiah*, in December 1952. This performance of *Messiah* was very important because it not only demonstrated Heeren's strong musical leadership, but it also effectively replaced the vespers services that had been instituted by the Winters during the previous administration. These two professors were just the beginning. In the September 1955 edition of *The Tie*, Heeren wrote an article in which he provided a sort of state of the school address, including a listing of ten full-time faculty.[28] These faculty, as listed in the 1956–57 *SBTS Academic Catalog*, were as follows: Forrest Heeren (dean, music administration, choral and vocal techniques), Walter Dahlin (conducting, music history, instrumental methods), Paul Jenkins Jr. (organ, service playing), Hugh T. McElrath (voice, hymnology, musicology), Donald Packard (theory, composition), Mary Raper (piano, theory, music literature), Charme Riesley (voice), Farrold Stephens (voice, vocal literature), Mabel Warkentin (piano, theory, methods [music education]), and James Wood (voice, repertoire).

In his article, Heeren described how the SCM had grown in faculty, resources, and students. Heeren shared that the SCM faculty had grown to ten full-time professors, three part-time instructors, six resident artists, and a full-time assistant. Heeren also described how the curriculum was continuing to develop, eliminating duplication of fields and creating new courses in expanded areas.[29] Heeren described the "ample" piano practice facilities along with organ equipment including a four-manual Aeolian-Skinner, four two-manual Moller practice organs, a Baldwin and

---

25. Heeren, interview, 102.
26. Heeren, interview, 100.
27. Heeren, interview, 101.
28. Heeren, "SCM Begins Twelfth Year," 3.
29. Heeren, "SCM Begins Twelfth Year," 3.

Hammond electric organ, and a three-manual Schlicker recital and teaching organ.[30] Heeren noted the SCM's growing library holdings: "hundreds of books, vocal and instrumental scores, multiple copies of choral materials, and phonograph records have been added to the library to accommodate the graduate program."[31] His hopes were that the SCM would be able to meet the graduate standards of the National Association of Schools of Music (NASM), along with standards required by the American Association of Theological Schools (ATS).[32]

Duke McCall, President 1951–1982

---

30. Heeren, "SCM Begins Twelfth Year," 3.
31. Heeren, "SCM Begins Twelfth Year," 3.
32. Heeren, "SCM Begins Twelfth Year," 3.

Forrest Heeren, Dean 1952–1981; and Mrs. Phyllis Heeren

DEGREE CHANGES

In the 1953–54 SCM catalogue, Heeren updated his title which had been changed to dean of the SCM rather than director because the SCM was now officially connected to the seminary. Two bachelor's degrees were now offered, the bachelor of sacred music and bachelor of sacred music education. The prerequisites for both degrees remained the same as in the previous administration and the requirements for both were incredibly similar with only the exception of the third year of courses which an extra elective course in Christian education each semester along with the ability for more flexibility for instrumental applied students.[33] The three-year course map for the BSM included the following:

First Year

---

33. SBTS, *Academic Catalog (1953–54)*, 37–39.

Ponder Anew What the Almighty Can Do

First Semester	Hours in Class	Credit
Theory Ia	6	4
Diction (Vocalists Only)	(1)	(1)
Religious Education	2	2
Choir Methods	2	2
New Testament	5	5
Applied Music Major	1	2
Applied Music Minor	2	1
(Class Piano or Voice)		
Choir (3); Oratorio Society (2)	5	1
Vocalists	24	18
Instrumentalists	23	17
Second Semester		
Theory Ib	6	4
Diction (Vocalists Only)	(1)	(1)
Conducting	3	2
Choir Methods	2	2
Religious Education or Theology	2	2
Hymnology	3	3
Applied Music Major	1	2
Applied Music Minor	2	1
(Class Piano or Voice)		
Choir, Oratorio Society	5	1
Vocalists	25	18
Instrumentalists	24	17

Second Year

First Semester	Hours in Class	Credit
Theory IIa	5	4
Advanced Conducting	2	2
Music History and Literature	3	2
Vocal Literature and Interpretation	2	2

The School of Church Music, 1952–2000

(Sacred Solos)		
Religious Education	2	2
Applied Music Major	1	3
Applied Music Minor	½	1
(If class piano, 2 hours in class)		
Choir, Oratorio Society	5	5
	20 ½	17

Second Semester

Theory IIb	5	4
Advanced Conducting	2	2
Music History and Literature	3	2
Instrumental Methods	2	2
Anthem Repertory	3	3
Applied Music Major	1	1
Applied Music Minor	½	1
(If class piano, 2 hours in class)		
Choir, Oratorio Society	5	1
	21 ½	18

Third Year

First Semester	Hours in Class	Credit
Theory III (Counterpoint)	4	4
Vocal Pedagogy	2	2
Service Playing and Accompanying (Instrumentalists Only)	(2)	(1)
Elective	4	4
Religious Education	2	2
Applied Music Major	1	3
Applied Music Minor	½	1
Choir, Oratorio, Ensemble	6	1 ½

Vocalists	19 ½	17 ½
Instrumentalists	21 ½	18 ½

Second Semester

Analytical Technique	2	2
Arranging II	2	2
Vocal Pedagogy	2	2
Service Playing and Accompanying (Instrumentalists Only)	(2)	(1)
Church Music Administration	2	2
Elective	2	2
Applied Music Major	1	3
Applied Music Minor	½	1
Choir, Oratorio, Ensembl	6	1 ½
Vocalists	17 ½	15 ½
Instrumentalists	19 ½	16 ½

[34]

In order to graduate with the master of sacred music degree, students had to fulfill prerequisites embodying the musical diversification that Heeren sought to build into the degree:

> To qualify for full graduate standing, each applicant for admission to the master's course is required:
>
> A. To have a B.A. or B.S. degree with a major in music or a B. Mus. degree from an accredited college or conservatory.
>
> B. 1. For a major emphasis in theory:
>
>   a. To have a minimum of 24 semester hours in theory courses, at least 4 hours of which should be in counterpoint.

34. SBTS, *Academic Catalog (1953–54)*, 34–36.

2. For a major emphasis in composition:

   a. To have an undergraduate major in theory, including counterpoint.

   b. To submit with the application an original composition in one of the developmental forms.

3. For a major emphasis in musicology:

   a. To have an average of 85 in college work

4. For a major emphasis in church music administration:

   a. To have completed satisfactorily approximately 60 semester hours of music for the Bachelor's degree.

5. For a major emphasis in organ: [not changed from previous requirements]

6. For a major emphasis in piano:

   a. To have an undergraduate major in piano or to present a recital on the senior level (at discretion of faculty)

7. To have a background of repertory representing all periods of piano literature.

Level of difficulty is suggested by the following:
Bach: 3-part Inventions
    Preludes and Fugues (Well-Tempered Clavier)
    French and English Suites
Haydn and Mozart sonatas
Beethoven Sonatas Op. 2, 10, 14, 27, 28, 31
    Schumann Fantasy pieces, Op. 12: Papillons
    Chopin Nocturnes, Waltzes, Preludes
    Brahms Intermezzi
    Debussy Children's Corner Suite
    Contemporary pieces such as:
Bartok: Mikrokosmos

Prokofieff: Visions Fugitives

    Barber: Excursions

      8. For a major emphasis in voice:

          To have performed a senior recital comprising representative examples of Italian, French, German, and English songs.

  C. To demonstrate, by examination, skills and capacities in the following fields:

    1. Harmony: written, aural, and keyboard

    2. Proficiency in sight-singing, and in melodic, harmonic, and rhythmic dictation.

    3. Counterpoint (for theory and composition majors).

    4. The history and literature of music and the study of musical forms, analytical or applied.[35]

More Degree Changes

One of the ways that Heeren worked to bring the SCM into a more equal footing with the school of theology was to eliminate the bachelor's degree and begin offering doctoral degrees. To accomplish this, Heeren continued to add faculty with terminal degrees who could bolster the school's reputation and desirability to potential students. One notable addition came in June of 1958 when he hired Dr. G. Maurice Hinson as head of piano studies.[36] The addition of the doctoral degree offering was announced in the 1955–56 *SBTS Academic Catalog*, one full year before the admission of the first students. The year-long buffer was in place so that several other necessary changes could be made prior to offering the doctor of sacred music degree (DSM). One of these necessary changes came to the master of sacred music curriculum (MSM). Although Heeren's previous catalog descriptions retained basic elements from the previous administration's wording, Heeren took the time to make more significant changes in keeping with his philosophy. One of these changes involved faculty recitals and concerts. A faculty recital series was scheduled each year on campus as well as faculty concerts in various SBC churches. Based on archival programs and interviews, Maurice Hinson performed more of these concerts than any other

---

35. SBTS, *Academic Catalog (1953–54)*, 20–22.
36. "Two Added to Music School Faculty," 3.

SCM faculty member.[37] Faculty and students continued to keep demanding choral performance schedules. In addition to semester-ending concerts, there were constant performances of large choral-orchestral works such as Handel's *Messiah*, Brahms' *Requiem*, and Mendelssohn's *Elijah*.[38]

Heeren had originally created "Regulations" that appeared to have some connection to the previous administration's "Regulation for Continuance in the School of Church Music." However, Heeren specifically noted how evaluations would be made concerning how students kept the "Regulations." Areas for evaluation included student juries, recital attendance, course sequences, minimum grades, and proficiency examinations.[39]

Maurice Hinson, faculty 1957–2015

---

37. "Programs: School of Church Music," quoted in Carle, "History of School of Church Music," 139.

38. "Programs," 140.

39. SBTS, *Academic Catalog (1958–59)*, 81.

THE DOCTOR OF SACRED MUSIC DEGREE

The final change made during the year before offering the DSM was the elimination of the bachelor of sacred music degree (BSM). Previously, if a MSM student had performed weakly during proficiency exams prior to entry, they would be added to the bachelor's level course corresponding to their area of needed remediation. Now that the bachelor's courses were gone, tutorial courses were introduced so that entering MSM students had a means to satisfy their remediation requirements.[40] When the doctor of sacred music was formally offered, the 1958–59 *SBTS Academic Catalog* stated the purpose of the degree:

> The purpose of doctoral studies is to provide for exceptional students an opportunity to prepare themselves adequately for positions of leadership and teaching in various facets of the church music field. The course leading to the degree of Doctor of Sacred Music emphasizes a high level of attainment in the academic, research and applied areas of music study.[41]

The need for trained leaders in churches had been a clear motivation for establishing a master's degree in sacred music. A need was also perceived for more people that could teach and train those who would train these needed church worship leaders. What better place could take up that godly call than the school of church music at Southern Seminary, under the leadership of Forrest Heeren?

Entrance exams for doctoral studies in church music were always considered rigorous at Southern Seminary. Throughout their existence, it became routine for prospective doctoral students, even recent master's degree graduates of the seminary, to take up residence for study and preparation for at least one year before taking their examinations.[42] Although "Preliminary Exams" were given later in the degree as the SCM's version of comprehensive exams, the entrance exams were considered particularly difficult. One masters and doctoral graduate from the late 1970s was Dr. Tim Sharp, who served as the executive director of the American Choral Directors Association from 2008–20. Sharp recounted in an interview that they [SCM faculty] knew that once someone was accepted into the

---

40. SBTS, *Academic Catalog (1956–57)*, 71–72, 77–79; SBTS, *Academic Catalog (1957–58)*, 70–71, 76–78; SBTS, *Academic Catalog (1958–59)*, 81–82, 88–90.

41. SBTS, *Academic Catalog (1958–59)*, 85.

42. Sharp, interview, September 1, 2021.

program, the person would finish the program. Sharp told how other schools would allow students to progress through the entire program and then have comprehensive exams at the end. This meant that a student could be ousted at the end. He recollected, "But the way we all termed it in those days was if you pass the [entrance exams] and get into the program, you will complete the program. It meant there was a pretty big learning curve between the master's and doctoral levels, so we had to get ready for what we knew were pretty intensive entrance exams to the DMA (successor to the DSM)."[43] The 1958–59 *SBTS Academic Catalog* indicated this concerning the entrance exams for the DSM:

> The applicant will be given an entrance examination of a comprehensive nature which will undertake to discover (1) the adequacy of the student's cultural background; (2) his ability to think clearly and write correctly; (3) his technical training in music; theory, church music methods and administration, hymnology, music history and literature, pedagogical and technical aspects of performing media; and (4) his aptitudes for graduate work and his purpose in undertaking it. The written comprehensive examination will be supplemented by a 45-minutes audition in the student's major applied music medium, conducting and sight-singing.[44]

After forty-four hours of study had been completed along with four major recitals or two recitals and a major research project/dissertation, "Preliminary Exams" were given to doctoral music students toward the end of their program.[45]

The catalog provided this description:

> The candidate will be required to take preliminary examinations in the areas of his special study, not earlier than the completion of his first full year of graduate study in this institution, or afterward not later than the end of his third year of candidacy.
>
> The examinations, written in nature, will be given according to a fixed schedule three times each session. These examinations as a whole must be passed satisfactorily if the student is to continue as a candidate for the degree. If the student fails his written examinations he may, upon recommendation of his committee of

---

43. Sharp, interview.
44. SBTS, *Academic Catalog (1958–59)*, 85.
45. SBTS, *Academic Catalog (1958–59)*, 87.

Instruction, and by permission of the faculty, be permitted to take the examinations once again.[46]

The "Preliminary Exams" given as one of the conclusions to the degree, not only functioned as a needed assessment vehicle, but they also added to the perceived compatibility between the SCM and other SBTS doctoral programs. To the rest of the seminary, these exams were simply the SCM's comprehensive examinations, similar to ones given at the end of the coursework stage within the PhD program.

THE CONTROVERSY OF 1957–58

A full account concerning this historically significant event in seminary history which occurred during the McCall administration is fully examined in Gregory Wills's book *The Southern Baptist Theological Seminary 1859–2009*, so the following only touches on the event's impact on the SCM.[47] Controversy arose when thirteen professors in the school of theology openly challenged President Duke McCall's ability to lead the seminary. Former dean of the school of religious education, Allen Graves, "believed that one of the greatest fomenters of rebellion against McCall, though not in highly visible ways, was the then venerable professor of homiletics, J. B. Witherspoon."[48] Witherspoon and the other twelve vocally resented how under the leadership of Fuller and now McCall was diversifying the seminary's role beyond what they thought was its proper task. By proper task, the rebellious professors considered the seminary's goal to be instruction in "the body of divinity" which included Old Testament, New Testament, theology, and church history.[49] Interestingly, despite the fact that one of the group's main points of contention involved the existence of schools in the seminary beyond the school of theology, the rebellious group attempted to recruit professors from each of the other schools to bolster their cause. Only one church music professor was invited to join but declined. This anonymous (at the time) church music professor said of the incident, "I had good reason to ally myself with their cause. However . . . I declined the

---

46. SBTS, *Academic Catalog (1958–59)*, 87.
47. Wills, *SBTS 1859–2009*, 351–404.
48. Graves, interview by Carle, June 24, 1984, in "History," 151.
49. Graves, interview, 151.

invitation to join them though I was thoroughly in sympathy with most, if not all, their grievances."[50]

Heeren instructed his faculty to keep out of the conflict.[51] Ultimately McCall dismissed all thirteen faculty and remained as president to lead Southern for nearly thirty years. McCall's strong support of Heeren and the SCM had been reciprocated and afterwards the SCM went on to enjoy a long period of sustained growth.

NOTABLE FACULTY, PROGRAM, AND FACILITY ADDITIONS

From 1960 until the end of his deanship in 1981, numeric growth experienced in the student body seems to indicate that Heeren's philosophy of church music and worship leadership training was in lock-step with the prevalent worship culture of many Southern Baptist churches. Many of the faculty hired by Heeren between the mid-1950s and 1978 were influential teachers and mentors for a generation of Southern Baptist worship leaders. Some of these faculty include G. Maurice Hinson, piano (1957); Jay Weldon Wilkey, voice (1963); J. Phillip Landgrave, voice, church music methods, and composition (1965); Donald P. Hustad, organ and philosophy of church music (1966); Richard R. Lin, voice, choral methods, and conducting (1967); Martha Powell, music bibliography, and music librarian (1969); G. Douglas Smith, instrumental ensembles, applied brass, and conducting (1975); Ronald E. Boud, organ (1977); Ronald A. Turner, voice, choral methods, applied voice, and church music methods (1977); and Boyd M. Jones II, organ (1978).

These faculty hires represent Heeren's desire to remain at the forefront of church music education by offering students course preparation for growing trends in church worship, such as Smith's hiring for instrumental/orchestra music and Landgrave's focus on the (then) new field of contemporary church music. Heeren's diversification of the foundational master of church music degree into a variety of focus options may have contributed to growth of the student body, but achieving better facilities also played a significant role. In 1970, Cooke Hall was opened. Under Heeren's leadership, the SCM moved to an attractive and functional location that connected to the rear of the Alumni Chapel. The new building included classrooms,

50. McElrath, interview by Carle, August 7, 1985, in Carle, "History," 152.
51. Heeren, interview, 153.

studios for private lessons, administrative offices, rehearsal halls, and practice rooms—everything needed for a growing music school. Moving the SCM from across campus to a new facility near the main worship and concert space of the seminary was a significant step in bringing the facilities of the SCM in line with achieving Heeren's goals for the school.

When Heeren retired in 1981, reflections on his leadership confirmed the significant and fruitful impact of his time as leader of the SCM. The July 1981 edition of *The Tie* printed a column in honor of his retirement. This column told of a "resolution" presented to Heeren by the faculty of the SCM, praising their colleague as a person who had "fulfilled his calling in an extraordinarily creative manner."[52] The column went on to recount how when Heeren was appointed as the dean in 1952, the SCM had "approximately 40 students enrolled, most of whom were not college graduates," and how the school in 1981 had over 350 full-time residential students enrolled in master and doctoral degrees and how the school was accredited by three associations: NASM, ATS, and the Southern Association of Colleges and Schools (SACS).[53] The article concluded by sharing of a musical festschrift presented to Heeren, including performances by various musical groups from the seminary at a special service in Alumni Chapel.[54] This growth in the student body would continue through much of the deanship of his successor, Milburn Price.

Milburn Price

When Heeren retired after nearly thirty years of continual growth, the SCM looked for new leadership. They found the next dean in Milburn Price, who was serving as the chairman of the music department at Furman University, located in the city of Southern Seminary's birth—Greenville, South Carolina. Price was forty-three years old and like Heeren, came with both academic and ministerial credentials.

Price was born in the small community of Electric Mills, Mississippi, a town that disappeared from existence when its hospital and major industrial employers closed.[55] Price's mother was a public-school music teacher

---

52. "Heeren Ends 29-Year Tenure."
53. "Heeren Ends 29-Year Tenure."
54. "Heeren Ends 29-Year Tenure."
55. Hardy, "New School of Church Music Dean."

whom Price confessed, "Always had me singing in public."[56] As a boy, Price auditioned for the Apollo Boys Choir of Dallas. He was selected to be part of the twenty-five-person choir and spent the ages of ten and eleven touring throughout the United States, singing concerts and doing homework on a bus.[57] During his middle and high school years, Price became "sidetracked" by sports.[58] His diversion from music became the source of partial scholarships to the University of Mississippi.[59] "Indeed, just weeks before entering college, Price was still trying to decide on a career: law, sports journalism, coaching, or music. Music soon won out, however."[60] After earning his bachelor's degree in music from the University of Mississippi, Price continued on, earning a master's degree in music history and literature from Baylor University and a doctorate in church music (DMA) from the University of Southern California, with an emphasis in voice and conducting.[61] After earning his doctorate, Price moved to Greenville, South Carolina, and the department of music at Furman University, where he later became the chair of the department.[62] *The Tie* alluded to Price's early calling to ministry while announcing his new deanship. An article recounted how, when Milburn Price was studying toward a bachelor of music degree more than 20 years before, he thought he was "headed toward the music ministry in a church."[63] The article continued, "A few years later, while working on a graduate degree in music at Baylor, he 'felt a call to the teaching ministry related to church music.' He will be installed as dean during the 1981 Church Music Institute, October 19–22, on the seminary campus."[64]

While in his role as administrator and faculty at Furman, Price served as part-time and interim music minister for several Baptist churches in the Greenville area. Price's other notable musical activities and honors included conducting the Greenville civic chorale and receiving awards from the American Society of Composers, Authors, and Publishers (ASCAP) for

---

56. Hardy, "New School of Church Music Dean."
57. Hardy, "New School of Church Music Dean."
58. Hardy, "New School of Church Music Dean."
59. Hardy, "New School of Church Music Dean."
60. Hardy, "New School of Church Music Dean."
61. Hardy, "New School of Church Music Dean."
62. Hardy, "New School of Church Music Dean."
63. Hardy, "New School of Church Music Dean."
64. Hardy, "New School of Church Music Dean."

his choral arrangements and compositions.[65] Price's compositions included "texts and music for several hymns, including three selections in the new Baptist Hymnal [1975]."[66] Price also completed a revised edition of William J. Reynold's *A Survey of Christian Hymnody* under a new title, *A Joyful Sound: Christian Hymnody.*[67]

In 1970, under Heeren's leadership, Cooke Hall had been constructed to be the new home of the school of church music. Ten years later, the SCM had outgrown its facilities. In Price's words, "This building was designed to accommodate a maximum of 170 music majors. Last year there were 291 degree-earning students."[68] Price attributed the "phenomenal growth of the School of Church Music" to the "increased importance and excellence of the program."[69] Price's comments were noteworthy, and positive. In 1980, there were indeed 291 full-time residential church music students enrolled in masters and doctoral church music degrees, but the total number of church music students was actually greater—nearly 350.[70] The number of students studying and rehearsing in the modestly-sized Cooke Hall made life in the SCM crowded and challenging.[71]

Price's goals also included the desire to capitalize on the SCM's relationship with community arts organizations like the Louisville orchestra. Price told an interviewer from the *Louisville Courier Journal*, "We have the resources to produce an absolutely first-rate choir."[72] The newspaper writer continued, "He hopes the seminary choir will enjoy a close relationship with the orchestra, similar to that between the famous Westminster College Choir and the New York Philharmonic Orchestra and the Philadelphia Orchestra."[73] It is interesting to note that even forty years later, the goals of SCM leadership still displayed a desire to replicate successes of the Westminster choir program.

---

65. Hardy, "New School of Church Music Dean."
66. Hardy, "New School of Church Music Dean."
67. Hardy, "New School of Church Music Dean."
68. Hardy, "New School of Church Music Dean."
69. Hardy, "New School of Church Music Dean."
70. "Heeren Ends 29-Year Tenure."
71. "Heeren Ends 29-Year Tenure."
72. Hardy, "New School of Church Music Dean."
73. Hardy, "New School of Church Music Dean."

BROAD ACCEPTANCE OF THE SCM

The SCM had struggled through its beginning years to achieve acceptance from the faculties of the school of theology and school of Christian education. By the time Milburn Price arrived on campus, this bias had all but dissolved. In an interview, Price described the relationship between faculty:

> We were very much integrated (during my deanship) despite whatever isolation Frances (Winters) felt during those early years. In those early years it was a new thing for a seminary to have a music program, so I guess everyone was having to become accustomed to that. But during the first years when I was there, I found there to be a very healthy relationship among the faculty. The theology faculty would come to music performances. Shortly after moving to Louisville, I became part time minister of music at Crescent Hill Baptist Church, where a number of seminary faculty member were members. So, I became acquainted with and interacted with them both in church and in seminary, which . . . made two sets of relationships. . . . easy to start becoming a part of that community.[74]

Curriculum and Faculty Expansion

In Price's first year, he commented that he desired to keep the positive enrollment growth and musical excellence going as it had been established by his predecessor, Heeren.[75] Due to student overcrowding, Price's initial goals included undertaking an expansion of Cooke Hall. The expansion completed during Price's tenure was the Cooke Annex, the portion of Cooke Hall that physically connects the original Cooke Hall to the rear of the Alumni Chapel, which includes an elevator, offices, basement practice rooms, and a second-floor organ practice room.

In terms of curricular change, Price also planned to add or expand some of the SCM's degree track offerings, music education, conducting, church music-drama, and instrumental music.[76] To oversee the church music education program, Price immediately brought Betty Bedsole on board. Price recounted in an interview,

---

74. Price, phone interview by author, August 9, 2021.
75. Hardy, "New School of Church Music Dean."
76. Hardy, "New School of Church Music Dean."

> We had an opening in music education or in church music education. In our searching around for a faculty member there, we discovered Betty Bedsole, who at that time was minister to children at First Baptist Church of Dallas, Texas . . . I became convinced that she was the person for our vacancy in music education when I saw her do a workshop on children's music education at the Southern Baptist Music Conference.
>
> And so we brought Betty on faculty with the understanding that she would get a doctoral degree in music education, which she did at the University of Illinois. And out of that the music education curriculum broadened.[77]

A second area of academic instruction Price expanded was that of conducting. Price commented that conducting was spread out among a variety of faculty members.[78] Price believed that Heeren had a perspective that conducting was something anybody could do, so the SCM did not need a conducting specialist.[79] Price felt that when retirements allowed, the SCM needed to have a person who would be the centerpiece for conducting and would be involved in heading up the program.[80] In the meantime, Price conducted the seminary choir for a few years. When Richard Lin and Donald Hustad retired, Price consolidated conducting into one position. At this point John Dickson joined the faculty. Price recounted, "I felt that the person who came into head up the conducting program needed to be the conductor of that flagship ensemble. So I turned over the seminary choir to John and I became conductor of the oratorio chorus."[81]

As far as expanding other degree areas, Dr. Doug Smith had been hired in 1975 as the first church music faculty to focus on instrumental music (apart from piano and organ) and Carl Gerbrandt had served to instruct and direct drama and its use in the church. A few years into his deanship, Price hired two professors to teach this popular facet of church music ministry: Ragan Courtney and Mozelle Clark Sherman. According to *The Tie*, Courtney was a graduate of New York's Neighborhood Playhouse School of Theater, and was widely known as a professional writer, actor and director, composing the musicals "Celebrate Life" and "Beginnings," and

77. Price, interview.
78. Price, interview.
79. Price, interview.
80. Price, interview.
81. Price, interview.

authoring the play, "Mountain Life."[82] The plan was for Courtney to work with Mozelle Sherman, Robert Hughes, and Raymond Bailey to develop the field of Christian drama.[83]

Mozelle Clark Sherman came to Southern from the fine arts faculty of Grand Canyon College in Phoenix, Arizona. She had extensive training in drama, communication arts, music composition, voice, and music theory. Sherman completed her master of music in voice from Indiana University and earned her PhD at the University of Wisconsin in Madison. While at Indiana University, Sherman studied with notable soprano and *bel canto* expert Ana Kaskas.[84] Sherman's focus at Southern Seminary was to grow the field of church music drama and work with other professors who taught in the areas of drama, telecommunications, oratorio, and youth musicals.[85] Concerning church music drama Price commented that he was grateful for Heeren's foresight in exploring the field. Heeren's early exploration into the field allowed Price to further develop the curriculum by adding more depth and breadth—helping the overall curriculum for church music to become the well-rounded course of study the entire faculty desired.[86]

It is worth noting that this issue of *The Tie* also announced the hiring of a number of theology and ministry faculty who later became well-known. Among the non-musical professors who joined the faculty in 1984 were William L. Hendricks, E. Glenn Hinson, Pamela Scalise, Danny Roy Stiver, and Molly Marshall-Green. A particularly noteworthy church music hiring in 1984 was Lloyd Lee Mims, who would later be appointed as the last dean of the SCM.[87]

---

82. "Seminary to Welcome Dozen New Profs," 3.
83. "Seminary to Welcome Dozen New Profs," 3.
84. "Seminary to Welcome Dozen New Profs," 3.
85. "Seminary to Welcome Dozen New Profs," 2.
86. Price, interview.
87. "Seminary to Welcome Dozen New Profs," 3.

Hugh T. McElrath, faculty 1949–1992 (standing); Donald Hustad, faculty 1966–1986 (sitting)

Phillip Landgrave, faculty 1965–2016

Richard Lin, faculty 1967–1983

Martha Powell, music librarian

Doug Smith, faculty 1975–2010

Price's Contributions

Milburn Price's twelve years as dean of the school of church music are remembered by many alumni from his era as the "glory days" of the SCM. When Price arrived, the SCM had nearly 350 church music students.[88] During Price's deanship the number of students surged far higher, then began to wane. However, by the 1988–89 academic year, there were still 539 total students enrolled in degree programs offered by the SCM.[89] Of these students, 422 were pursuing the master of church music (MCM) degree, sixty-four sought to earn the master of divinity in church music (MDivCM), and 35 were actively earning their doctor of musical arts (DMA).[90] It is no wonder that one of Price's initial goals included an expansion of Cooke Hall. "A major need right now is for this building to expand," Price said.[91] Cooke Hall was built so that a wing could be extended toward Lexington Road to provide for more space. He said he would like to get started

88. "Heeren Ends 29-Year Tenure."
89. SBTS, "Special Task Force."
90. SBTS, "Special Task Force."
91. Price, interview.

on that program as soon as possible.⁹² In comparison to enrollment figures of the SCMW at SBTS, these enrollment numbers of the SCM certainly suggest why many of those involved in the school remember these years as a "Camelot" time. Though the numbers were high and sustained through several years of the early and mid-1980s, student enrollment numbers in following years went into decline.⁹³ This situation will be discussed further in chapters 5 and 6.

When asked what he believed to be his most significant contributions while serving as dean, Milburn Price mostly cited curriculum development which he believed would better prepare students to serve the churches of the SBC. His first recollection was of the establishment in 1984 of the new degree, master of divinity with an emphasis in church music.⁹⁴ Price placed more emphasis on the master of divinity in church music as a degree option to try to encourage students towards a depth of theological understanding to their seminary education.⁹⁵ The theological depth of the degree came through combining of the core curriculum for the master of divinity degree and the music courses for church music.⁹⁶ Price believed this degree to be a very important curriculum development and an important development in helping prepare students for ministry because the coursework would broaden the scope of their theological preparation in addition to trying to provide a strong music foundation.⁹⁷

Price also felt satisfaction for his addition of a course that became a required class for degrees offered in the SCM, philosophy of music ministry. In an interview Price related,

> When I went to Southern, I began teaching a course called Philosophy of Music Ministry. I felt the topics we discussed were ones with which ministers of music needed to be acquainted. And so, I claimed as my own the teaching of the philosophy of music ministry class over those twelve years—I taught every student who came through the church music program. The philosophy of music ministry [course] was dedicated toward integrating a sense of musicianship and spirituality so that there was a healthy balance

---

92. Hardy, "New School of Church Music Dean."
93. SBTS, "Special Task Force."
94. SBTS, *Academic Catalog (1984–85)*.
95. Price, interview.
96. Price, interview.
97. Price, interview.

in the perspective of students when they left seminary to go into a position of ministry in a church.[98]

Price's course reflected a growing scholarly concern that church musicians and worship leaders understand and view their callings as ministers beyond the role of musician.

Though not specifically recalled by Price in his interview, the creation of this course may have been influenced by a ground-breaking work written by another SCM faculty member which became used as a textbook in church music programs at Christian schools and seminaries across the country. During Price's first year as dean, SCM organ faculty, well-known Billy Graham musician, and scholar Dr. Donald P. Hustad had published the first edition of his book *Jubilate: Church Music in Worship and Renewal*.[99] *Jubilate* became the standard for late-twentieth-century texts articulating a biblically-informed philosophy of church music. In his book, Hustad surveyed the anthropological and liturgical role of music as art and as a means of communication, arbiter of authority, and vital tool for Christian worship from Bible times through to the present day. Though Hustad's work was not intended specifically as a biblical theology of worship, this book was pivotal in helping launch a movement in scholarly confessional institutions to theologically validate the role and value of music as an element and medium for congregational worship.

MOHLER'S PRESIDENTIAL APPOINTMENT BRINGS TRANSITION TO SCM

As previously addressed in this dissertation, President Ellis Fuller believed in two commitments for SBTS: Southern "should be committed to the highest scholarship and to producing effective gospel preachers for Southern Baptist Churches."[100] Fuller's problem, according to SBC historian Greg Wills, was that his method of raising the level of scholarship of Southern Seminary involved the hiring of young, progressive faculty who had been educated in liberal American and European universities.[101] This trend ultimately conflicted with producing theologically orthodox preachers for SBC

---

98. Price, interview.
99. Hustad, *Jubilate!*
100. Wills, *SBTS 1859–2009*, 331.
101. Wills, *SBTS 1859–2009*, 332.

churches. During Fuller's short presidency, the faculty grew from eleven faculty to twenty-seven to keep up with the quantum leap in the seminary's student enrollment, which grew from 520 to 1009.[102]

Skipping ahead a few decades to the late 1970s and early 1980s, Paul Pressler and Paige Patterson led a plan designed to restore conservative values, preaching, and seminary education. Pressler and Patterson accomplished this feat by building a coalition of conservative Southern Baptists who voted for conservative platforms and denominational leaders in both the 1979 and 1980 conventions.[103] The new conservative majority sought to correct the SBC's slide into theological liberalism. The president of Southern Seminary during these events, Roy L. Honeycutt (1926–2004), was unwilling to make the changes required by this new denominational leadership. Ultimately, the SBTS board of trustees replaced Honeycutt with then thirty-three-year-old Dr. R. Albert Mohler Jr. Wills documents this transition fully in his book *Southern Baptist Theological Seminary 1859–2009*.

An article in the May/June 1993 edition of *The Tie* reported the administration transition as occurring in a meeting moments before adjournment by a trio of trustee resignations.[104] Southern Seminary's board of trustees ushered in a new era at its semi-annual meeting April 19–21 by bidding farewell to retiring President Roy L. Honeycutt and welcoming his successor, Mohler.[105] Mohler had been elected in March at a called meeting of the board in Atlanta. Besides delivering a series of devotionals at his first board meeting, Mohler did not participate formally in any of the deliberations.[106] Mohler assumed the presidency on August 1, 1993. *The Tie* mentioned the new prevailing atmosphere that was apparent in the Board meeting: "In contrast to the contested decisions and protracted debates of recent years, most business items sailed through sessions of the full board with minimal discussion. Opposition within the board has steadily dwindled since conservatives gained a clear majority in 1990 and began to assume leadership of key offices and committees."[107]

Another poignant retrospective description of Mohler's appointment appeared in the fall 2018 edition of the *Southern Seminary Magazine*. One

---

102. Wills, *SBTS 1859–2009*, 333.
103. Wills, *SBTS 1859–2009*, 437.
104. Wills, *SBTS 1859–2009*, 437.
105. Wills, *SBTS 1859–2009*, 437.
106. Wills, *SBTS 1859–2009*, 437.
107. "Seminary Board Meeting Marks Beginning of Era."

statement from the article read as follows: "Southern remained faithful to Boyce's vision until the early 20th century, when theological liberalism—the trickle down from German higher criticism—gradually replaced the school's confessional fidelity and held sway until Mohler's election as president in 1993."[108] The article continued, "In his opening convocation on August 31, 1993, Mohler began the difficult work of restoring the founder's vision with an historical address titled, 'Don't Just Do Something; Stand There!' calling for institutional faithfulness to the seminary's confession of faith, the Abstract of Principles."[109] A new day had clearly come to Southern Seminary, a day whose impact would be felt in many places, including the school of church music.

Mohler's election by the board of trustees triggered a series of faculty departures including the provost, two vice presidents, and two deans—one of them was Milburn Price.[110] The May/June 1993 edition of *The Tie* reported on Price's resignation this way: "As Southern Seminary prepares for the upcoming school year and a new presidential administration, the school will be facing key changes in its top administrative posts." The article continued, "Milburn Price, dean of the School of Church Music since 1981, will become dean of the School of Music at Samford University in Birmingham, Alabama. Previously Price chaired the music department at Furman University in Greenville, S. C."[111]

Though Mohler had tried to assure Price that "music is not on anybody's 'deal with it' list" and "you don't need to worry about anything. I really hope you stay," he [Price] recounted that he felt called to Samford.[112] The faculty of the SCM held a sense of nervousness because they felt that Price was "abandoning the ship."[113]

> Faculty at that time felt like he [Price] was abandoning the ship. There was enormous concern because the dean of the School of Christian Education did the same thing at the same time. There were enormous questions about whether the School of Social Work could survive. And so, then we saw somebody as golden, as committed, and as incredibly gifted as Milburn Price decide to

---

108. Robinson, "Three Changes in Theological Education," 52.
109. Robinson, "Three Changes in Theological Education," 52.
110. "Five Administrators Leave Positions."
111. "Five Administrators Leave Positions."
112. Price, interview.
113. Mims, interview.

leave. You know, we felt like even though he said his leaving was couched in a calling to Samford, we didn't believe it. We did not believe it.[114]

It was into this time of significant institutional and denominational transition that Lloyd Mims began serving as the interim dean of the school of church music.

Lloyd Lee Mims

Born in Bradenton, Florida, Lloyd L. Mims earned his bachelor of music education and master of music degrees from the University of Southern Mississippi in 1973 and 1976, respectively. Like many church musicians and worship leaders during the 1970s, Mims served in the local church as a combination minister of music and youth. Serving Bethany Baptist in Prentiss, Mississippi, during his undergraduate years and then full time afterwards at Collins Baptist Church in Collins, Mississippi, Mims also served as music specialist for the Mississippi Baptist Convention before coming to Louisville in 1979 to pursue his doctor of musical arts (DMA).[115]

In addition to service in local churches, Mims's background was also filled with lots of musical training and performances in both classical voice and string orchestra. Mims wielded a lyric and flexible baritone voice. Before coming to Southern, he won the 1977 Metropolitan Opera Auditions for his district, ultimately finishing as a regional finalist.[116] His vocal performing achievements paled when compared to his wife, Marilyn Williamson Mims. Marilyn, who also studied voice at the University of Southern Mississippi, with Jay Wilkey at Southern, and with Virginia Zeani at the University of Indiana Bloomington, won the national Metropolitan Opera national council auditions in 1986. This win propelled her to an operatic career at the Met which lasted until 1995. She received a diagnosis of endometriosis in 1995, at which point she became Artist in Residence at Southern. Despite her diagnosis, she gave birth to a daughter, Virginia, in 1997; Virginia was named in honor of Marilyn's beloved voice teacher from Indiana University.[117]

---

114. Mims, interview.
115. Mims, curriculum vitae.
116. Mims, curriculum vitae.
117. Palm Beach Atlantic Faculty Directory.

When Price left in 1993, Mims was an associate professor serving as chair of the voice department. After serving as interim dean of the SCM for 1993–94, he eventually was appointed dean during the 1994–95 academic year. Mims's service as interim lasted for one and a half years while Mohler decided who he wanted to serve as the full-time dean. "He kept trying to hire Terry York, but Terry kept turning him down. Finally, I think he got tired of dealing with it and just decided that I was okay. Literally that I was okay."[118] Terry York had completed his DMA at NOBTS and had served as the Sunday School board's music and worship consultant and coordinator for the 1991 *Baptist Hymnal*. In 2006, York left Lifeway Christian Resources to become professor of church music at Baylor University.

Milburn Price, Dean 1980–1993

Mims's Goals for the SCM

Due to the feelings of instability within the faculty of the SCM, Mims believed his mission to be one of providing stability as the school navigated its

118. Mims, interview.

way through a period of questioning its future.¹¹⁹ After Mims took the reins of the SCM, another necessary part of Mims's mission revealed itself—he needed to find a way to stem the tide of declining student enrollment.¹²⁰ As someone who, as a student, remembered the "glory days" of the late 1970s and early 1980s, Mims could see the enrollment decline happening before his very eyes. During Mims's tenure as dean, enrollment numbers in the SCM dropped from 329 full-time enrolled residential students (FTE) in 1993 to 207 FTEs in the year 2000.¹²¹

Mozelle Clark Sherman, faculty 1984–2016

MULTIPLE FACTORS CONTRIBUTING TO DECLINE IN ENROLLMENT

The "glory days" of the SCM, with its amazingly high enrollment numbers, were fueled by a superior faculty, an effective curriculum, a well-earned reputation of musical excellence, and a constituency of churches who trusted the SCM to provide quality graduates to lead their churches in

---

119. Mims, interview.
120. Mims, interview.
121. SBTS, "Special Task Force."

music and worship. The numeric success of the Heeren and Price years was undeniably aided by a strong congruence between the school's programs and the musical values and prevailing worship culture of many SBC churches. By the time Mims took the helm of the SCM, the prevailing worship culture in many SBC churches had shifted. Regarding the conservative resurgence of the SBC and its impact on the worship culture of SBC churches, former Samford University worship professor Eric Mathis noted, "The Controversy was the impending consequence of numerous issues and differences among Southern Baptists. When studied cumulatively, the worship practices and theologies held by conservative and moderate Southern Baptists function as signifiers for the deep and painful fragmentation that existed within and ultimately eroded the Southern Baptist Convention."[122] Mathis's evaluation continued, "Over time the differences among Southern Baptist became most visible in their worship gatherings, where the prayers, musical selections, Scripture passages, sermons, and response times of conservatives could not have been more different than, or opposed to, those of moderates, and vice versa."[123] According to Mathis, the result of this opposition was two Southern Baptist ways of worshiping: a conservative way and a moderate way.[124]

These "two ways" to worship became a contest where the enrollment of the SCM was the clear loser. Moderate churches that preferred a style of worship which matched the job competencies of SCM graduates would no longer consider Southern graduates because of their disagreements with Mohler and SBC conservatives. Conservative churches, who supported Mohler and who desired Southern graduates as their pastors, had generally moved to a newer worship style—a worship style they perceived SCM graduates as being ill-prepared to lead.[125]

Former faculty John Dickson (served 1985–2000) remembered a conversation with Mohler in which he (Dickson) told Mohler that he did not hold Dr. Mohler responsible for the enrollment drop, nor did he believe that his (Mohler's) changes did anything more than hasten the numeric decline that would have eventually occurred at the SCM.[126] Dickson based his opinion on the clear changes he observed in worship culture among the

---

122. Mathis, "Campaigning in House of God," 13.
123. Mathis, "Campaigning in House of God," 13.
124. Mathis, "Campaigning in House of God," 13.
125. Dickson, teleconference interview by author, August 31, 2021.
126. Dickson, interview.

majority of SBC churches. Dickson thought that the graduates produced by the SCM, along with their skill sets and understanding of worship, were becoming more and more outliers in the landscape of SBC worship.[127] These unique challenges were certainly laid on Lloyd Mims's shoulders. How would he lead the SCM through this new period of challenge?

ADDRESSING ENROLLMENT CHALLENGES WITH NEW CURRICULUM

There was no clear solution for Mims as he attempted to address declining student enrollment in the SCM. One of the challenges he faced was the curriculum. The standard degree in the SCM, the master of church music, had become, during the Heeren and Price years, as much of an academic option for those choosing to pursue a graduate music degree as it was a preparation for ministry in local churches. Some students came to Southern simply for a top-tier musical education—and many of these students were women. As the seminary turned back toward its theological roots, grounded in Reformed theology, preparing ministers for service in local SBC churches became reestablished as the seminary's fundamental purpose. For most within the conservative resurgence, with its emphasis on biblical inspiration and a conservative hermeneutic, this change also meant that only male pastors could lead the church and its worship.

Just as the master of divinity was the basic degree for pastors serving in the local church, the master of church music was the foundational degree preparing church musicians for vocational ministry in local churches. As the primary degree offered by the SCM to prepare vocational ministers in the church, the master of church music could no longer be viewed as the most appropriate course of study for female students. Mims's solution to this was to create two new degree tracks, the master of arts in worship leadership and the master of music. In an interview Mims related that at the time, "there was concern about women in ministry that raised so many red flags among the faculty in the music school that they wanted to offer an opportunity to bring in more students without that being a question. The MA (master of arts) and MM (master of music) were not degrees in ministry. And so, you know if a female wanted to get in those degrees, there was no question that they were ministry degrees, etc."[128]

127. Dickson, interview.
128. Mims, interview.

Although Mims resigned in 2000, just before these planned degrees became available to students, the curriculum for the master of arts in worship was described in the 2000–2001 catalog just as he intended:

> Although is it not as comprehensive as the 91-hour Master of Divinity with a worship track, the Master of Arts in Worship is designed to provide the student a solid background in biblical studies and Christian life and thought, combined with a core of studies in the field of worship.
>
> The worship and music studies portion of the curriculum involves the integration of music and worship, but a baccalaureate degree and proficiency in music are not prerequisites for this degree. Students choosing the Master of Arts in Worship should seek academic counseling from the Associate Dean of the School of Church Music and Worship.[129]

The curriculum indicated for master of arts in worship was as follows:

31980	Written Communication	0

Scripture and Interpretation (9 hours)

20200	Introduction to the Old Testament I or	
20220	Introduction to the Old Testament II	3
22200	Introduction to the New Testament I or	
22220	Introduction to the New Testament II	3
27700	Biblical Theology of Worship	3

Theology and Tradition (12 hours)

25100	Introduction to Church History I	3
25120	Introduction to Church History II	3
27020	Introduction to Christian Theology I	3
27040	Introduction to Christian Theology II	3

Ministry Studies (5 hours)

40010	Formation for Christian Ministry	2
32100	Personal Evangelism	3

---

129. SBTS, *Academic Catalog (2000–2001)*, 77.

The School of Church Music, 1952–2000

Supervised Ministry Experience (4 hours)
44994	Supervised Ministry Experience: Worship I	
44995	Supervised Ministry Experience: Worship II	2

Worship Studies (12 hours)
40200	The Worshipping Church	3
41085	Introduction to Hymnology	2
40222	Christian Worship in Contemporary Culture	3
Restricted Electives:		4
30200	Worship in the African-American Church	3
41100	Hymnology II	
41110	Baptist Hymnody	3
31510	Dramatized Scripture	2
40230	Leadership in Contemporary Expressions of Corporate Worship	2

Music Studies (4 hours)
41150	Introduction to Music Ministry	2
Music Ministry restricted electives (41000–41340)		2

Ensembles (4 semesters)   0

Electives in Church Music and Worship   2

Total Master of Arts in Worship Requirements   48

[130]

The master of music with an emphasis in church music degree that was created specifically "for laypersons only"[131] was described as follows:

> The degree Master of Music with an emphasis in Church Music is designed for laypersons (those not called to vocational ministry) who feel additional training in a specialized area of music ministry would make them more useful for service in the local church. The

---

130. SBTS, *Academic Catalog (2000–2001)*, 77.
131. SBTS, *Academic Catalog (2000–2001)*, 83.

degree comprises three specific components: (1) Biblical and theological studies to give a firm grounding in the foundational core of all ministry in the church, (2) Applied studies to allow the student to become a better performer in the church, either in a solo, choral, or instrumental capacity, (3) Specialized church music studies, in one of nine tracks, to help the student focus on a particular area of music ministry where his/her gifts might best be utilized in the church. These tracks are Children's Music Ministry, Youth Music Ministry, Instrumental Music Ministry, Teaching Ministry in the Church, Solo Ministry in the Church, Church Music Drama Ministry, Conducting, Composition, and Worship Studies.

Entrance requirements are: (1) acceptance by the seminary based on standards set up by the institution regarding laypersons, (2) a baccalaureate degree with a major in music form an institution with both N.A.S.M. and regional accreditation (students without such a degree, or its equivalent, may not pursue this degree), (3) each student will take Music Placement Examinations during orientation to determine his/her general music competence and candidacy into a particular applied emphasis, (4) any deficiencies discovered in the Music Placement Examinations will necessitate the completion of the appropriate pre-graduate areas of study that are prerequisites to all master's-level church music study at the seminary.

The curriculum indicated for the master of music with an emphasis in church music was as follows:

31980	Written Communication	0

Foundational Studies (14 hours)

20200	Introduction to the Old Testament I or	
20220	Introduction to the Old Testament II	3
22200	Introduction to the New Testament I or	
22220	Introduction to the New Testament II	3
27020	Introduction to Christian Theology I or	
27040	Introduction to Christian Theology II	3

Applied Studies (18 hours)
Emphasis One: Voice, Piano, Organ, or Instrumental
Solo Applied Area   8

Related Applied Area (4 hours of courses, not ensembles)
    Pedagogy of Major Area   2
    Elective (Youth Track requires 41125; Instrumental
    Trace requires 51660; Church Music Drama Track Requires   2
    41320)
Minor Applied Area (taken after proficiency exam is passed)
Vocalists take piano, pianists take organ, organists take voice,
Instrumentalists take voice or piano)   2
Ensembles (four semesters)   4
Recital Laboratory (four semesters)   0

Emphasis Two: Conducting or Composition
Solo Applied Area   4
Emphasis Applied Area   4
Related Applied Area (applied area electives)   4
Minor Applied Area (taken after proficiency exam is passed;
Vocalists take piano, pianists take organ, organists take voice,
Instrumentalists take voice or piano)   2
Ensembles (four semesters)   4
Recital Laboratory (four semesters)   0

Church Music Studies (15 hours)
41085   Introduction to Hymnology or
40200   The Worshipping Church   3
52600   Graduate Conducting   2
Elective in Composition, Arranging, or Analysis   2
Elective in Musicology   2

Ministry Track Courses (6 hours)
Children's Ministry Track
41150   Music Ministry w/ Preschoolers & Children   2
Elective in Children's Ministry   2
Elective in Children's Music Ministry   2

Youth Music Ministry Track

41170	Music Ministry w/ Adolescents & Adults	2
52650	Choral Techniques	2
	Elective in Youth Ministry	2

Instrumental Music Ministry Track

41135	Church Music Literature for Instruments	1
41230	Church Music Instrumental Administration	1
41242	Handbell Methods	1
51670	Seminar in Advanced Instrumental Writing	2
	Elective in Instrumental Music	1

Teaching Ministry in the Church Track

41125	Church Music Literature for Voices	1
	Additional Pedagogy in Applied Area	2
	Additional Literature electives in Applied Area	3

Solo Ministry in the Church Track (approval required)

Additional Applied Study	2–4
Additional Literature electives in Applied Area	2–4

Church Music Drama Ministry Track

41300	Producing & Staging Church Music Drama	2
52580	Church Music Drama Literature	2
	Elective in Church Music Drama	2

Conducting Track

52650	Choral Techniques or	
58800	Orchestra Instrumental Pedagogy	2
	Additional Applied Area electives	4

Worship Studies Track

40200	The Worshipping Church	3
	Elective in Worship Studies	3

Total Master of Arts in Worship Requirements 47
[132]

The third new degree program that came as a result of Mims's leadership was the master of divinity (MDiv) with emphasis in worship. This MDiv was an update of the older but still offered degree, master of divinity with emphasis in church music.[133] The degree description was as follows:

> The Master of Divinity is the foundational professional degree program for persons in ministry. The program of study leading to this degree is designed to provide the student with comprehensive knowledge in biblical studies and Christian life and thought studies. In addition, it will help the student develop the specific skills necessary for effective ministry.
>
> The worship track curriculum combines the cohesiveness of required courses with considerable choice and flexibility. The extent of choice depends upon competency attained in pre-seminary study and the sequence of study chosen by the student.
>
> Students choosing the worship track should seek academic advisement through the office of the Associate Dean of the School of Church Music and Worship.[134]

The curriculum indicated for the master of divinity with an emphasis in church music was as follows:

31980	Written Communication	0
	Scripture and Interpretation (18 hours)	
20200	Introduction to the Old Testament I	3
20220	Introduction to the Old Testament II	3
22200	Introduction to the New Testament I	3
22220	Introduction to the New Testament II	3
20400	Elementary Hebrew	3
22400	Elementary Greek	0
20440	Hebrew Syntax and Exegesis or	
22440	Greek Syntax and Exegesis	3

132. SBTS, *Academic Catalog (2000–2001)*, 83.
133. SBTS, *Academic Catalog (2000–2001)*, 78.
134. SBTS, *Academic Catalog (2000–2001)*, 78.

Theology and Tradition (12 hours)

25100	Introduction to Church History I	3
25120	Introduction to Church History II	3
27020	Introduction to Christian Theology I	3
27040	Introduction to Christian Theology II	3

Worldview and Culture (6 hours)

28500	Introduction to Christian Philosophy	3
29250	Survey of Christian Ethics	3

Ministry and Proclamation (17 hours)

30000	The Ministry of Proclamation	3
30020	Preaching Practicum	3
32100	Personal Evangelism	3
40010	Formation for Christian Ministry	2
40301	The Practice of Ministry	3
42210	Team Ministry Relations	3

Ministry Studies (5 hours)

40010	Formation for Christian Ministry	2
32100	Personal Evangelism	3

Supervised Ministry Experience (4 hours)

44994	Supervised Ministry Experience Worship I	2
44995	Supervised Ministry Experience Worship II	2

Worship Studies (22 hours)

23960	Worship & Min. in the New Testament	3
31510	Dramatized Scripture	2
40200	The Worshipping Church	3
40222	Christian Worship in Contemporary Culture	3
41085	Introduction to Hymnology	2

Drama Elective (31500–31610, 41300, 50970, 52580	2–3
Worship Electives (26800, 30200, 41060, 41100, 41110)	5–6

Music Studies (4 hours)

41150	Introduction to Music Ministry	2
Church Music Literature (41125 or 41135)		1
Church Music electives (41000–41490, 50000–50370, 51110–58930; many courses have prerequisite stipulations)		4
Ensembles (50700, 50710, 50730, 50750, 50940, 50980)		2
Free Electives		3
Total Master of Divinity-Worship Track Requirements		91

[135]

One final curricular contribution should be listed during Lloyd Mims's term as dean: the course entitled "The Worshipping Church." This course was unique and important because it was created in 1993–94 in collaboration with the dean of the School of Theology at that time, Dr. David Dockery. This singular course is worth mentioning because of its existence as the only course in worship and because it was required for every student in every degree at Southern Seminary. The catalog described the course as follows:

> A study of Christian worship, its biblical roots, its historical development, the impact of the Reformation and the liturgical revival; a comparative study of contemporary denominational worship patterns, the selection of worship materials, planning orders of worship, inter-staff participation in worship in relation to preaching, evangelism, music, and the spiritual growth of participants.[136]

In 2009, along with several other significant changes to music and worship studies at SBTS, the Worshipping Church course was dropped from requirement for degrees offered in the school of theology (SOT).[137] It continued to be required in degrees offered through the Billy Graham school for missions, evangelism, and ministry (BGS) through 2019.[138]

---

135. SBTS, *Academic Catalog (2000–2001)*, 78.
136. SBTS, *Academic Catalog (2002–3)*.
137. SBTS, *Academic Catalog (2009–10)*.
138. See SBTS, *Academic Catalog* (from 1996 to 2009).

1994 Service to establish the Billy Graham school for missions and evangelism at Southern Seminary. Pictured left to right: Thom Rainer, R. Albert Mohler Jr., David Dockery, Lloyd Mims

Lloyd Mims's deanship in many ways served as the closing bookend to the "Glory Days" of the SCM. Mims's first few years continued to produce performances of musical excellence for which the SCM had become known: The oratorio chorus and seminary orchestra performing Mozart's *Requiem*, Walton's *Belshazzar's Feast*, Handel's *Messiah*, Mendelssohn's *Elijah*, the seminary orchestra performing Mahler's First Symphony and Shostakovich's Tenth Symphony, seminary choir serving as the featured group at the Southern Regional American Choral Directors' Association (ACDA) convention, male chorale performing Verdi's *Aida* with the Kentucky Opera, productions of *Amahl and the Night Visitors* and *Smoke on the Mountain*, and the world-premiere of the musical *Two from Galilee*.[139]

---

139. Mims, speech to SCM reunion.

THE SCHOOL OF CHURCH MUSIC, 1952–2000

Lloyd Mims, Dean 1994–2000

John Dickson, faculty 1985–2000

Mims's Departure

Although every dean of the SCM (Heeren, Price, and Mims) vocally proclaimed the SCM's purpose as preparing church musicians and worship leaders for the churches of the SBC, the SCM demonstrated much of its understanding of self-worth through musical performances of mostly classical works.[140] As evidenced by his work on adding new degree programs right up to his departure, Mims's work to bring stability to the SCM continued throughout his deanship. Adding courses and even degrees were helpful but did not appear to be serving as the long-term solutions needed to bring the SCM's student enrollment back to stability and strength. Mims reminisced, "I just did my best to stay the course, to keep the curriculum alive, to infuse as much practicality and spiritual calling into it as possible so that it didn't call attention to the fact that we had dropped to so few numbers because nobody wanted our trained seminary musicians anymore."[141]

Mims's departure was reported in the August 2000 issue of *Towers*: "The seminary is also looking for a new dean for the School of Church Music and Worship. Thomas Bolton is serving as the interim dean in place of Lloyd Mims, who resigned to become dean of the School of Music and Fine Arts at Palm Beach Atlantic College [now University] in Florida."[142] In the article, President Mohler is reported as saying, "We will greatly miss Lloyd and Marilyn Mims as they follow God's call to another place of service." Mohler continued, "Lloyd has served with great faithfulness as dean of the School of Church Music and Worship, and he leaves a legacy of lives and ministries shaped by his personal gifts and warm spirit."[143] After twenty years of serving on Southern's campus, Mims's time came to an end. The baton was now passed to the next and final dean of the SCM, Dr. Thomas Bolton.

---

140. Mims, speech to SCM reunion.
141. Mims, interview.
142. "Williams Changes Positions, Mims Resigns," 8.
143. "Williams Changes Positions, Mims Resigns," 8.

5

The School of Church Music and Worship, 2000–2009

CHANGES IN THE SCM

In March 2000, *The Tie* released a special supplement in the form of a large magazine. Among the changes announced in this supplement, Lloyd Mims reported coming changes to the school of church music.[1] In addition to the recent re-naming of the SCM to the "school of church music *and Worship*" [emphasis added] (SCMW), Mims reported the addition of a bachelor of science degree in biblical studies with a major in music at Boyce College, a "soon-to-be established Doctor of Ministry in Worship," and a follow-up announcement for the forthcoming MA in worship.[2] Mims also announced a new structure for the SCMW that would include three divisions: (1) an "academy of music," (2) an "institute of worship," and (3) a "conservatory of church music."[3] Mims wrote,

> These new degrees, as well as demands of the churches have led us to restructure the School of Church Music and Worship. Elsewhere in this publication you will see more specific news about the restructuring. The dean will still oversee the entire school and the associate deans will direct the work of all master's level and doctoral programs, respectively. However, the Academy will be guided by a faculty member (as of yet unnamed) who will oversee

1. Mims, "School of Church Music and Worship Report," 24.
2. Mims, "School of Church Music and Worship Report," 24.
3. Ellsworth, "School of Church Music Restructures," 25.

the baccalaureate work in Boyce College. The Institute of Worship will be guided by a faculty member specifically in charge of promoting new conferences and events; these offerings will widen the curriculum now available through the school. All degrees in worship will emanate from the Institute of Worship. The conservatory of church music will continue to proffer all the music degrees of the school.[4]

Later in the publication, Mims elaborated on the changes stating, "The biggest difference is that we are offering more degrees with worship as the driving force, yet we are still continuing to offer the degrees we've always offered that give priority to music. . . . we're embracing a much wider array of church music education."[5]

The changes to the doctor of ministry (DMin) in worship focused on altering the residency requirements. Instead of a one-year residency, the coursework moved to a modular format. This change represented part of a larger transformation as the article stressed that SCMW degrees would now "emphasize a praise and worship approach to music."[6] In a related article, Daniel Block, a professor of Old Testament Interpretation at the time, states, "There's more to worship than music . . . music is important, but worship begins with a revelation of God."[7] Daniel Akin, vice president for academic administration at the time, explains, "Southern Seminary is trying to build on the best of its past tradition in the music school while at the same time charting a forward course for our churches of the 21st century."[8] Akin continues, "We recognize that music styles change with each new generation and we accept the responsibility of providing ministers of music and worship who can effectively minister to those congregations."[9] After many years of relative stability during the deanships of Heeren and Price, Lloyd Mims's administration appeared to be buffeted by one significant change after another. Though he served as the architect for many adjustments and curricular innovations, Mims would resign two months later, in May 2000. Mims's efforts positioned the SCMW after his departure for further changes to be instituted by its next leader, Dr. Tom Bolton.

4. Mims, "School of Church Music and Worship Report," 24.
5. Ellsworth, "School of Church Music Restructures," 25.
6. Ellsworth, "School of Church Music Restructures," 25.
7. Block, quoted in Ellsworth, "School of Church Music Restructures," 25.
8. Akin, quoted in Ellsworth, "Southern's School of Church Music Restructures," 25.
9. Akin, quoted in Ellsworth, "Southern's School of Church Music Restructures," 25.

The School of Church Music and Worship, 2000–2009

Acting Dean Thomas Bolton

When he was asked in the spring of 2000 to serve as interim dean, Tom Bolton was already serving as professor of church music and worship. Bolton had previously joined the faculty of the SCM in 1996. Before coming to Southern, Bolton had taught for sixteen years at Ouachita Baptist University (OBU; 1973–89).[10] While serving at OBU, Bolton taught music history courses for both undergraduate and graduate students, graduate courses in research and bibliography, music literature courses, vocal diction, opera workshop, private voice lessons, choral arranging, and directed the chamber singers.[11] When Bolton left OBU to serve as minister of music at the First Baptist Church of Little Rock, Arkansas, in 1989, he "just felt a calling into full-time ministry."[12] At FBC Little Rock, Bolton had directed a significant worship ministry within a 4,000-member church. After his choir and orchestra led a 20-minute musical segment during a national event where President Mohler spoke, Bolton was approached by Mims to join the faculty at Southern.[13] "I really felt that God was putting together the two former parts of my life, the academic part and the ministerial part," he said regarding the time of his hire.[14]

Bolton described his interview process as one that needed to have the approval of many different factions of interest: "I had to go through interviews with Dr. Mohler, Dr. Akin, music people, and I had to give a 25-minute recital."[15] After passing these hurdles, Bolton discovered that the SCMW was still slightly different from his expectations. He later recounted,

> Well again, it was academically and musically excellent. I thought my coming was accepted well by the faculty. There had been a huge turnover in faculty two years before, and I didn't realize that this was so fresh. When I was hired, it [the Conservative Resurgence in the SBC] wasn't really discussed. In Arkansas, we don't have a whole lot of CBF-type churches, you know; Baptist is basically conservative, that's all. We didn't have politics in the church, you know, so I wasn't up on that. Suddenly I moved into the bull's eye of church politics. I was looked at as being brought in by Mohler,

10. Bolton, curriculum vitae.
11. Bolton, curriculum vitae.
12. Bolton, interview by author, September 8, 2021.
13. Bolton, interview.
14. Bolton, interview.
15. Bolton, interview.

and so I was looked at rather askance at times, but especially by people outside the Southern community—like churches that I would attend.

When I came to interview, I was put through the grill by current faculty, and even senior faculty who were included in on this, and Hugh McElrath was one of them. . . . he and I became great friends because he found out that I was a good musician. I have a PhD in musicology—that's his field. But I also had a performing degree in voice, not in ministry really—I didn't go to seminary. All of my ministry experience was just the school of hard knocks, but that seemed to be okay for them. So I was accepted. Dr. McElrath said, "How did you get here?" because they were expecting something different, being brought in by Dr. Mohler. But we [faculty] had a great relationship.[16]

Although the music faculty may have originally appeared suspicious of Bolton's hiring, as per his account, the initial skepticism faded into friendship. Four years later, after the departure of Mims and Dickson, Bolton was positioned to serve in a different capacity.

In the September 2000 supplemental edition of *The Tie*, Bolton introduced himself to the Southern Seminary community as acting dean by way of his report from the SCMW. Bolton praised God's grace through a number of favorable reports, including a sixty percent increase in enrollment for the SCMW. The actual numbers from the 1999–2000 academic year to the 2000–2001 academic year showed a growth in total enrollment from 207 to 223.[17] Though these numbers were far from encouraging, Bolton also had more blessings to herald: the hiring of Carl "Chip" Levering Stam (on faculty 2000–2011) as the founding director of the new Institute of Christian Worship, the beginning of the Seminary Academy of Music [now the Seminary School of the Arts] which was directed by Southern DMA alumnus, Vernon Cherrix, and the initial class of students enrolled in the master of arts in worship degree.[18]

Though Bolton was originally named "acting dean," the appointment soon became permanent. The SCMW's outlook had been cloudy during Mims's leadership. Bolton's deanship seemed to promise brighter days to come.

---

16. Bolton, interview.
17. SBTS, "Special Task Force," 5.
18. Bolton, "School of Church Music and Worship Report," 27.

ACCREDITATION AND CURRICULA FOCUSING ON WORSHIP

During the first decade of the 2000s, the SCMW under Bolton attempted to stem the tide of declining enrollment through the addition of several new degree options. Southern Seminary, along with the SCMW, answered (and still answers) to a number of accrediting agencies, including ATS and SACS. The SCMW also had to provide accreditation reports to NASM, which establishes national standards for undergraduate and graduate degrees and other credentials for music and music-related disciplines.[19] The SCMW's 2004 report to NASM provided a clear accounting of these degrees. NASM requires institutions to meet a list of fourteen criteria for membership:

> (1) The institution shall offer regular classes in such areas as theory, history, and appropriate repertories of music, as well as instruction in performance. (2) Shall maintain a curricular program in musicianship skills at levels appropriate to the needs of its students. (3) Shall offer instruction in and opportunities for ensemble performance. (4) The institution shall offer at least one complete curriculum. (5) [Criteria skipped in source document.] (6) Institutions offering graduate programs must have graduate students in residence. (7) All policies regarding the admission and retention of students, as well as those pertaining to the school's evaluation of progress through its educational program, shall be clearly defined in literature published by the institution. (8) All tuition, fees, and other charges, as well as all policies pertaining thereto, shall be clearly described in the institution's published literature. (9) Faculty members shall be qualified by educational background and/or professional experience for their specific teaching assignments. The institution shall list its faculty in its published literature. (10) The institution shall have facilities and equipment adequate to the needs of its educational program. (11) The institution shall have library space and holdings adequate to the needs of its educational program. (12) The institution shall be licensed or tabled to operate as required by local and state legal codes. The institution shall meet all legal requirements to operate wherever it conducts its activities. Multipurpose institutions . . . shall be accredited by the appropriate regional or institutional accrediting agency. (13) The institution shall provide . . . all coursework or educational services to support its educational programs or demonstrate that any cooperate or contracted coursework or educational services are

---

19. See https://nasm.arts-accredit.org.

provided by an outside institution or organization having accreditation as an entity by a nationally recognized accrediting agency. (14) The institution demonstrates commitment to a program of continued self-evaluation.[20]

The SCM had successfully met these criteria since first earning accreditation in December 1971.[21]

In the SCMW's NASM consultative review for accreditation renewal in 2004, particular attention was given to the newest degree, the master of arts with emphasis in worship. The introduction to this report provides context:

> In recent years, many churches have seen a growing interest in the area of Christian worship. Those seeking to be leaders in Southern Baptist and other evangelical churches have felt the need to become knowledgeable in the various areas that relate to the planning and leadership of biblical worship. The faculty of the School of Church Music and Worship has sought to broaden the scope of our curricula in Music and Worship by strengthening the "worship" component of our Church Music degrees and by providing some specialized degrees in worship that do not necessarily require full proficiencies in the traditional church music areas (vocal, choral, and keyboard). Notice that in the year ___, [original document leaves this blank, but was officially changed in 1996] even the name of the school was changed from The School of Church Music to The School of Church Music and Worship, reflecting an interest in being intentional about the study of Christian worship as it relates to Church Music.
>
> Some of this realignment of our focus has meant a serious study of how folk, jazz, and popular musical styles can be used with spiritual authenticity and professional excellence in the context of corporate worship. The new emphasis has also included an increased attention to the biblical moorings for Christian worship and a desire to study how Christians down through the ages have understood the Bible's instructions.
>
> In a very real sense, the "worship" degrees offered by the School of Church Music and Worship are interdisciplinary programs. The students are concentrating their academic studies in the field of

---

20. Crookshank, "Basic Criteria for Membership."
21. SBTS, "History Report (2004)."

worship, but doing so in the broader context of music ministry and rigorous theological education.[22]

The 2004 NASM accreditation team focused on how this new "worship" degree would comply with established NASM standards. The NASM team reported on the (1) proficiencies required for entrance to the program; (2) research and professional tools required in the program; (3) required grade-point-average; (4) residency requirements; (5) allowance for transferable credits; (6) minimum number of credit hours required beyond the baccalaureate; (7) the presence of a comprehensive review at or near the end of the degree; (8) final project requirements; (8) and Southern's approaches to develop breadth of competence for students in the new program.[23] Other standard review considerations involved the credentialing of faculty, availability of adequate classroom space, instructional resources, such as a keyboard lab, building facilities, and budgeted finances set aside for students in the degree.[24] The final pages of this review document included the SCMW's rationale for adding the degree, which has been sufficiently articulated in the previous block quotation.[25]

Curriculum for the Master of Arts in Worship

The curriculum for this new worship degree included many of the same course requirements found in the master of church music degree. The main differences between this degree and previously established church music degrees were fewer music skills courses and more courses treating the theology, history, and methodology of Christian worship. Bolton's intention was to direct student training towards practical and useful application in the local church.[26] The curriculum for the master of arts in worship leadership, as noted in the 2004 NASM report is as follows:

Biblical and Theological Studies
    20200 Survey of Old Testament I or II   3 credits

---

22. SBTS SCMW, introduction to "NASM Consultative Review (2004)."
23. SBTS SCMW, "NASM Consultative Review," 2–4.
24. SBTS SCMW, "NASM Consultative Review," 5–11.
25. SBTS SCMW, "NASM Consultative Review," 12–14.
26. Bolton, interview.

22200	Survey of New Testament I or II	3 credits
25100	Introduction to Church History I	3 credits
25120	Introduction to Church History II	3 credits
27000	Survey of Systematic Theology	3 credits
32100	Personal Evangelism	3 credits
40010	Formation for Christian Ministry	2 credits
	Theological Elective	3 credits
	Total Biblical and Theological Studies	**23 credits**

Major Area (Worship courses with significant emphasis in music)

40200	The Worshipping Church	3 credits
40230	Leadership in Contemporary Expressions of Corporate Worship	2 credits
41085	Introduction to Hymnology	2 credits
44994	Supervised Ministry Experience I: Worship	2 credits
44995	Supervised Ministry Experience II: Worship	2 credits

Electives in WORSHIP — 2 credits

30200	Worship in the African American Church	3 credits
31510	Dramatized Scripture	2 credits
41100	Hymnology II	2 credits
41110	Baptist Hymnody	3 credits
41115	Music of the Praise and Worship Movement	2 credits
	Total Major Area	**13 credits**

(Worship with significant music emphasis)

Studies in Church Music

41150	Introduction to Music Ministry	2 credits
40235	Contemporary Worship Ensemble Lab	1 credit

Electives in Church Music Studies — 3 credits

41070	Writing Songs for Worship	2 credits
41100	Hymnology II	2 credits
41110	Baptist Hymnody	2 credits
41125	Church Music Literature for Voices	1 credit
41135	Church Music Literature for Instruments	1 credit
41136	Church Instrumental Music Administration	1 credit

41150	Music Ministry w/ Preschoolers & Children	2 credits
41170	Music Ministry w/ Adolescents & Adults	2 credits
41242	Handbell Methods	1 credit
41300	Producing & Staging Church Music Drama	2 credits
41310	Sound, Lighting, & Recording Techniques	2 credits
41320	Acting for Singers	2 credits
41340	Electronic Notation and Sequencing	2 credits
51680	Composing, Arranging, and Publishing For Today's Church	2 credits
	Ensembles (4 semesters) (no credit)	(no credit)
Total Studies in Church Music		6 credits

TOTAL HOURS   48 credits

27

Though some musical requirements that had always been required were dropped for the new MA degree, they were not abandoned. After some faculty expressed concern that a student pursuing the MA might graduate with a degree in worship but without the ability to read music, it was decided that all MA students should be required to take proficiency examinations in voice and keyboard (or guitar) and if deficiencies were revealed, then the student would have to do remedial study in that area.[28]

Though the SCMW initiated several new degrees during Mims's term as dean, the master of arts in worship leadership represented the most significant change to the curriculum as it necessitated not only the creation of a new curriculum and the creation of a new degree, the SCMW was also obliged to hire a new faculty with expertise in this area. The faculty hired to lead in this new course of study was Carl (Chip) Stam.

CARL ("CHIP") LEVERING STAM

Of all the hires made by any dean of the school of church music, Carl Stam was likely the most historic because Stam was the professor charged with founding the degree program studying worship. He was not only a

---

27. SBTS SCMW, "NASM Consultative Review," 16–17.
28. SBTS, "History Report," 9.

nationally known choral conductor, but a prominent worship leader and music minister known for crafting biblically grounded worship using new idioms. Stam was hired by Mims during the closing days of his deanship, thus his time at Southern coincided with Bolton's administration. Concerning Stam's hiring, Mims relates, "I visited Chip for two years before [he was hired] and he turned us down. A year later and he still said no, but I guess God got ahold of him because he called me back a couple of weeks later and said, 'You know, I really need to look more deeply at this opportunity' and you know God impressed on his heart to say yes."[29] Stam was hired by Mims in the spring of 2000 and began his service on the seminary faculty in August of that year, just after Mims resigned. Stam expressed in a conversation that he was excited to be coming to work with Mims and Dickson, however Stam's time at SBTS was to be spent in other company.[30]

Stam was pursued for two years due to his "unicorn qualities." By "unicorn qualities," Mims referred to Stam holding graduate degrees in both music and theology.[31] Stam had come to SBTS from Notre Dame University where he had been successfully promoted form the rank of instructor, to assistant professor of music, associate professional specialist and director of choral music.[32] Before coming to Notre Dame, Stam had served as a choral conductor and at one point as the interim director of choral activities at the University of North Carolina at Chapel Hill.[33] While at UNC-Chapel Hill as a graduate student and adjunct professor, Stam served as the pastor of worship and music at the Chapel Hill Bible Church.[34] At Southern Seminary, Stam's teaching assignments included teaching the core worship courses in the new degree: The Worshiping Church, Leadership in Contemporary Expressions of Worship, Christian Worship and Contemporary Culture. Stam also taught courses in choral conducting as well as directing choral ensembles. This work included teaching conducting seminars, and choral techniques, and directing the oratorio chorus.[35]

Stam's ministry was not confined to Southern's campus. In addition to directing the Kentucky Baptist men's chorale for over ten years, Stam also

---

29. Mims, phone interview by author, August 26, 2021.
30. Stam, conversation with author, April 19, 2001.
31. Mims, interview.
32. Stam, curriculum vitae.
33. Stam, curriculum vitae.
34. Stam, curriculum vitae.
35. Stam, curriculum vitae.

served as the minister of music and worship at Clifton Baptist in Louisville from 2002 until his death in 2011.

If the core mission of many previous SCM professors found its identity in cultivating the art and artistry of the student musician for use in the church, Stam's tenure as a teacher and trainer of worship leaders demonstrated a different quality. For example, Mike Cosper, the founding worship pastor of Sojourn Community Church writes, "Chip taught me nearly everything I know about worship."[36] There are many worship pastors and worship leaders who might make the same confession. "Stam indeed influenced the thoughts of people during his time—several churches and institutions, and thousands of people around the country."[37] In addition to his students in the academy and those whom he led in weekly worship, Stam was a pioneer using electronic media to share his devotional scholarship concerning worship. In 1995, Stam began to publish a "widely popular, web-based weekly devotional that shared interesting and challenging quotes about the nature of worship and prayer in the life of the Christian church called 'Worship Quote of the Week.'"[38] Though Stam's weekly emails (around five to six thousand at its height) fell into dormancy some years ago, friend and fellow worship scholar, John D. Witvliet curated and published a collection of over 300 of Stam's devotions: *Worship in the Joy of the Lord: Selections from Chip Stam's Worship Quote of the Week*.[39] In Stam's "Worship Quotes of the Week," he would begin with a title (usually self-crafted which encapsulated the essence of the quote), a fairly large quote, usually from a well-known theologian, Bible scholar, or church musician, and finally the bibliographic information on the work from which Stam found the quote.[40] Stam's weekly quotes demonstrated his continual diverse attempts to teach and inspire those leading music and worship in the local church towards biblical worship rather than to settle for the musical and cultural trends of popular religious expression.

Stam's teaching and influence brought worship leader training at SBTS into the wider conversation about Christian worship that was occurring more broadly in evangelical Christian culture. As contemporary forms of worship were overtaking more traditional ones in the corporate worship

---

36. Taylor, "Carl ('Chip') Stam (1953–2011)."
37. Hanbury, "Southern Story: Carl 'Chip' Stam," 3.
38. Stam, "Worship Quote of the Week."
39. Witvliet, *Worship in Joy of the Lord*.
40. Witvliet, *Worship in Joy of the Lord*, 4.

life of American churches, including Southern Baptist churches, a new movement of worship scholars and practitioners including Stam were asking questions of churches who were changing their worship. Questions like the following were timely ones for Baptist church leaders to answer: "What does it mean to be a pastoral musician? Are traditions always bad? Can a worship leader actually 'usher' a congregation into the courts of God?" In the experience of many Southern Baptist worshipers, the answers to these questions were most often being provided by those representing mainstream praise and worship or the church growth movement. Their answers did not appear to many as being consistent with Stam's answers—answers that were found through thoughtful consideration of Scripture.[41]

Author and theologian David Peterson and church music icon Harold Best were two important prophetic voices that called evangelical churches to worship biblically amidst the stylistic paradigm shift of contemporary worship in the 1990s. Peterson's 1992 book *Engaging with God: A Biblical Theology of Worship* presented the concept that based on Scripture, Christian worship happened in the way that God wants and on the terms he alone can stipulate. For many non-Reformed SBC congregations, Peterson's book was their first introduction to covenantal worship and the regulative principal of worship.[42] Harold Best published his well-known book *Music through the Eyes of Faith* in 1993. Best's pastoral demeanor and scholarly attention to detail helped give his book wide appeal for pastors, worship leaders, and church musicians. Best used his book to explore topics relevant to SBC churches struggling for unity in the midst of tensions concerning the style of music in their worship services. In lectures and speaking engagements at churches, conferences, and the academy, Best observed, "Most contemporary churches say they are text-driven but don't actually worship that way. We need a humbling of music in worship."[43] These two authors were among those who helped to give rising young leaders like Stam scholarly "ammunition" to focus evangelical Christians on biblical worship consisting of corporate response to Scripture rather than focusing on musical styles. Best was quoted as having said of and to Stam, "The interesting thing about you, Chip, is that you just keep growing and growing in your humble servanthood, your ability to take flack, your ability to face things that are

---

41. Best, Cosper, and Stam, "Discussion of Worship and Church Music."
42. Peterson, *Engaging with God*, 20.
43. Best, Cosper, and Stam, "Discussion of Worship and Church Music," episode 3.

anomalous in the church, and the servant spirit you have in articulating the truth of biblical worship."[44] Best was right.

Chip Stam, faculty 2000–2011

The Passing of Chip Stam

Early in 2007, Stam was diagnosed with non-Hodgkin's lymphoma. During the first two years of Stam's battle with cancer, he seemed to be winning. However, his struggle became increasingly difficult and on May 1, 2011, Stam "saw Jesus face to face for the first time."[45] Stam himself wrote in one of his final "Worship Quotes of the Week," "I am preparing to die (again, whether that's near or far) and crying tears of great joy and satisfaction. If you aren't trusting in Jesus alone for hope in this life and the next, you cannot possibly understand the peace that passes understanding. Come to Jesus."[46]

Stam's wife Doris shared, "He died peacefully while Clara and I sang Psalm 23, 'The Lord is My Shepherd.' Though Chip had been unresponsive for several days, I have no doubt he was singing with us, and then beheld

44. Best, Cosper, and Stam, "Discussion of Worship and Church Music," episode 8.
45. Taylor, "Carl ('Chip') Stam."
46. Taylor, "Carl ('Chip') Stam."

the face of his Creator, joining in the worship of Christ with heavenly beings in song, a beaming smile on his face!"[47]

Of the many tributes offered in speech and in writing for the life and ministry of the worship-leading theologian named Chip Stam, one particularly poignant epitaph came from his two dear friends, prominent Southern Seminary professors Tom Schreiner (New Testament) and Bruce Ware (systematic theology):

> To the end of his life, one characteristic stood out above all others, and this was his unflinching confidence in the God who, in His great love, had sent His Son to die in his place and pay the penalty for his sin. For all of us who have been with Chip over these past four years of his battle with cancer, Chip has displayed to us how to die well as the fruit of trusting God well. Chip lived the reality of the gospel and exhibited a peace that passes human understanding as his heart was filled with joy over the greatness and grace of God's gift of salvation. We visited Chip many times during his ordeal with cancer, and on every occasion, we came back encouraged and strengthened in our faith. Chip wanted to live to an old age, but he gave his life to God, trusting him for his life and death. Therefore, visits with him and Doris and the family were never gloomy affairs. The joy of knowing Jesus was refracted through his sufferings. May this be said of us.[48]

Carl Stam's life and death had a profound impact on worship students, Southern Seminary, and the school of church music. In fact, some faculty felt that Stam's death, in some ways, paralleled the passing of the school of church music and Worship.[49]

SOBERING NUMBERS

In the SCMW's faculty meeting held on Wednesday, September 11, 2002, Bolton shared that he had been compiling information for the NASM report and found the numbers "sobering."[50] Bolton shared with the faculty that the enrollment was down 27 percent from the previous year. According

---

47. Stam, "Tigger in a Tuxedo."
48. Schreiner and Ware, quoted in Taylor, "Carl ('Chip') Stam."
49. This sentiment was shared independently by two interviewees: Greenway, teleconference interview by author, September 6, 2021; Stewart, phone interview by author, October 13, 2021.
50. SCMW, faculty meeting notes, September 11, 2002, 2.

The School of Church Music and Worship, 2000–2009

to meeting notes, "Some students that have not yet finished their degree did not return this semester. Other students have cut back on coursework."[51] He shared that though the master of church music degree was still the highest populated degree, its enrollment was gradually declining while the master of arts in worship degree enrollment was steadily rising.[52] All of these factors contributed to a reduction in the number of classes taken within the SCMW.

Later that same school year, during a faculty meeting held on March 19, 2003, Bolton distributed a graph to the faculty that indicated the cost of educating a student in the SCMW was over $10,000 as compared to the cost of educating a student in any of the other schools in the seminary, which ranged from $2,500–$3,600.[53] At that time, there was an active search on to fill two open faculty positions. These faculty searches were cancelled and an applied music fee was added to student tuition. If enrollment remained stable, the two mitigation strategies implemented by Bolton were meant to reduce the cost of educating worship students by $1,363.[54] This move represented a proverbial drop in the bucket, but it was also a good faith effort by Bolton to do what he could to address the serious cost disparity in educating music and worship students with that of other seminary students. Other changes would be needed.

During the faculty meeting on April 2, 2003, Bolton proposed a number of solutions aimed at chipping away the mountainous fiscal challenge facing the SCMW. Bolton's resolve to consider all possibilities was reflected in his willingness to alter the Church Music Institute (CMI). The CMI had been a time-honored tradition of the SCMW since it was introduced by Forrest Heeren in 1962. Bolton, unwilling to completely dissolve the CMI, suggested that it be dropped to every third year rather than every year.[55] The CMI was a conference aimed at equipping and encouraging church musicians and alumni of the SCM that had been a mainstay of the SCM and SCMW for over forty years. Bolton transparently commented to the faculty, "I don't think I'm getting a return for the money we invest."[56] In discussion of this point, one faculty remarked that they (the SCMW) should be

---

51. SCMW, faculty meeting notes, 2.
52. SCMW, faculty meeting notes, 2.
53. SCMW, faculty meeting notes, 1.
54. SCMW, faculty meeting notes, 1.
55. Crookshank, personal notes, SCMW faculty meeting, April 2, 2003.
56. Crookshank, personal meeting notes.

careful that they were not so responsive to what churches wanted that the SCMW lost its prophetic role. By that he meant that part of the role of the SCMW was to "reach a standard that's higher than the average church can do."[57] To this remark, faculty member Dr. Greg Brewton interjected, "We're perceived as being not in touch with what churches are doing. Our students today, at Southern and Boyce [College] are really into authentic whatever. If they can't evangelize, they don't want any part of it."[58] The CMI was not held during the 2003–04 academic year and never held again, quietly passing away with other traditions that had been established during the previous era.

Tom Bolton, faculty, Dean, 1996–2012 (piano, foreground); Esther Rothenbusch Crookshank, faculty, 1994– (background)

THE CHANGING LANDSCAPE OF CHURCH MUSIC AND WORSHIP

The worship style landscape had been changing among Southern Baptist churches. By the early 2000s, this change became observable even within the students of the SCMW. Changes in the worship culture of the SBC

---

57. Crookshank, personal meeting notes.
58. Crookshank, personal meeting notes.

resulted in changes in the job competencies required for those leading worship ministries in the SBC. In turn, these changes required the curriculum for worship leader training at the SCMW to change. Though political and theological changes in the SBC did have some effect on the SCMW, the changes in the SCMW were not so clearly driven by either the conservative resurgence in the SBC or by the appointment of Mohler to the presidency of Southern Seminary. The larger changes in worship culture driving transition within worship leader training had their origins in the church growth movement. These changes, which were slow at first, had rapidly accelerated by the 2000s. What exactly is the church growth movement and how did it come to change the basic understanding of worship in Western evangelicalism?

The North American society for church growth's definition provides a starting point for understanding the topic:

> Church growth is that discipline which investigates the nature, expansion, planting, multiplication, function, and health of Christian churches as they relate to the effective implementation of God's commission to 'make disciples of all peoples' (Matt. 28:18–20). Students of church growth strive to integrate the eternal theological principles of God's Word concerning the expansion of the church with the best insights of contemporary social and behavioral sciences, employing as the initial framework of reference the foundational work done by Donald McGavran.[59]

How could a methodology for missions become a cultural movement in the United States that would impact the worship culture of Southern Baptists and the training of the worship leaders for SBC churches? A basic understanding of the history of the church growth movement can provide some answers.[60]

Donald McGavran

In the 1930s, Donald McGavran, widely considered to be the "father of the Church Growth Movement," served as the executive secretary-treasurer of the India Mission of the Disciples of Christ, who at that time sponsored

---

59. Rainer, *The Book of Church Growth*, 20.

60. The topic of the church growth movement represents a subject too vast to address in this dissertation. However, a basic knowledge of the church growth movement may help to frame some of the issues contained in the story of worship leader training at Southern Seminary.

eighty missionaries.[61] As the administrative head, overseeing monies and mission endeavors of a significantly sized missions organization with a fifty-year history of service to the Indian subcontinent, McGavran was struck by the reality that none of their congregations were growing. McGavran investigated the mission efforts of other denominations in central India and found that 136 out of 165 mission stations also claimed no numeric growth.[62] This epiphany caused McGavran to question, "What *does* make churches grow? More importantly, what makes many churches *stop* growing? How is it possible for Christians to come out of ripe harvest fields empty-handed?"[63] For the next seventeen years, McGavran continued the work of vocational missions. In his time-period and denominational context, McGavran worked with agencies—many of which might today be considered humanitarian rather than evangelistic. McGavran's duties included caring for those with leprosy, teaching in schools, working in hospitals, providing food for the hungry, and helping with rural construction projects.[64] After reflecting on his seventeen years of observation and labor, McGavran was called upon more and more to serve in the role of evangelical consultant. Ultimately McGavran tested his developing theories upon similar mission work projects in Africa. McGavran's observations and insights were written down in his first book *Bridges of God*. Though the book appeared to be well-received, McGavran's writing did little to change the opinions and strategy assumed by his mid-twentieth century main line Protestant missions organization. In McGavran's words, "The static view of missions, the shift of the focus from the growth of the Church to good deeds done by Western churches and to interchurch aid had been too complete for one book to change the trend."[65]

Even though no significant changes appeared on the horizon for McGavran's mission organization, his work did not go unnoticed. Through the remainder of the 1950s, McGavran was asked to apply his knowledge to a variety of missions projects set on different continents.[66] By 1965, McGavran was hired as the founding dean of the Fuller Theological Seminary School of World Mission.

61. Wagner, preface to *Understanding Church Growth*, viii.
62. McGavran and Hunter, *Church Growth Strategies*, 16.
63. McGavran and Hunter, *Church Growth Strategies*, 16.
64. McGavran and Hunter, *Church Growth Strategies*, 16–17.
65. McGavran and Hunter, *Church Growth Strategies*, 17.
66. McGavran and Hunter, *Church Growth Strategies*, 18.

During the 1960s, with the help of his colleagues Alan Tippett, C. Peter Wagner, Arthur Glasser, and Ralph Winter, McGavran systematized his ideas into a full-formed methodology and published the book regarded by many as the foundational text of the church growth movement: *Understanding Church Growth*.[67] By now, the questions and conclusions McGavran cultivated as a vocational missionary were being reinterpreted and reapplied to North American churches. Pastors and church leaders from many denominations marginalized the church growth movement as a gimmick but McGavran was undaunted. According to McGavran, "It was no gimmick to get more people and money into the church, its [church growth's] foundation was theological."[68] In the heart and mind of McGavran, church growth represented nothing less than complete faithfulness to fulfilling the Great Commission.[69]

Gains and Criticisms

Similar to McGavrans's sentiments, other church growth practitioners saw this philosophy and methodology as the primary lens through which the Great Commission might be fulfilled in every culture and setting. Through its use, church growth adherents have continually sought to combat discouraging statistics such as those shared by David Olson in his book *The American Church in Crisis*. Olson cites 2008 data provided by the Barna Group showing yearly decreases in church membership and attendance from every corner of North American Christianity.[70]

The church growth movement gained significant traction as a global movement of evangelical ecumenism during the late 1960s and early 1970s.[71] Through key historic events such as the 1966 World Congress on Evangelism in Berlin and the 1974 International Congress on World Evangelization in Lausanne, Switzerland, the church growth movement gained high visibility through the contributions of plenary speakers and published papers.[72] These international developments were strengthened by growing friendships between large and aggressively growing megachurches in North

---

67. McGavran and Hunter, *Church Growth Strategies*, 18.
68. McGavran and Hunter, *Church Growth Strategies*, 19.
69. McGavran and Hunter, *Church Growth Strategies*, 19.
70. Olson, *The American Church in Crisis*, 21–29.
71. Rainer, *The Book of Church Growth*, 42.
72. Rainer, *The Book of Church Growth*, 42.

America, the development of global witness training programs published by groups such as Evangelism Explosion, the Billy Graham Evangelistic Association, Campus Crusade for Christ, and by efforts from the Sunday school board of the SBC to create a synergy that propelled the church growth movement to the forefront of the American church.

As accolades mounted for the church growth movement, so did criticism. In his book *The Book of Church Growth: History, Theology, and Principles*, Thom Rainer recounts some of the colorful statements uttered by the movement's detractors. Though many of these criticisms might be easily discounted, the most significant critiques were aimed at CGM's theology—or lack thereof. One critic stated that church growth was a theology of evangelism that "reduced the Christian commitment to an inoffensive appeal avoiding the suggestion that to become a Christian one must turn from a social order that perpetuates injustice."[73] One of McGavran's associates, C. Peter Wagner, recounts a response to the church growth movement that criticized CGM as being "precariously deficient as a strategy for evangelism," particularly theologically.[74] As CGM was becoming increasingly accepted by Pentecostals, Wagner also obtained serious criticism from a reviewer who believed Wagner's theology of CGM to be "dangerously close to Pelagianism."[75] Though many opinions attacked what were perceived as theological deficiencies, advocates of CGM believed (and still do) that they held unassailable positions as the righteous stewards of the Great Commission.

The church growth method did not originate with theologians. CGM was born from missionaries trying their best to discover, in the field, the best methods possible to fulfill the Great Commission within international contexts. It should not be surprising that many of CGM's practitioners worked in hindsight to fill the theological holes besetting their seemingly effective methods. Gailyn Van Rheenan, professor of missions at Abilene Christian University, posits that CGM "assumes theology but ineffectively employs it to analyze culture, determine strategy, and perceive history."[76] Despite his criticism, Van Rheenan lauds CGM for promoting a focus on personal ministry and redirecting believers to focus on the church's "missionary

---

73. Rainer, *The Book of Church Growth*, 45.
74. Rainer, *The Book of Church Growth*, 45.
75. Rainer, *The Book of Church Growth*, 46.
76. Van Rheenen, "Reformist View," 167.

nature."[77] Charles Van Engen, a former biblical theology of mission professor at Fuller Seminary, called on CGM supporters whether on the field, in churches, or serving in institutional settings to work together to create a full and complete biblical theology of church growth.[78] Craig Van Gelder, former professor of congregational mission at Luther Seminary, even attempted to persuade early adopters of CGM to transition their allegiance to a parallel movement called the Gospel and Our Culture Movement.[79]

Criticisms of CGM and Current Models

Despite efforts from first- and second-generation leaders of the CGM to justify their work theologically through use of statements like the Lausanne Covenant, many pastors and church leaders had their understanding of evangelism and church growth shaped simply by applications of CGM that were less concerned with theology. Gary McIntosh, a close friend and associate of McGavran, identified two distinct divisions of CGM which he identified as "Classic" and "Popular."[80] It may be that many pastors and church leaders have been introduced to CGM through the more popular iterations of McGavran's concept. Some of these more recent versions appear to have shed the "classic" practitioners' concern for theological integrity in favor of what frequently draws pastors and church leaders to adopt CGM ideologies, growing numbers of people in their worship services. Many of these newer practitioner-pastors have also discovered the relative fame that accompanies the phenomenon of the mega church. The Hartford Institute for Religion Research defines a megachurch as a Protestant congregation that has an average weekly attendance of 2,000 or more members in its services.[81] In order to maintain their large gatherings, many megachurches have adopted a style of music and liturgy that has become known as "attractional."[82]

"Attractional" represents one of the newer monikers employed by current CGM practitioners to describe the methods and styles used in their churches to become attractive to potential attenders. Billy Hornsby's book

77. Van Rheenen, "Reformist View," 169.
78. Van Engen, "Centrist View," 123–47.
79. Van Gelder, "Gospel and Our Culture View," 75–102.
80. Engle and McIntosh, *Evaluating the Church Growth Movement*, 19.
81. Allen, "What is a Megachurch."
82. Nieuwhof, "Three Ways the Attractional Church Needs to Change."

The Attractional Church: Growth through a Refreshing, Relational, and Relevant Church Experience makes good use of the word. The book cover biography describes Hornsby as the teaching pastor and "staff coach" for a large church located in Birmingham, Alabama. The biography also indicates that he "directs a nationwide church-planting organization, Association of Related Churches, and trains pastors in leadership with EQUIP as the Senior Consultant for Europe."[83] In describing his church's CGM goals, Hornsby uses a significant metaphor to point pastors and church leaders to see how their church can become an attractional church. Hornsby challenges pastors to see the gospel as their "product," Jesus as the "Manufacturer," their local church as the "model," the building, music, staff, and service as the "dealership," and the worship service as the "showroom floor."[84] For pastors and church leaders desperate to grow the number of worshipers in their church, transforming their churches into "attractional" churches may appear to be the answer—despite its appealing more to cultural paradigms rather than biblical ones. As late as 2018, popular CGM consultant and author Rich Birch boldly proclaimed to his readers that "if you're looking for theological discussions around church growth, this book (Birch's book) will leave you wanting more."[85] Birch represents a current example of McIntosh's "popular" form of CGM, one that simply cuts to the chase to help churches adopt "practical systems to drive growth at (their) church."[86]

CHANGES COMING TO WORSHIP LEADER TRAINING

Between 1980 and 2019, worship leader training at Southern Seminary was subject to the same changes in musical and cultural trends that were also impacting churches. Though the observations and mission theories of Disciples of Christ Church missionary McGavran, who served in India during the 1930s and 1940s, might seem far removed from Louisville, Kentucky, they were not. Throughout the twentieth century, the numbers of people identifying as church members declined as the musical styles of rock and popular music swelled.[87] The church growth movement recognized these two trends, synthesizing them in a way that changed the way that Protestants

---

83. Hornsby, *The Attractional Church*, jacket bio.
84. Hornsby, *The Attractional Church*, 23–26.
85. Birch, *Church Growth Flywheel*, 33.
86. Birch, *Church Growth Flywheel*, cover.
87. Rainer, *The Book of Church Growth*, 159.

and evangelicals worshiped forever—including Southern Baptists.[88] As the paradigms of the church growth movement became normative in Southern Baptist congregations, changes in the styles of music also changed.[89] As the preferred music style in churches transitioned, the job competencies necessary for helping churches produce their worship followed suit. As the job competencies for worship leaders developed, music and worship educators at Southern Seminary continually faced pressure to adapt their curricula to a new constituency.[90] Tom Bolton and the faculty of the SCMW worked tirelessly for nearly a decade, trying to turn around the run-away costs and declining enrollment of the SCMW. As during Mims's deanship, Bolton's efforts would not bring back the glory days of the school of church music. By the end of 2008, Southern Seminary's administration decided that stronger measures were needed.

The Special Task Force on the Future of the School of Church Music and Worship

In 2008, a series of letters were issued by the office of President Mohler to several faculty, alumni, administrators, and trustees requesting their participation in a special task force to consider the future of church musician and worship leader training at Southern Seminary. Part of the letter reads as follows:

> Over the past twenty years, our churches have experienced a radical revolution in church music and worship. As The Southern Baptist Theological Seminary seeks to fulfill our mission assigned to us by the churches of the Southern Baptist Convention, we want to ensure that we are doing all that we can do in order to meet the real needs of our churches and to maximize the stewardship of our institutional mission and responsibility.
>
> To that end, recognizing the magnitude of the changes that have been experienced, I'm establishing a Task Force on the Future of Church Music at Southern Seminary in order to provide a

88. Ruth and Lim, *Lovin' on Jesus*, 3–7.
89. Rainer, *The Book of Church Growth*, 226–36.
90. A common thread discovered in the staff meeting notes between 1997 and 2002 reveals deans and faculty who were constantly trying to attract students to a program whose reputation for excellence was also considered to be stylistically out of the norm for increasing numbers of SBC congregations. Nearly every interview subject also revealed the same concern.

base of research and analysis from which we can draw appropriate conclusions about the future shape of this institution and its programs....

The School of Church Music and Worship has been a part of this institution for over half a century, representing excellence in training and music education. We need your help to make certain that this institution is poised for the future, even as we cherish and honor the past.[91]

Tom Bolton was all too familiar with the issues at hand. When the task force met, Bolton also found familiarity in the faces of graduates, fellow faculty, administration, and trustees who had answered Mohler's invitation. Some of the task force members were more supportive than others, however all knew that the very existence of worship leader training may be at stake.[92]

Task force members were provided with a packet which included lots of data. This data took the form of various tables and graphs, all of which painted a discouraging picture of the SCMW's future. According to the data, the SCM had a total of 539 students during the 1988–89 academic year. In the 2008–09 academic year, there were only 167 students.[93] The additional degrees added during the Mims and Bolton administrations appeared to have done little to stem the tide of a diminishing student population as the drop in student enrollment was felt across all degrees offered by the SCMW.[94] Adding salt to the proverbial wound, during this same time period the other schools in the seminary all experienced enrollment increases.[95]

Another telling statistic presented to the task force were charts and graphs testifying to the larger impact of worship culture change in the United States as compared to efforts in SBC seminaries to train worship leaders. Though declining numbers at SBTS were discouraging, the other SBC seminaries that offered worship leader training fared no better. SWBTS's school of church music had an enrollment of 260 during the academic year 1988–89 but by the 2007–08 academic year had fallen to 120 students.[96] During the same time period, NOBTS's church music and worship student

---

91. Mohler, letter to task force members, December 12, 2008; the copy utilized belongs to Angela Starnes Swain, professor of Music and Worship, MBTS.

92. Swain and Swain, teleconference interview by author, May 12, 2022.

93. SBTS, "Special Task Force," 5.

94. SBTS, "Special Task Force," 6–10.

95. SBTS, "Special Task Force," 12–27.

96. SBTS, "Special Task Force," 29.

The School of Church Music and Worship, 2000–2009

enrollment went from 49 students to only 11.⁹⁷ Perhaps just as discouraging is the fact that Gateway Baptist Theological Seminary had dropped their church music degrees several years previously while Southeastern Baptist Theological Seminary (SEBTS) and Midwestern Baptist Theological Seminary (MBTS) had at that time modest offerings in the way of church music and worship leader training.⁹⁸ The task force enrollment numbers made it appear that the worship culture of many SBC churches, a worship culture that had been shaped by the impact of the church growth movement, had changed churches to the point that few desired a seminary graduate with excellent music and theological preparation to lead their worship ministries.

The next segment of the Special Task Force Report included a financial analysis. These metrics were perhaps even more bleak than the ones indicating enrollment trends. The report notes, "In the 2007–2008 Actuals, the direct revenues attributable to the School of Music were insufficient, but a substantial margin, to cover even the direct expenses incurred by the School of Music.... The School of Music, therefore, did not make any contribution toward the net expenses incurred in the functional categories."⁹⁹ The report continues, "The budgeted 2008–2009 direct revenues attributable to the School of Music are also insufficient, by a substantial margin, to cover even the direct expenses budgeted to be incurred, but at a smaller margin when budgeted amounts for three open faculty positions not to be filled are subtracted."¹⁰⁰ This point led to the conclusion: "The School of Music, therefore, will not make any contribution toward the net expenses that will be incurred in the function categories listed."¹⁰¹ One enrollment acronym that recurred frequently in the financial report was "FTE" or "full-time equivalent." Perhaps the most condemning statistic for the SCMW included this term and was saved for the last point of the financial report: "The direct expenses per FTE student in the School of Music in 2009 of $12,266 was 2.6 times the average direct expenses incurred for all SBTS students, even though students are charged the same tuition rates for all masters level courses."¹⁰² These statistics seemed compelling enough to condemn the SCMW as a temporary part of SBTS's mission whose time had

97. SBTS, "Special Task Force," 29.
98. Swain and Swain, interview.
99. SBTS, "Special Task Force," 33.
100. SBTS, "Special Task Force," 33.
101. SBTS, "Special Task Force," 33.
102. SBTS, "Special Task Force," 34.

now come. However, a larger-scale administrative overhaul was underway at SBTS that would ultimately save worship leader training at Southern. Though no longer a free-standing school, the task force's findings led to a reorganization that transitioned the SCMW into a department serving as part of another school, the School of Church Ministries.

THE SCHOOL OF CHURCH MINISTRIES

During the 2009 spring meeting of the Board of Trustees, the Board approved the creation of a new school that combined the SCMW and the school of leadership (itself a new iteration of the school of Christian education) into the School of Church Ministries.[103] Though the task force reports gave enrollment and financial figures leading to a needed administrative transition, the subsuming of the SCMW into a new school that included divisions of leadership and Christian education and their respective degrees was framed as being a natural reflection of what was happening in the majority of SBC churches. Russell D. Moore, then the dean of the School of Theology explained, "We spent much time talking with pastors and ministers of music, to find that music ministers are, in the vast majority of cases, doing everything from discipleship to evangelism leadership to Christian education to family ministry."[104] Moore continued,

> This new school will provide a pioneering curriculum training ministers to serve in multiple roles at once. It will also create a new faculty synergy, combining their strengths to train multi-competent ministers who are leaders in family ministry, worship ministry, men's ministry, women's ministry, youth ministry, children's ministry, Christian education and discipleship.[105]

An especially popular combination needed in the local church was cross-training in the areas of worship leadership and youth ministry. Randy Stinson served as dean of the new school, transitioning from dean of the School of Leadership. Tom Bolton retired, along with the majority of the faculty from the SCMW, and Greg Brewton was appointed to serve as the area coordinator over music and worship.[106] Of this significant administrative transition President Mohler stated,

103. Robinson, "Southern Launches New School," 40–41.
104. Robinson, "Southern Launches New School," 40.
105. Robinson, "Southern Launches New School," 40–41.
106. Robinson, "Southern Launches New School," 41.

The School of Church Music and Worship, 2000–2009

> We are very proud of the history of both the School of Church Music and Worship and the School of Leadership and Church Ministry. Both have served well, both have distinguished histories and both bring a great deal to this new school. The reality is that we are experiencing vast changes in the landscape of higher education and these reflect similar changes in the lives of our churches. We are absolutely determined that Southern Seminary be on the front lines of innovation and making certain that we are still serving the needs of our churches."[107]

Though worship leader training at Southern Seminary was transitioning into governance by another school within the seminary, Mohler displayed an intent to continue supporting the SCMW's mission.

While Mohler and even long-time music and worship faculty members couched these significant changes with incredibly positive expectations, not everyone was convinced that the administrative shift was a positive occurrence. In an article published by another Baptist publication, information from the same press announcement was told in a different way. The article entitled, "Southern Seminary Closing School of Church Music" opened with, "Southern Baptist Theological Seminary is closing its 65-year-old School of Church Music and Worship, combining it with the School of Leadership and Church Ministry into a new School of Church Ministries."[108] This article also quoted Mohler: "The bottom line is there has been a substantial drop in the number of music students at the graduate level in Southern Baptist Convention seminaries."[109] The article also makes note that the music faculty would drop from eleven to four full-time faculty and that these staff reductions would take place by attrition.[110]

No matter what the seminary attempted to communicate regarding the administrative transition of the SCMW into the School of Church Ministries, the perception of many from outside the seminary community[111] was that Southern Seminary President Mohler had "killed" and disbanded the school of church music.[112] I can attest anecdotally to a pervasive and

---

107. Robinson, "Southern Launches New School," 41.
108. Allen, "Southern Seminary Closing School of Church Music."
109. Allen, "Southern Seminary Closing School of Church Music."
110. Allen, "Southern Seminary Closing School of Church Music."
111. The seminary "bubble" is a colloquial term used by several interviewees to describe the culture and influence of SBTS or any other institution with their immediately surrounding constituency.
112. Crider, phone interview by author, August 13, 2021.

persistent misunderstanding on the part of many who seemed to believe that the seminary ceased worship leader training in 2009. According to Jason Stewart, Kentucky Baptist Convention music and worship specialist and SCM alumnus, in 2015 this misconception was still a part of the conversation among Kentucky Baptist ministers of music.[113] Part of the continuing mission of those who serve and study in the department of biblical worship (DBW) is to graciously prove that the opposite is true.

After the creation of the school of church ministries in 2009 by the merging of the old SCMW with the school of church Leadership, the SCMW no longer existed as an entity of Southern Seminary, but its mission continued as the "division of biblical worship." School of church ministries dean Randy Stinson believed that the initial name change to "division" of biblical worship might stir up more negative sentiments than necessary; therefore, Stinson ultimately changed the name to "department of biblical worship."[114]

By all accounts, the academic year of 2009–10 was a memorable year for worship leader training at Southern Seminary. By May 2010, the sixty-five-year-old SCMW was no longer a school. The Church Music Institute had been permanently cancelled and the oratorio chorus and seminary orchestra had been disbanded.[115] Several of the remaining faculty had retired; Tom Bolton retired as dean but continued as professor until full retirement in 2012. This left Maurice Henson as senior professor along with four full-time faculty members: Ronald Turner, Sandra Turner, Esther Crookshank, Carl Stam, and newly appointed music and worship division chair, Greg Brewton. Carl Stam passed away shortly after the SCMW's transition to the DBW, and Sandra Turner did not return the following year, leaving only three full-time faculty total. Southern Seminary's entity for worship leader training had been administratively pruned but was still seeking answers for how to connect with its constituency and rebuild its enrollment. A radical change had been made. This time, however, in contrast to the last major SCMW transition of 2000, hope of recovery for many seemed more difficult to find.

---

113. Stewart, interview.
114. Crider, interview.
115. SBTS, "Self Study," 7.

6

The Division/Department of Biblical Worship, 2009–19

INSTITUTIONAL MERGER I: THE SCHOOL OF CHURCH MINISTRIES, 2009–13

In 2015, the department of biblical worship included a timeline within the self-study undertaken by and included in the DBW's report to the commission on accreditation for NASM. This timeline provided a synopsis of the curricular developments for music and worship training undertaken by Southern Seminary since the previous report that was submitted in 2005. Dr. Greg Brewton, who was the department chair at the time, prepared much of the report, which was submitted on February 20, 2015.[1] NASM required five information points to be fulfilled within the self-study: (1) Degrees for which renewal of final approval for listing is sought. [There were none.] (2) Degrees for which plan approval and final approval for listing are sought at the same time. [There were none.] (3) Degrees for which plan approval is sought: master of arts in worship leadership, professional track. (4) Degrees for which final approval for listing is sought: master of arts in worship leadership (music); master of divinity in worship leadership (music); master of church music. (5) Degrees for which renewal of plan approval is sought: bachelor of science in biblical studies (worship [music]

---

1. SBTS, "Self Study."

and pastoral studies); bachelor of science in biblical studies (worship and music studies).[2]

The information provided for NASM's inquiries represented the most significant changes ever made to worship leader training curriculum at Southern Seminary. These changes did not take place all at once, nor did they take place in a vacuum. Rather, many other smaller events between 2009 and 2015 combined to create a significant change in music and worship studies at Southern Seminary.

Events Impacting the Division of Biblical Worship

In addition to the notable and previously mentioned items from 2009, there were other factors at work that impacted the state of the DBW. In April of 2009, Dr. Mohler established the Academy of Sacred Music as a forum for concerts and lectures. This academy, a subset of the DBW, was directed by Dr. Esther Crookshank.[3] In addition to the large administrative change which came through the SCMW's transition to the division of biblical worship in 2009, all of the degree programs offered by the new DBW were revised.[4] One of these revisions was the termination of the doctor of musical arts degree (DMA) including the closing of new admissions to DMA entrants.[5] Two years after the DMA was terminated, the PhD in Christian worship degree was launched in 2011.[6] This curricular revision required reapproval from accrediting agencies like NASM, SACS, ATS.

A tangential occurrence, but nonetheless impacting the work of the DBW, Boyce Music Professor Nathan Platt resigned following the spring semester of 2010 to serve as worship pastor of a local church in Michigan.[7] Platt's vacancy was filled by R. Scott Connell [to be addressed later in this chapter]. Connell was hired as the program director for the newly revised bachelor's degrees in worship studies offered by Boyce College, the undergraduate institution of Southern Seminary.[8] Although a clear administrative distinction exists between all Southern Seminary schools, degrees,

2. SBTS, "Self Study."
3. SBTS, "Self Study," 11.
4. SBTS, "Self Study," 12.
5. SBTS, "Self Study," 8.
6. SBTS, "Self Study," 8.
7. SBTS, "Self Study," 12.
8. SBTS, "Self Study," 12.

and coursework and those of Boyce College, the worship leader training degrees offered by the DBW and Boyce College were more unified. In fact, NASM considered [and still considers] the music and worship degrees at SBTS and Boyce College as representing one unified entity.[9] May of 2010 also saw the retirement of Dr. Tom Bolton and a medical leave for Professor Stam, who would pass away the following May from his illness.[10]

Significant changes were in motion for worship leader training at Southern Seminary. Many graduates, former faculty, and those in the alumni community of the SCMW were mourning the losses of all they had known and loved.[11] To many from this constituency who were attached to former generations of the SCMW, the new changes represented the "footsteps of doom" for worship leader training at Southern Seminary.[12] This was an unfortunate misunderstanding and far from the truth. The drastic changes in the curricula for worship leader training were made in response to the changes in worship culture and the needs of Southern Baptist churches—changes made to ensure worship leader training continued at Southern Seminary. The job competencies needed for worship pastors in SBC churches had changed significantly from those job competencies required for ministers of music who had entered ministry thirty years earlier. In 2009 and 2010, the administration of Southern Seminary was seeking to redesign the worship leadership training curriculum in order to better prepare students for the job requirements that were currently found in the majority of SBC churches.[13] In order to understand this dynamic, a short excursus examines these changing job competencies.

JOB COMPETENCIES FOR MINISTERS OF MUSIC, 1960S–80S

As indicated previously, SBTS has, from its very beginning, valued congregational worship and the training of those who lead local churches in corporate worship. Especially in the decades after World War II, the need for and prevalence of full-time leaders of church music and worship grew.[14]

9. SBTS, "Self Study," 9–12.
10. SBTS, "Self Study," 12.
11. Stewart, phone interview by author, October 13, 2021.
12. Stewart, interview.
13. Crider, phone interview by author, August 13, 2021.
14. Bearden, "Competencies for Minister of Music," 15–20.

These worship leaders generally went by the title "minister of music" and filled the roles of spiritual leader, administrator, music educator, and performer.[15] Professor James C. McKinney of SWBTS wrote in 1967 of job competencies that a minister of music needed to possess in a series of articles published in the former Baptist Sunday school board publication, *The Church Musician*. McKinney's four role descriptions are worth quoting in full:

> As a Spiritual Leader, the minister of music must be "thoroughly grounded in (1) hymnology; (2) the uses of music in worship, proclamation, and Christian growth; (3) the manner and forms of worship for various church groups; and (4) the history of music in the Christian church.
>
> The minister must have skills and knowledges beyond those required of other musicians. As a Music Educator, the minister of music must have specific music skills and be able to use music methods and materials for each age group in the church. In addition, he must have a working knowledge of learning theories, group dynamics, and interpersonal relations all for the purpose that the program participants may worship, witness, and minister through music.
>
> As an Administrator, he must be able to (1) enlist, supervise, and train volunteer "workers" and music program employees; (2) purchase and maintain music and music supplies, musical instruments, robes, and electronic equipment; and (3) plan the overall program of church music as a part of the total church life. In addition, the church music administrator must be able to deal with such matters as music budget preparation, music facility design, public relations and publicity, and special projects (radio programs and telecasts that use music).
>
> As a Performer, the minister of music should function as a competent conductor, both chorally and instrumentally, with in-depth knowledge of church music literature and performance practices. Skills in music analysis and arranging, basic keyboard execution, and a knowledge of the problems and possibilities of accompanists and the organist are needed. Vocally, the minister of music must sing adequately enough to demonstrate a good vocal sound to the choir and have a solid knowledge of vocal pedagogical techniques."[16]

---

15. McKinney, "Person and Work of Church Musician," quoted in Bearden, 43.

16. McKinney, "Person and Work of Church Musician," 43–45.

It is significant that in the mid-1960s, the leading church musicians in the denomination viewed congregations as being in need of ongoing music education, with a skilled musician at the helm whose musicianship could be emulated. Thus, according to one of the leading Southern Baptist church musicians, the four roles of spiritual leader, music educator, administrator, and skilled performer were of greatest importance for the worship life of a healthy church.

In the decades following the opening of the SCM, more and more churches needed ministers of music who were trained in areas identified by McKinney. Much of this urgency was driven by congregations use in worship of large musical ensembles who required competent leadership. Instruction and encouragement from denominational leaders such as McKinney filled the needs of congregations who were attempting to respond to the growing worship needs of their churches.

During the remainder of the 1960s and 1970s, other studies were published that specified worship leader job competencies in Southern Baptist churches. These studies mostly focused on the philosophy and vision needed by ministers of music to perform their job, though some studies also addressed practical job competencies. One of these studies was Loren R. Williams's *A Study of Church Music Ministry in Southern Baptist Churches: Implications and Suggestions for Program Utilization* (1967), which "revealed a need for more and better trained music leadership for the churches," including better piano and organ training and the ability to work with a wide range of instruments.[17]

In 1971, an SBC church music department committee chaired by LeRoy McClard produced a project providing a list of church music leader qualities. The qualities listed included (1) personal qualities such as Christian commitment, loyalty to the church, dependability, love for people and music, and an outgoing personality; (2) training and experience in general leadership, including general and specialized (but unspecified) music skills; and (3) a knowledge of the assigned responsibilities, including the constituency and the organizational procedures.[18] In 1971, Cecil M. Roper produced a study for the church music department of the Sunday school board that focused on the background and training of SBC ministers of music. Roper's study recommended curriculum guidelines for SBC colleges and seminaries that he believed should be created by a committee selected from the music faculties of representative schools, local churches,

17. Williams, "A Study of Church Music," quoted in Bearden, 45.
18. McClard et al., "Church Music Program," quoted in Bearden, 47–48.

and the SBC church music conference. Roper cited the decline of music education in public schools as a driving factor behind the need for greater attention to the musical education aspects of music ministry in the local church, including increasing the music education component in church music degree curricula.[19] In addition to these published studies, there were also numerous lecture presentations on the subject given in locations such as the SBC church music conference and Ridgecrest music week.[20] These events represented large gatherings of both professional and volunteer music and worship constituents from SBC churches across the nation. Due to the inherent social aspects of these gatherings, addressing the large crowds provided significant impacts for the spread of ideas beyond the influence of many written studies. From the 1940s through the 1970s, the worship culture of SBC churches was both musically rich and pastorally demanding. Ministers of music who served during this worship culture required job competencies with significant musical, relational, and administrative skill.

In 1980, the same year that Milburn Price became dean of the SCM, Donald Roland Bearden, a master of church music graduate from NOBTS completed an extremely thorough study of job competencies required for SBC ministers of music.[21] Bearden's dissertation, the first on the subject, laid a foundation for congregational understanding of the position of minister of music as well as providing the impetus for three more dissertations on the subject appearing in 2003 (Barnett), 2007 (Flahardy), and 2016 (Sheeks).[22] Part of Bearden's mixed-methods study[23] included a survey of ministers of music, denominational leaders, and church music professors. The goal of his project was to identify a set of common job competencies that could be agreed upon by church music professionals, churches, and the academy. Survey participants were asked approximately one week in advance to prepare for their interviews with Bearden by carrying out the following: "(1) Determine the major areas in the church's music ministry (several suggested areas were listed); (2) List goals for each area of primary

---

19. Roper, "Training, Attitudes, and Influences of Southern Baptist Music Directors," quoted in Bearden, 50–51.

20. Bearden, "Competencies for Minister of Music," 45–46.

21. Bearden, "Competencies for Minister of Music," abstract.

22. Barnett, "Comparative Analysis of Critical Competencies"; Flahardy, "Essential Leadership Competencies"; and Sheeks, "Skills Necessary for Evangelical Church Music Ministry."

23. Creswell, *Qualitative Inquiry and Research Design*, 215.

significance; (3) Decide how goal achievement could be determined; (4) List these goals in order of importance or urgency."[24]

Bearden's study revealed a variety of insights. The goals for music ministry most often mentioned by survey participants from every category of church music professional "fit into the area of musical skills and knowledge."[25] The goals included goal 2 (to develop in choir members traits of loyalty and commitment, and reinforce theological truths); goal 4 (to develop a music education program which promotes consistent growth in its members; goal 5 (to develop a program for training the congregation in hymnody and hymn singing); goal 6 (to have choir members who use correct vocal technique); goal 8 (to develop skills in basic musicianship of all members of the church music program); goal 9 (to provide musical experiences for members of the church music program which result in fulfillment and joy; and goal 14 (to develop choir members sensitivity to choral blend, balance, and musical interpretation).[26]

Bearden's research included three different interview formats designed respectively for (1) church music professionals representing small, medium, and large churches; (2) college and seminary church music professors; and (3) denominational worship leaders. Bearden concluded that for all three groups the primary goals for their music and worship ministries (in 1980) all involved highly developing the musical skills, musical appreciation, and musical fulfillment of the congregation.[27] Though these goals seemed to reflect the philosophy upon which the SCM was founded in 1944, Bearden also realized that even by 1980, the majority of church music training curriculum had not kept up with the evolving job competencies required for SBC ministers of music.[28] To this point Bearden wrote, "There exists today a great need for strengthening of the church music program in Southern Baptist colleges. . . . A recent examination of college catalogs from a representative number of Southern Baptist colleges shows little evidence of significant change in the church music programs since 1964."[29]

By the turn of the new millennium, the goals for music and worship ministries in local churches had changed even more significantly. By the early 2000s, many churches had begun to choose job titles like "worship

24. Bearden, "Competencies for Minister of Music," 54.
25. Bearden, "Competencies for Minister of Music," 65.
26. Bearden, "Competencies for Minister of Music," 64.
27. Bearden, "Competencies for Minister of Music," 65–66.
28. Bearden, quoted in Boer, "Comparative Content Analysis," 8.
29. Bearden, quoted Boer, 8.

pastor" rather than "minister of music." What exactly was the difference between a minister of music and a worship pastor? How were these differences impacting worship leader training at SBTS?

FROM MINISTER OF MUSIC TO WORSHIP PASTOR

Monique Ingalls, in her groundbreaking dissertation on the contemporary worship movement (2008), described a significant change in church music and worship leadership that began to occur within evangelical churches at the end of the twentieth century:

> Perhaps the most important structural change in church worship that the adoption of contemporary worship instigated was the shift from "music minister" to "worship leader" . . . "Worship leaders," who generally served as lead vocalist and guitarist during musical worship, were trained in popular styles and were often expected to give verbal exhortations and spontaneous prayers. As charismatic ideas about worship became widespread among evangelicals, the worship leader was seen as being responsible for leading the people into a moving experience of the presence of God.[30]

For Ingalls, it was the spread of charismatic theology and practices of worship into broader evangelical church life that changed the role of the person in leadership from skilled musician modeling vibrant singing to a person leading worshipers into the presence of God. In his dissertation on worship leader competencies a decade later (2019), worship scholar-pastor Ken Boer observed, "While pastors in previous eras viewed themselves as responsible for leadership of the entire service, including prayer, Scripture reading, and selection of music, many pastors today delegate these responsibilities to worship leaders [and worship pastors] and focus their energies on the sermon."[31] Both Ingalls and Boer point to important differences that have developed in corporate worship leadership over the last few decades.[32]

Worship historian Lester Ruth remarked that to many church attenders, contemporary worship music and praise and worship music features bands instead of orchestras, projected images on screens instead of printed hymnals.[33] Other facets, Ruth remarks, have "flipped several classic liturgical

30. Ingalls, "Awesome in This Place," 1.
31. Boer, "Comparative Content Analysis," 2.
32. Boer, "Comparative Content Analysis," 1.
33. Ruth and Lim, *Lovin' on Jesus*, 1.

The Division/Department of Biblical Worship, 2009–19

presumptions on their head for a generation of young Christians."[34] These "flipped presumptions" shifted the job title of most worship leading church musicians from "minister of music," the term originated by John Finley Williamson and his Westminster choir in the 1930s, (see chapter 3 of this dissertation) to that of "worship leader" or "worship pastor." In 2001, a report published by the North American Mission Board of the SBC (*Southern Baptist Congregations Today: A Survey at the Turn of the New Millennium*) determined that 11.7 percent of SBC churches always used praise teams in their worship services while 6.9 percent used them often and only 44.3 percent never used them.[35] Job titles and musical leadership models were clearly changing within the denomination. A broadening and transition in job competencies logically followed.

The change in job titles was not simply a shift in nomenclature; it described a shift that was occurring within the tasks and goals of worship in local churches. Most worship pastors, unlike ministers of music, placed greater job emphasis on contemporary music styles. This change increased the responsibility for most aspects of both worship planning and worship leadership. The additional worship leading responsibilities often included the leading of public prayer and spoken transitions. This meant that worship leaders needed to have sensitivity towards the congregation's *emotional* involvement in the worship service [emphasis added].[36] Marty McCall, former creative arts pastor at McClean Bible Church (a church of over 20,000 members in the suburbs of Washington, DC) described the roles of the modern worship pastor in his worship blog in 2018 as including "singer, musician, arranger, band director, event planner, scheduling genius, walking song library, tech and leadership liaison, rehearsal manager, organizer, producer, stage hand, peacemaker, encourager, confronter, comforter, budget manager, administrator, employee, and boss."[37] Though many of the responsibilities overlapped between minister of music and worship pastor, the lens of responsibilities and skills needed to serve as a worship pastor often require a different outlook. This new outlook created a fresh impetus to redefine the job competencies held by ministers of music from earlier years.

---

34. Ruth and Lim, *Lovin' on Jesus*, 1.
35. Jones, "Southern Baptist Congregations and Worshipers," 38.
36. Boer, "Comparative Content Analysis," 1.
37. McCall, "Worship Leaders Get a Mentor," 3n10.

Defining the Roles of Worship Pastors

Over the last several years, worship theologians, worship leaders, and church musicians have attempted to define the role of a modern worship pastor. John Witvliet, the director of the Calvin Institute of Christian worship and professor of worship, theology, and congregational ministry studies at Calvin University and Calvin Theological Seminary, supplies four self-identities of those who lead worship: (1) craftspeople who shape and deliver something as art; (2) directors or coordinators who recruit volunteers, proofread orders of service, and work with sound technicians; (3) performers on stage whom others watch; 4) spiritual engineers whose creativity, personal testimony and charismatic personality can turn an ordinary moment into a holy moment.[38] Paxon Jeancake, director of worship at Covenant Church in Palm Bay, Florida, and writing contributor for The Gospel Coalition writes of the worship pastor's role in his book *The Art of Worship: Opening Our Eyes to the Beauty of the Gospel*. Jeancake writes that because gospel-centered worship has three dimensions of leadership, theology, and community, the worship pastor must "think like a theologian, labor like an artist, and shepherd like a pastor."[39] Author, composer, speaker, teacher, and former worship pastor Greg Scheer believes that worship leaders and pastors generally fall into five categories: performer, creator, therapist, teacher, and director.[40] Boer synchronized his survey of these and other defining qualities of the modern worship pastor in a taxonomy of worship leader roles. Boer's taxonomy of roles included personal faith, theology, liturgy, art, corporate pastor, pastor of volunteers, engager of public leadership, director/coordinator, evangelist, tech director, and teacher.[41]

Boer's Summary of Worship Leader Competencies

In Boer's dissertation, he compared worship leadership curricula from several SBC undergraduate college, university, and seminary programs with the job descriptions from many SBC churches seeking candidates for open worship pastor positions. The uniqueness of Boer's research came through its three parameters, "(1) the desired characteristics of worship leaders, (2) within the Southern Baptist Convention (3) in both churches

---

38. Witvliet, *Worship Seeking Understanding*, 262, quoted in Boer, 48–49.
39. Jeancake, *The Art of Worship*, 37–44, quoted in Boer, 49.
40. Scheer, *Essential Worship*, 269, quoted in Boer, 50.
41. Boer, "Comparative Content Analysis," 54.

and undergraduate worship programs."[42] As Boer created his list for comparison between curriculums and job descriptions, he summarized the worship pastor competencies which churches desired from their worship pastor candidates as indicated by their job descriptions. Boer then synthesized and ranked these qualities. The quality most highly desired by churches for their worship leaders was found to be "the Worship Leader's Heart."[43] For churches and worship scholars, the personal character and integrity of the candidate for ministry were of primary importance. The next competency Boer listed was that of interpersonal skills for ministry.[44] Among the interpersonal skills needed, Boer identified both the worship pastor's relationships with worship ministry volunteers and church members. Of primary importance for Boer, however, were the relationships between worship pastor and senior pastor.[45] Boer's third criterion was the worship pastor's ability to mentor future leaders.[46] Fourth was the worship leader's ability to wisely plan corporate worship; planning corporate worship includes the worship leader's task of selecting music and planning the service order.[47] Boer points out that in addition to his findings, a 2016 study, "Skills Necessary for Evangelical Church Music Ministry," noted that worship planning and design was determined to be "very important" by eighty-one percent of the study's respondents.[48] The fifth highest rated job competency indicated for worship leaders was the worship leader's theological understanding.[49] Due to the great importance inherent to the role, Boer's study found that a large majority of churches seeking worship leaders are significantly concerned with the theological understanding of the individual who fulfills these tasks. Following these top five qualities, as the sixth criterion, came the job competencies to lead singing.[50] Boer's list encompasses eleven more criteria, including the following: ability to lead through speaking and prayer,[51] contemporary vocal and instrumental

---

42. Boer, "Comparative Content Analysis," 93.
43. Boer, "Comparative Content Analysis," 67.
44. Boer, "Comparative Content Analysis," 69.
45. Boer, "Comparative Content Analysis," 70.
46. Boer, "Comparative Content Analysis," 71.
47. Boer, "Comparative Content Analysis," 71.
48. Boer, "Comparative Content Analysis," 72.
49. Boer, "Comparative Content Analysis," 73.
50. Boer, "Comparative Content Analysis," 75–76.
51. Boer, "Comparative Content Analysis," 76–77.

leadership,[52] choral leadership,[53] instrumental conducting and orchestra,[54] knowledge of music theory,[55] songwriting,[56] training children and youth in musical skills,[57] non-verbal communication skills,[58] drama and visual arts,[59] culturally-driven leadership,[60] worship technology,[61] and administration.[62]

Boer's insights are important because, as he argues in his dissertation, very few studies have used categories derived from churches rather than schools.[63] Boer also discovered that schools of music generally created and justified their curricula solely based on NASM standards rather than the concerns of churches or schools.[64] Bearden's study from 1980 included interviews from active music ministry professionals, but only Boer examined existing curricula. In 1980, the NASM standards and job competencies for church music ministry positions displayed general congruence, but by 2019 this was clearly no longer the case. The drastic administrative transitions at SBTS in 2009 led to a soul-searching on the part of those at Southern who were committed to training worship leaders for the churches of the SBC. Though many competent leaders had tried valiantly for several years to adapt and revise the curriculum of the former SCM, their efforts appeared to be too little too late. By 2011, with the lowest number of full-time residential worship students since the 1940s,[65] SCM dean Randy Stinson looked outside for help, with three new hires. He found it in Joseph R. Crider, Charles T. Lewis, and R. Scott Connell.

---

52. Boer, "Comparative Content Analysis," 78–79.
53. Boer, "Comparative Content Analysis," 80–81.
54. Boer, "Comparative Content Analysis," 81–2.
55. Boer, "Comparative Content Analysis," 82–84.
56. Boer, "Comparative Content Analysis," 84–85.
57. Boer, "Comparative Content Analysis," 86.
58. Boer, "Comparative Content Analysis," 86–88.
59. Boer, "Comparative Content Analysis," 88–89.
60. Boer, "Comparative Content Analysis," 89–91.
61. Boer, "Comparative Content Analysis," 91–92.
62. Boer, "Comparative Content Analysis," 92–93.
63. Boer, "Comparative Content Analysis," 93.
64. Boer, "Comparative Content Analysis," 93.
65. Carle, "History of School of Church Music," 56; and SBTS, "Special Task Force," 5.

The Division/Department of Biblical Worship, 2009–19

FACULTY ADDITIONS

Scott Connell and the Reenergizing of Undergraduate Worship Leader Training

In 1955, under Forrest Heeren, the SCM discontinued offering the bachelor of sacred music.[66] Because of the vision and direction of the SCM of that time, Southern chose to cease offering undergraduate degrees in church music. Years later, in 2007 with the maturing of Boyce College into an accredited undergraduate institution, a degree was added: bachelor of science in biblical studies: music ministry.[67] At that point Nathan Platt, a recent DMA graduate from the SCMW was appointed the coordinating professor for the Boyce College music program—"basically a one-man-show," to quote a contemporary alumnus of his, Matthew Swain.[68] As part of the administrative reorganization that brought about the consolidation of the SCMW and the School of Leadership into the School of Church Ministries, the music and worship studies for Boyce College transitioned to Cooke Hall to benefit from a shared proximity to the seminary music and worship studies program as well as the excellent facilities.[69] As dean of the School of Church Ministries, Stinson was interested in integrating the curriculums for the programs represented in his new school and he rightly realized the crucial connection between the flourishing of graduate worship studies and that of a growing undergraduate program. The key person who helped these plans come to fruition was Connell.

On October 11, 2010, a news release announced that Boyce College had named Scott Connell as its new instructor of music and worship leadership. In July of that year, Connell had visited Southern's campus as a prospective student. In a meeting in which Connell expressed to Michael Wilder his concern that worship pastors should be trained theologically, Wilder encouraged Connell to pursue a PhD through the School of Church Ministries. This conversation "sparked a series of meetings that culminated in Southern offering Connell his position as instructor of music and worship leadership at Boyce."[70] Connell had previously served as a senior pastor, church planter, associate pastor, minister of music and youth, and

---

66. Carle, "History of School of Church Music," 125.
67. Boyce College, *Academic Catalog (2007)*.
68. Swain and Swain, interview.
69. Swain and Swain, interview.
70. Hayes, "Southern Story: Scott Connell," 12.

Christian school principal.[71] His background completely fit the culture and vision of Stinson. Stinson remarked, "I am personally excited about Connell being a part of the SBTS team. He embodies the threefold commitment of the School of Church Ministries in the areas of biblical worship, family discipleship, and pastoral leadership. He is a pastor who leads worship, not a *mere church musician* [emphasis added], which is central to our new direction."[72] Stinson was not interested in hiring "mere church musicians." In Crider and Lewis, it turned out that Stinson again found exactly the people he wanted.

Crider and Lewis Come to Southern

Over the course of a weekend in the middle of the spring semester of 2011, Stinson, dean of the newly formed School of Church Ministries, assembled Timothy Paul Jones (associate professor of leadership and church ministry), Michael Wilder (associate professor of leadership and church ministry), Greg Brewton (associate dean of worship leadership and coordinator of music and worship studies), Charles Lewis, and Joseph Crider just outside of Louisville at General Butler State Park.[73] Over two days this group met, resembling a local church staff and "looking at and dreaming about" the curriculum they wanted to reshape in the SCM.[74] Stinson, Jones, Wilder, and Brewton were all SBTS faculty who had made the transition from their respective former schools into the new school. Lewis and Crider, on the other hand, were not yet faculty. Lewis was serving as the minister of music and worship at First Baptist Church of West Palm Beach, Florida, and teaching adjunctively at Palm Beach Atlantic University, while Crider was serving as an associate dean of the School of Arts and Sciences at Liberty University in Lynchburg, Virginia. Crider recollected, "We just got together and dreamt about what a school of church ministries would look like in theological education."[75] As lifelong practitioners of church music and worship and coming from outside the traditions of the SCMW, Crider and Lewis were hired to help turn the proverbial ship around.

---

71. Hayes, "Southern Story," 12.
72. Hayes, "Boyce College Brings Pastor, Worship Leader on Board."
73. Crider, interview.
74. Crider, interview.
75. Crider, interview.

The memorial issue of *The Towers* magazine (May 23, 2011) honored recently deceased professor Carl "Chip" Stam, who had passed on May 10. Though the edition clearly focused on Stam's legacy, buried on a page towards the back of the magazine a headline read, "SBTS adds new music and worship profs to SCM."[76] In this article, in addition to accolades emanating from their respective pastors and deans, Stinson added,

> Joe Crider and Chuck Lewis share our vision. They are able to train up those who will be not only accomplished musicians but pastors who lead worship. These men are respected in the scholarly guild, but they are also two of the most effective worship leaders in our denomination, who know what it is, week by week, to lead the people of God in worship. I could not be more thrilled to see these two men joining us in spending the next decades of their ministry training up the next generation of worship pastors."[77]

Lauded as "two prominent worship leaders in the Southern Baptist Convention," Crider and Lewis were described as being "part of a major step forward in the seminary's School of Church Ministries' vision for training worship pastors equipped for the challenges of the 21st century."[78]

Crider came to Southern with over twenty years of vocational ministry experience. His local church ministry experience, included service as the worship pastor of Second Baptist Church in Springfield, Missouri, and First Baptist Church, Roanoke, Virginia.[79] He served these churches while teaching at Southwest Baptist University in Bolivar, Missouri, and Liberty University in Lynchburg, Virginia, respectively.[80] While at Liberty, Crider served as the associate dean of the college of arts and sciences and a professor of music and humanities.[81] During his tenure at Southern, Crider would continue to serve local churches as the worship pastor of Highview Baptist Church in Louisville, and then LaGrange Baptist Church in LaGrange, Kentucky.[82]

Lewis also spent over twenty years serving in vocational ministry in local churches before coming to SBTS, including First Baptist Church in

---

76. Griffin, "SBTS Adds New Profs to SCM," 14.
77. Griffin, "SBTS Adds New Profs to SCM," 14.
78. Griffin, "SBTS Adds New Profs to SCM," 14.
79. Crider, curriculum vitae.
80. Crider, curriculum vitae.
81. Crider, curriculum vitae.
82. Crider, curriculum vitae.

West Palm Beach, Florida. While serving FBC West Palm Beach, Lewis also served as an adjunct professor at Palm Beach Atlantic University under the leadership of former SCMW dean Lloyd Mims. At Southern, in addition to spearheading theory and aural skills courses, Lewis was best known for his leadership and direction of Southern's premiere vocal ensemble, Doxology.[83]

Sometime in the summer of 2011, before the academic year began, Crider, Lewis, and Brewton went back again to General Butler State Park for another retreat, but this time, in addition to creating new curriculum, the purpose was also spiritual in nature.[84] In an interview, Crider related,

> We did devotions, we prayed, we sought the Lord, we prayed on our knees, we cried out to God. It was a very, very intensely spiritual time, but we also looked at every part of the curriculum—we basically started with a clean sheet of paper. We said, okay, if we could build our own curriculum to produce the most effective worship pastors, what would it look like? We had one of those huge pieces of flip paper and with all the pages and we created this fictional person called Dob W (an acronym for Department of Biblical Worship)."
>
> We drew a stick figure with a head, heart, hands, and feet representing different aspects of a student. Then we just spent time talking about what classes Dob W would need to have, with the hands representing musical skills, the heart being the heart of a pastor and ministry side of things, the head being the theological and biblical understandings of worship, and the feet being the missional/evangelical community-related aspects of a worship leader.
>
> We spent time with each of those areas figuring out what classes we should offer. Then we went through what we felt were the best books to use in those classes, what texts would best represent those things, and began to develop every aspect of the curriculum and then we went back to the school. For the first few faculty meetings of the School of Church Ministries we were approving curricular changes right and left.[85]

The curriculum changes developed by Crider, Lewis, and Brewton at this retreat would eventually turn into the curriculum changes reported by Brewton in the 2015 NASM Self-Study Report.

---

83. Lewis, curriculum vitae.
84. Crider, interview.
85. Crider, interview.

The Division/Department of Biblical Worship, 2009–19

THE FAITHFUL LABOR OF GREGORY B. BREWTON

Though most changes occurring in worship leader training at Southern were driven by new faces, one specific veteran professor contributed to positive changes ushered in by the new team of faculty: Gregory B. Brewton. Brewton was a product of Forrest Heeren's SCM, earning his master of church music degree in 1980 during a period of peak enrollment for the SCM.[86] After serving local churches in music and worship ministry for over twenty years, Brewton and his family returned to Louisville in 1998 for Brewton to pursue the doctor of musical arts (DMA). Little did Brewton know the magnitude of transitions coming to the SCMW and the role he would play in them. In 2000, after Brewton completed his coursework for the DMA, both Mims and Dickson departed Southern to teach in different institutions: Mims becoming the dean of the school of fine arts at Palm Beach Atlantic University and Dickson to Texas Tech University as the director of choral activities. The holes left by their departures had significant ramifications for two students in particular, Matthew Swain and Greg Brewton.[87] Both Swain and Brewton were DMA students intending to study voice with Mims and conducting with Dickson. After Mims and Dickson departed, Swain and Brewton were left without primary professors in their areas of study. Both felt they had little recourse but to change their degrees to ones that could be completed with the remaining faculty.[88] That meant stepping back from their research degrees (DMA) to the doctor of music ministry degree (DMM), which was a professional doctorate containing fewer academic credentials.

After the two graduated in 2001, Swain, feeling called to service in the local church, departed Louisville to serve a church in Savannah, Georgia.[89] Interestingly, Swain later accepted the position of professor of music and worship at MBTS in Kansas City, moving back into the academy to direct both the undergraduate and graduate worship programs at MBTS.[90] Brewton, on the other hand, had been serving local churches in Louisville and remained connected to Southern Seminary as an adjunct professor. The decision to remain in Louisville meant that when the opportunity presented

---

86. "Heeren Ends 29-year Tenure."
87. Swain and Swain, interview.
88. Swain and Swain, interview.
89. Swain and Swain, interview.
90. Swain and Swain, interview.

itself, Brewton was positioned to coordinate the Boyce College music and worship degrees (before Platt) and later to serve as the department chair for the Division (and then Department) of Biblical Worship.

Brewton's time at Southern was qualitatively different than many music and worship faculty. As opposed to being hired for an open position after a national search, Brewton came as a student and patiently waited his turn—when opportunity arose and need was great, he was there to take on the necessary work. He routinely served in the background, simply grateful for any opportunity he could get to serve the seminary by teaching and mentoring students.[91] While many of the church musicians and worship leaders trained by the former SCM were locked into a philosophy and style from a bygone era, Brewton always looked forward, embracing new ideas and new methods.[92] When Crider and Lewis spearheaded significant change in the DBW, Brewton was excited to join in the renewal of enthusiasm and purpose rather than departing in disappointment. It was in this spirit that Brewton humbly continued with the administrative title and responsibilities of department chair for biblical worship while at the same time stepping back, allowing Crider to take the lead in the department's renewal. Brewton understood the unfortunate circumstances of holding a professional doctorate (DMM) rather than the more esteemed research doctorate (DMA). When his lack of academic credentials kept him for many years from acceptance into the full faculty at Southern, he did not complain; he simply carried on teaching, directing, serving, and mentoring the students God placed in his path.

In September of 2021, Brewton contracted the COVID-19 virus. Within two weeks, he passed away at Baptist East Hospital in Louisville at the age of sixty-five.[93] President Mohler called Brewton "one of the most faithful, kind, committed, and gifted teachers of his generation and he shaped hundreds of worship leaders and musicians in the service of the church. . . . he was always ready to help and to lead."[94] Mohler's accolade was not an exaggeration. Though many connected to the Southern Seminary community may only recognize Brewton from his final years from his direction of the seminary's premiere vocal ensemble, Doxology, the legacy

---

91. Swain and Swain, interview.
92. Crider, interview.
93. Robinson, "SBTS Mourns Loss."
94. Robinson, "SBTS Mourns Loss."

The Division/Department of Biblical Worship, 2009-19

he left was far greater than the contributions of one role. This perspective was eloquently articulated by former provost Dr. Matthew Hall:

> Few professors have demonstrated greater dedication to their students than Greg Brewton. He held his students to the highest standards, expecting the very best of them. But those standards were undergirded by the irrepressible joy he took in teaching and the consistent love and care he showed for the lives of students and alumni. His ministry among us was one of God's kindest blessings.[95]

No history of worship leader training would be complete without documenting Dr. Greg Brewton and his pastoral impact on the hundreds of students and faculty he bettered for the sake of Christ's kingdom, including the author of this book.

CRIDER IMPLEMENTS CURRICULUM CHANGES

There were consistent curriculum changes at different intervals throughout the history of worship leader training at Southern Seminary. The majority of the changes made over the years were usually small changes, such as adding a class here or there or re-writing the syllabus of a particular course due to changes in NASM requirements. As pointed out by Boer in his research, most curriculum changes made by any music school or department have been made as a reaction to changes from the accreditation body. The changes made by Crider, Lewis, and Brewton in conjunction with other staff and administration in 2011 were more significant. Rather than starting with and keeping the degree corpus, the new curricula were written from the ground up.[96] Crider described many of the curriculum changes:

> All the band lab courses on rhythm instruments, those labs were inserted to be in place of previous classes. There were some classes that were offered before that they were making the music majors take that were just that—more classical types of things students were being made to take because they always had been. We got rid of several required classes in the old degree program and that made quite a bit of room for our new degree program. Still, our MA in worship was in the upper 60s in hours, maybe 67–68 hours. Wow, that was really robust—almost double what a normal Master

---

95. Robinson, "SBTS Mourns Loss."
96. Crider, interview.

of Arts in anything would be. I mean, most Master of Arts degrees are 30–36 hours and ours was really, really robust in comparison.

Some classes were brand new additions, but some were remodeled and redeveloped, like the Worshiping Church class Greg and I did. We had to make it more accessible to other non-music students because the other schools were going to be requiring it. Rather than aesthetics with a dive into philosophy, we wanted our curriculum to start with our theology to form our philosophy and inform our methodology. That was one of our mantras, the other was that we were training pastors who lead worship.[97]

Crider's thoughts demonstrate his assessment of the curriculum used by the SCMW to train worship leaders. Using the biblical metaphor, new wine needed new wineskins.

Crider's perception was consistent with every other new leader that appeared over the life of the SCMW. As has been noted, new leaders generally viewed their predecessors with respect, but also with a hint of criticism towards a perceived preoccupation with performance and lack of practical preparation for church ministry. In 2011, this perspective was not only understood but clearly articulated. As Crider and other interviewees have noted, for a long time, the perception of many was that the SBC seminaries (SBTS, SWBTS, SEBTS, MBTS, and NOBTS), had "divorced their curriculum" [but not intentionally] from the way that SBC churches were worshiping. Constituent churches believed that they [seminaries] had trained a generation of church musicians for "a world that just simply didn't exist anymore."[98] Crider disclosed, "We felt strongly that the only way that our students and eventually our graduates were going to make an impact on local churches was if they themselves had significantly developed their own spiritual walk and personally understood the transformative nature of corporate worship."[99] Although Crider and Lewis brought spirit-driven and meaningful changes to the DBW's curriculum, the enrollment did not immediately rebound. Sustained enrollment growth needed one more significant administrative change. That change would come in the leadership of Dr. Adam Greenway.

---

97. Crider, interview.
98. Crider, interview.
99. Crider, interview.

The Division/Department of Biblical Worship, 2009–19

Adam Greenway and Institutional Merger II: The Billy Graham School of Missions, Evangelism, and Ministry

By 2011, many significant changes had buffeted those who trained worship leaders at Southern Seminary. The SCM, SCMW, and now DBW had, in the span of three years, transitioned from being a free-standing school within Southern Seminary to being a department belonging to the new School of Church Ministries. In 2013, the DBW changed its administrative alignment again. Under the administrative support of dean Randy Stinson, Crider and Lewis had radically changed the curricula for training worship leaders—using guidance from their own practical experience along with input from several other notable worship pastors.[100] However, despite their hard work, enrollment in the DBW continued to slip. Between the 2010–11 and 2011–12 academic years, enrollment in seminary worship degrees fell from a total of 73 [not counting Boyce College degrees] to 53, a drop of twenty-eight percent.[101] In the following two academic years (2012–13 and 2013–14), the enrollment remained relatively stagnant at 49 and 50 FTE graduate worship students respectively. The 2013–14 academic year, however, included another administrative transition on the Southern Seminary campus that would impact the future of worship leader training.

During the 2013–2014 academic year, Dr. Mohler once again adjusted the administrative structure of Southern Seminary by combining the school of church ministries and the Billy Graham school of missions and evangelism. The new school would become the singular counterpart to the school of theology as the Billy Graham school of missions, evangelism, and ministry. The previous dean of the Billy Graham School (BGS), Zane Pratt, was appointed as the International Mission Board's vice president for global training. With the departure of provost Russell Moore to serve as the new head of the SBC Ethics and Religious Liberty Commission, the dean of the now dissolved SCM, Randy Stinson, was appointed to serve as Southern Seminary's new provost. The leadership of the new school fell to Dr. Adam Greenway.

Born in Avon Park, Florida, Greenway grew up fifteen minutes north of that community in Frostproof, Florida. A *cum laude* graduate of Samford University (1998), master of divinity graduate of SWBTS (2002), and

---

100. Crider, interview.
101. CWM degree information provided by SBTS Registrar Norm Chung.

PhD graduate from Southern (2007), Greenway was lauded in a SBTS press release (May 31, 2013) as a "consistent denominational leader" who had served in several roles within the Kentucky Baptist Convention including president.[102] Greenway had also served as a pastor, teaching professor, and seminary administrator.[103] Mohler remarked, "Our national search brought us right back home in this case, where the right man for the job was waiting, ready to take on this new challenge."[104] Later on October 1, 2013, President Mohler spoke to the significance of Greenway's installation:

> The Billy Graham School will celebrate its 20th anniversary later next year. It was 20 years ago that Dr. Billy Graham was present here in Louisville for the announcement of the establishment of that school as part of my inauguration. The Lord has greatly blessed this school over the years. This is the Lord's timing that as the Billy Graham School enters into its 20th year and as its aimed toward the future, Adam Greenway would be its dean.[105]

Greenway's four-point installation sermon offered four aspects for a "full gospel ministry."[106] Greenway's sermon functioned as an abstract for his deanship. Greenway pointed to the gospel's "divine origination" or that God is the ultimate source of everything known in creation, his identity as the author of redemption, and to his delight in reconciling people to himself.[107] The next point of his sermon pointed to the gospel's "divine declaration," and humanity's ultimate inability to pay the overdrawn account accumulated by their sins.[108] Thirdly, Greenway identified the gospel's "divine transaction" and how Christ became sin so that sinners might be reconciled to God.[109] Finally, Greenway appealed to the gospel's "divine mission" and the importance of God's mandate to all Christians to live out the Great Commission.[110] Greenway's sermon clearly articulated the need for *applied* theology and *applied* spirituality [emphasis added]. Applying

---

102. SBTS Office of Communications, press release, May 31, 2013.
103. Greenway, curriculum vitae.
104. SBTS, press release.
105. Irvin, "Installation Address."
106. Irvin, "Installation Address."
107. Irvin, "Installation Address."
108. Irvin, "Installation Address."
109. Irvin, "Installation Address."
110. Irvin, "Installation Address."

The Division/Department of Biblical Worship, 2009-19

the credo of this sermon to the department of biblical worship was to be a hallmark of Greenway's tenure as BGS dean.

FTE Progression from 2010 to 2019

DBW professors Brewton, Connell (Boyce College worship program coordinator), Crider, Crookshank, and Lewis served as a single unit for worship leader training at Southern Seminary and Boyce College for the better part of a decade. Under their leadership, the academic years from 2010 to 2019 demonstrated a pattern of growth in the number of FTE students. Although Southern Seminary considers Boyce College and the seminary separate entities, the faculty and curricula for worship leaders training have always been closely interrelated. For this reason, considering both undergraduate and graduate FTEs in worship provides a more complete understanding of the enrollment trends of the SCMW and DBW.

From 2010 to 2019, Boyce College, under the leadership of Connell, offered three different degrees for training worship leaders, the bachelor of science (BS) in Music, BS in worship and music studies, and BS in worship and pastoral studies.[111] The older music degree offering from Boyce College's earliest years as a fully credentialed private college, the BS in music, was the preferred degree chosen by students from 2010 through 2012.[112] However, by the 2012–13 academic year, enrollment in the two newer degrees, the BS in worship and music studies and the BS in worship and pastoral studies, surpassed the older degree. In conjunction with the rise in prominence of the newer degrees, 2012–13 also saw the FTEs for Boyce College worship degrees nearly double, from 25 FTEs in 2011–12 to 43 FTEs in 2012–13. Over the next three academic years (2013–14 through 2016–17), undergraduate worship training degrees saw consecutive increases. Connell's last two years as undergraduate program coordinator for undergraduate worship degrees saw FTEs rise as high as 80 and 81 students, respectively.

In 2018, Connell departed Boyce College to become the worship pastor at First Baptist Church, Jacksonville, Florida. With his departure, as with any transition, the enrollment growths over the following two years became a bit stagnant, with FTEs in 2018–19 and 2019–20 at 69 students, respectively. During Connell's time at Boyce College, he proved that a

---

111. See Boyce College, *Academic Catalog* for the following academic years: 2010–11; 2011–12; 2012–13; 2013–14; 2014–15; 2015–16; 2016–17; 2017–18; 2018–19.

112. The following relies on Boyce College, CMW enrollment statistics.

strong and pastoral leader, combined with strong curriculum that matched the worship culture of constituent SBC churches could combine to create an inviting Christian collegiate environment for families to send their undergraduate students to college. This was especially true for students who sought solid and relevant worship leader training at the undergraduate level.

As mentioned earlier in this chapter, Crider's and Lewis's first two years of service to Southern did not immediately yield the results of higher enrollments. During the first three academic years of the curriculum renewal (2010–13), the DBW offered over ten different degree programs.[113] In reality, the DBW offered three different degrees with different areas of specialization for each degree; a master of arts in worship leadership, a master of church music, and a master of divinity in worship leadership. The master of church music (MCM), which had been the majority degree for decades, slipped to a distant third place in degrees chosen by entering music and worship students. For instance, as late as 2010, the MCM still represented the majority-held worship degree with twenty students out of a total enrollment of 73. However, just two years later that number had dropped to only 9 MCM students. Looking forward to the academic year 2018–19, there were 12 MCM students compared to 96 total music and worship students. By the time the DBW got to 2020, there were only three degrees listed, the MA worship leadership, the master of church music, and the MDiv worship leadership, and by fall 2021 the master of church music was completely dropped from the degrees offered by the DBW.

Although during the first year of Crider's and Lewis's coming (2010–11) the DBW recorded an enrollment of 73 masters-level worship students, this number dropped to 53 in 2011–12. The next two years (2012–13 and 2013–14) also appeared to underperform with enrollments of 49 and 50, respectively. In 2014, however, the enrollment rebounded with a growth of nearly 40 percent to 81 FTEs. The strong enrollments continued in 2015–16 with 83 FTEs, 92 FTSs in 2016–17, 88 FTEs in 2017–18, and 96 FTEs in 2018–19.

When the enrollment growth of the undergraduate degrees offered by Boyce College are overlaid with the enrollments of the DBWs master's degrees, a strong pattern of enrollment growth is displayed for the decade of the 2010s. This figure clearly demonstrates the upward trending of worship

---

113. The following relies on SBTS, CMW degree enrollment statistics.

enrollment. It should be noted that these numbers do not represent doctoral enrollment of worship students. See table 1 below.

Both the Boyce College worship curriculum renewal and that of Southern Seminary each took approximately two years to demonstrate positive enrollment growth. However, both seemed to truly begin to develop significant effectiveness after the merging of the DBW into the BGS and the appointment of Greenway as dean. Both undergraduate and graduate degrees demonstrated their strongest efficacy when strong curriculum was combined with strong, spirit-led leadership. To this point, after the departure of Connell in 2018, the enrollment for Boyce worship degrees expectedly lagged.

The second decade of the new millennium brought about the most significant changes in worship leader training that Southern Seminary had ever encountered. Despite the challenges of declining enrollment and disconnected constituencies, the DBW turned things around between 2010 and 2019 under the driven and spirit-led leadership of the faculty and administration. After successive seasons of turbulent change, worship leader training at Southern Seminary had endured to meet the needs of the churches of the SBC.

TABLE 1. ENROLLMENT TRENDS IN WORSHIP LEADER DEGREE PROGRAMS 1988–2019

	Boyce College	Southern Seminary	TOTALS
2010–11	28	73	101
2011–12	25	53	78
2012–13	43	49	92
2013–14	53	50	103
2014–15	67	81	148
2015–16	81	83	164
2016–17	80	92	172
2017–18	69	88	157
2018–19	69	96	165

PONDER ANEW WHAT THE ALMIGHTY CAN DO

Chuck Lewis, faculty 2011–2019

Joe Crider, faculty 2011–2019

7

Conclusion

THE HISTORY OF WORSHIP leader training at SBTS encompasses a long and multi-faceted story of God-called and gifted men and women who felt themselves to be commissioned by God to teach, train, equip, and mentor those called to lead church music and worship in the congregations of the SBC. From humble and challenging beginnings, church music and worship leader training degree programs at SBTS grew to represent (in the early 1980s) nearly one third of the total seminary enrollment.[1] A momentous change in the theological and political culture of the SBC, the worship wars of the 1990s and 2000s, and the significant transition in the seminary administration which followed combined to break down the synchronization that had previously existed between SBC worship culture, job competencies for SBC worship leaders, and the seminary's church music and worship leader training curricula. As these factors became increasingly disjunct, the enrollment of students in church music and worship degrees at SBTS steadily declined, leading to a significant institutional reorganization in August 2009.[2]

In 2009 the SCMW (formerly SCM) was terminated, and its programs absorbed, first into the school of church ministries (2009–13) and then in the Billy Graham school for missions, evangelism, and ministry (2013–).[3] Each transition was accompanied by changes in philosophy, faculty, and

---

1. SBTS, "Special Task Force," 5.
2. SBTS, *Academic Catalog (2009–10)*.
3. SBTS, *Academic Catalog (2013–14)*.

curricula. Just as the original faculty of the SCM were called upon to construct and teach a curriculum that would prepare graduates to fulfill the job competencies of church music and worship leadership in 1944, so did the generation of seminary leaders and faculty in the years of the worship paradigm shift between 2000–2019.

PURPOSE OF RESEARCH

The purpose of this study was to follow the development of the degree programs in church music and worship leadership offered at SBTS, specifically during the period circa 1980 through 2019, with particular attention to the master of church music and master of arts in worship leadership. The end goal was to trace and document from primary sources the changes in key degree programs of the SCM, SCMW, division of biblical worship, and department of biblical worship at SBTS from 1980–2019, within the context of cultural mega-shifts and shifts in educational philosophy precipitating those changes.

My research examined the effects of four large trajectories (each embracing multiple variables) that impacted the changes in degree programs during this time: (1) cultural and musical trends affecting evangelical church music during the period; (2) musical and stylistic influences on Southern Baptist worship during the period; (3) denominational changes within the SBC; (4) institutional change and restructuring during the study period. The first three of these factors impacted the job competencies necessary for leading a successful music and worship ministry in a Southern Baptist church. Because the church music and worship leader training degrees at Southern Seminary were designed to train individuals to fulfill the competencies necessary to lead local church music and worship ministries in SBC contexts, the curricula had to adjust with the culture. By adjusting to prevailing evangelical worship culture, a domino-effect developed where the changes occurring in Southern Baptist worship culture impacted the job competencies necessary for church music and worship leadership, which then required major modifications in the curricula used for church music and worship leader training at SBTS. By examining the effects of these four variables, this project delved into the life of the institution during the critical era of 1980–2019—an era that had not yet received a thorough study.

CONCLUSION

RESEARCH QUESTIONS

The research questions guiding the study were as follows:

1. What were the cultural and musical trends at work in the United States between the years 1980 and 2019?
2. What were the musical and stylistic influences acting on worship in Southern Baptist churches in the examined time period?
3. What were the key changes occurring within the Southern Baptist Convention during the years of this study and how did these changes help to shape the worship culture of Southern Baptist churches?
4. What changes in educational philosophy (both broadly and specific to the training of church musicians and worship leaders) occurred at SBTS between 1980 and 2019 and how did these changes impact the requirements for pastoral and musical competencies in the church music and worship leadership training programs at the institution?
5. What institutional changes took place in The Southern Baptist Theological Seminary's administrative leadership during these years, and how did those changes serve as a catalyst for administrative changes within the SCM, SCMW, and DBW?

SOME CONCLUSIONS

Regarding Cultural and Musical Trends

Between the years of 1980 and 2019, cultural and musical trends were at work in the United States, influencing and shaping the styles of music and worship used in Southern Baptist churches. Lester Ruth posited that "by the latter half of the 1980s the popular branch of the church growth movement [as opposed to original academic theorists like Donald McGavran, Gary McIntosh, and C. Peter Wagner] was a well-established feature in the ecclesiastical landscape, affecting both mainline and evangelical constituencies."[4] Ruth points out that "the size and scope of the popular branch of Church Growth movement" grew out of publishers applying the words "Church Growth" to "anything that was vaguely speaking of growing a church."[5]

---

4. Ruth and Hong, *History of Contemporary Praise and Worship*, 247.
5. Ruth and Lim, *History of Contemporary Praise and Worship*, 248.

This popular branch of the CGM became important for the second wave of contemporary worship hitting churches in the United States during the late 1980s and 1990s because it "provided a steady, trans denominational backdrop advocating liturgical innovation throughout this period . . . Church Growth voices increasingly and specifically promoted band-based contemporary worship as the necessary step for congregational health and faithfulness."[6] The influences on SBC churches generated by this factor cannot be underestimated. The enrollment struggles for worship leader training at Southern Seminary during the 1990s and 2000s were largely understood to have been generated by the changes in worship culture, musical influences, and the culture they projected onto evangelical worship.[7]

Throughout the history of the Christian church, worship has been understood to be a service to God; Protestant Christians usually call their corporate worship gatherings worship *services*. According to theologians like David Peterson, "Worship of the living and true God is essentially *an engagement with him on the terms that he proposes and in the way that he alone makes possible.*"[8] Evangelism has always been a crucial part of the church's worshipful response to God's revelation through his Word. However, in the 1990s and 2000s, a branch of evangelistic methodology that spawned from the CGM began to hold sway over biblical theology of worship.

The CGM's methodology was driven by the practicalities of the church's evangelistic mission.[9] Unfortunately, the CGM also succeeded in nudging many churches' desire for evangelism into the realm of pragmatism. CGM pundits had been stressing corporate worship's role in fulfilling the Great Commission (Matt 28:18–20) as early as the 1980s.[10] However, as opposed to the praise and worship movement that preceded it, contemporary worship generated by CGM brought with it a different concept of worship.[11] Ruth wrote, "CGM, similar to other post-Enlightenment innovations like democracy and capitalism also use increasing numbers to indicate success."[12] He continued,

---

6. Ruth and Lim, *History of Contemporary Praise and Worship*, 248.
7. Bolton, interview, 2021.
8. Peterson, *Engaging with God*, 20.
9. Ruth and Lim, *History of Contemporary Praise and Worship*, 250.
10. Ruth and Lim, *History of Contemporary Praise and Worship*, 250.
11. Ruth and Lim, *History of Contemporary Praise and Worship*, 169.
12. Ruth and Lim, *History of Contemporary Praise and Worship*, 169.

Conclusion

> Thus, in contrast to Praise & Worship, which flowed with the momentum of seeking God's presence, liturgical pragmatism [in Contemporary Worship] gained its momentum from the goal of using the most effective means possible in worship. Less overtly concerned with the promise of God's presence, proponents of Contemporary Worship were mesmerized by an apostolic adaptability to become all things to all people in order to win the most people possible. . . . For Contemporary Worship [born out of CGM], the principal matter was a gap—namely, how the church could bridge the chasm that existed between worship and people so people could experience the grace of God.[13]

Those leading the way for CGM believed that corporate worship was the most likely place where the non-Christian would hear the gospel.[14] Worship even gained a colloquial term from many CGM adherents as the "port of entry."[15] James Emery White, senior pastor of Mecklenburg Community Church in Charlotte, North Carolina, and PhD alumnus of Southern Seminary wrote,

> To summarize, worship and church growth are biblically joined; worship is often the barrier which keeps non-churched persons from involvement in the life of the church; worship is the "front door" of the church, the first impression and introduction of the life of the church to people exploring church and the Christian faith as an option for their lives; and finally worship is the single most dominant reason for the initial choice of involvement in a particular local church.[16]

Due to the CGM adherents' concept that worship was the single point of entry for non-believers into the Christian faith, they stressed that worship's most significant value was how it communicated the gospel to non-believers.

For CGM adherents, communication referred to the style of communication in addition to its substance.[17] Even the father of CGM, McGavran had argued that "the gospel needs to be wrapped in the cultural forms of the people the church hopes to present it to."[18] Ruth excellently described

---

13. Ruth and Lim, *History of Contemporary Praise and Worship*, 169.
14. Ruth and Lim, *History of Contemporary Praise and Worship*, 250.
15. Ruth and Lim, *History of Contemporary Praise and Worship*, 250.
16. White, *Opening the Front Door*, 21, quoted in Ruth and Lim, *History*, 250.
17. Ruth and Lim, *History of Contemporary Praise and Worship*, 250.
18. Ruth and Lim, *History of Contemporary Praise and Worship*, 250.

how rock and other popular forms of music became the dominant style of worship in the 1990s and 2000s:

> As Church Growth advocates began to suggest that church desiring to grow should target North Americans who were attracted to forms of popular culture, these advocates therefore thought it critical to highlight emerging examples of Contemporary Worship as evidence that it was possible for Christianity and its worship of God to exist in a "pop" form too.[19]

Popular musical styles, leadership models, and methods for directing large group gatherings [such as corporate worship] entered churches in the years following 1980. Once these factors were entrenched, they did not go away. This significant ecclesiological and liturgical paradigm shift not only influenced Southern Baptist churches, but also those at Southern Seminary who by sacred calling were tasked with training worship leaders for those churches.

Greg Brewton, faculty 2002–2021

19. Ruth and Lim, *History of Contemporary Praise and Worship*, 251.

Conclusion

Regarding Changes in Seminary Leadership

Cultural and musical changes were not the only forces driving changes in worship leaders training at Southern Seminary between 1980 and 2019. These external changes were complemented by a significant internal transition—the coming of President R. Albert Mohler Jr. When the conservative trustees of Southern Seminary began looking for the successor to outgoing seminary President Roy. L. Honeycutt, one of the group's choices was then dean of Southern's school of theology, David Dockery.[20] However, Dockery realized that if he were in the list of finalists and failed to be appointed, then he would likely not have the new president's confidence and would not be able to remain dean. Therefore, he did not allow his name to be considered.[21] However, Dockery and several others recommended the editor of the Georgia Baptist newspaper, *The Christian Index*, Mohler, who was thirty-three at the time.[22] Although Mohler appeared too young to be considered, the trustees interviewed him because of his significant recommendations.[23]

Mohler earned both his MDiv and PhD degrees at Southern and during his doctoral studies had served in the seminary's development office, director of funding, and ultimately as assistant to Honeycutt.[24] Although Mohler had identified with moderates early on, after studying conservative scholarship, developing friendships with Timothy George and David Dockery, and researching the works of conservatives such as Carl F. H. Henry, Francis Schaeffer, and D. James Kennedy, Mohler had become "thoroughly conservative."[25] Despite being known during his student years as either liberal or moderate, some of the moderate and/or liberal faculty were aware of his new theological bearing.[26] Because Mohler was identified from the start of his presidency as a leader in the conservative movement, he was not warmly welcomed by either the Louisville community or Kentucky Baptist leaders.[27]

---

20. Wills, *SBTS 1859–2009*, 511.
21. Wills, *SBTS 1859–2009*, 511.
22. Wills, *SBTS 1859–2009*, 511.
23. Wills, *SBTS 1859–2009*, 511.
24. Wills, *SBTS 1859–2009*, 512.
25. Wills, *SBTS 1859–2009*, 512.
26. Wills, *SBTS 1859–2009*, 513.
27. Wills, *SBTS 1859–2009*, 513.

The story of Mohler's ascendancy to the presidency of Southern Seminary has been told from a variety of perspectives and has been thoroughly documented by scholars and historians. This study sought to connect the ramifications of Mohler's presidency on enrollment trends in worship leader training degrees at Southern Seminary. The most obvious connection might be observed through Mohler's impact on the SCM's constituent churches, and in turn, student enrollment in worship leader training degrees.

Regarding Denominational Influences and Enrollment Trends

In its 1985 report to ATS, Southern Seminary reported the largest enrollment in its history: 2,335 total enrollment and 1,675 full-time residential students (FTEs).[28] After 1985, enrollment began to steadily decline. By the 1997–98 academic year, five years into Mohler's presidency, Southern Seminary's enrollment had declined to a total enrollment of 1,350 with 851 FTEs.[29] The SCMW had also exhibited a steady decline from 1985 to 1998.[30] Although the SCM had enjoyed total enrollments as high as 539 during the 1988–89 academic year, during the 1997–98 academic year, the SCMW's total enrollment had fallen to 221.[31]

By the 1998–99 academic year, six years into Mohler's presidency, the seminary's enrollment numbers had turned. When the 2009 Special Task Force convened to discuss the future of worship leader training at Southern Seminary, the Seminary's total enrollment had grown to its highest enrollment in history, 2,562. The SCMW, on the other hand, had fallen to its lowest enrollment since the 1940s, with a total enrollment of 167 and only 80 FTEs.[32] Over the same time period that the seminary's enrollment had *grown* by nearly fifty-three percent, the SCMW's enrollment had *declined* by almost thirty-one percent.[33] If the enrollment for worship leader training degrees had only been subject to the same denominational and administrative influences affecting the rest of the seminary, worship leader training might have enjoyed a similar enrollment rebound. Due to the

---

28. Wills, *SBTS 1859–2009*, 545–46.
29. Wills, *SBTS 1859–2009*, 546.
30. SBTS, "Special Task Force," 5.
31. SBTS, "Special Task Force," 5.
32. Wills, *SBTS 1859–2009*, 511; SBTS, "Special Task Force," 5.
33. Wills, *SBTS 1859–2009*, 511; SBTS, "Special Task Force," 5.

CONCLUSION

worship paradigm shift brought on by the CGM as discussed earlier, this was not the case.

While the peaks and valleys of Southern Seminary's enrollment trend numbers may have been directly attributed to the coming of Mohler, the issue was not so clearly defined for worship leader training. Former SCM professor John Dickson relayed an account of a conversation he had with Mohler where Dickson reassured Mohler that he believed the SCM's enrollment decline was not his fault.[34] Even though many at the time blamed Mohler's coming as being the sole negative force impacting the SCM's enrollment decline, Dickson believed that the high enrollments in the SCM from the 1970s and 1980s were never sustainable.[35] Dickson identified the disparity between mainstream SBC worship culture and the more formal music and worship style represented by the SCM as the true culprit of enrollment decline.[36]

Although not totally to blame, the changes brought by Mohler's administration did help place Southern Seminary's worship leader training program in an "impossible conundrum."[37] Churches supporting Mohler and his changes knew the stylistic reputation of the SCM and the differences identified by Dickson. These churches, ones making up the majority of Southern Seminary's constituency, had also been largely shaped by the pragmatism of the church growth movement. These churches did not want graduates from the SCMW leading their church's worship, viewing them as musically irrelevant and out of touch with contemporary worship. On the other side, churches who preferred the musical style and culture for which the SCMW was known were generally less theologically conservative. These more moderate churches did not want a Southern Seminary graduate leading their church's worship because of their negative impressions of Mohler and his theological stance.[38] Many diverse conditions had seemingly conspired, providing no functional constituencies to bring new students into worship leader training at Southern Seminary.

As stated, the enrollment declines in worship leader training at Southern Seminary cannot be attributed to just one factor. Among the diverse factors contributing to the decline that peaked around 2010 were

---

34. Dickson, teleconference interview by author, August 31, 2021.
35. Dickson, interview.
36. Dickson, interview.
37. Bolton, interview; Stewart, interview.
38. Bolton, interview; Stewart, interview.

(1) denominational polity shifts in the SBC; (2) Mohler's strong leadership away from some of the traditional constituent churches of the SCM; (3) the growing prominence of contemporary worship in evangelical churches; and (4) ecclesiological effects of the church growth movement. These multiple factors combined in a proverbial "perfect storm," creating enrollment declines in worship leader training degrees at Southern Seminary that persisted from the 1985–86 academic year until a rebound finally occurred during the 2014–15 academic year.[39]

Regarding Changes in Educational Method

Over the life of the institution, broad changes have occurred in education philosophy and methodology that impacted the curricula pertaining to pastoral and musical competencies for church music and worship leadership training programs. One of the most significant such changes occurring between 1980 and 2019 was the advent of the internet, which gave way to distance learning and online education.

As stated by Southern Seminary professor, Dr. Timothy Paul Jones in *Teaching the World: Foundations for Online Theological Education*, many Christian educational institutions seemed to leap into online education simply as a practical means to gain revenue during unsure economic times.[40] According to Jones, by the period between 1980 and the 2010s, online education reached a benchmark where students used a computer connected to the internet alongside other media as part of their course assignments.[41] Many students during what Jones and his coauthors describe as this "Third Phase of Distance Education," might regularly "watch their lectures on videotapes or DVDs but also submitted assignments and interacted with professors and fellow students via email or discussion forums."[42] Due to their inherent skill-building components, these modes of distance learning have proved particularly challenging for many music and worship programs, including worship leader training at Southern Seminary. For many other types of degree programs, the use of online learning has not been so difficult. After 2000, the ATS still required MDiv students to

---

39. SBTS, "Special Task Force," 5; and SBTS Office of Registrar, "Enrollment History, 2001–2 through 2021–22."

40. Jones, introduction to *Teaching the World*, xv.

41. Jones et al., *Teaching the World*, 9.

42. Jones et al., *Teaching the World*, 9.

CONCLUSION

complete at least one-third of their coursework on campus.[43] By 2012, however, ATS began granting exceptions to that requirement, and by 2017 over one dozen accredited seminaries were offering fully online MDiv degrees and finding ways to apply the new rules to other degree offerings.[44]

Some schools quickly positioned themselves to take advantage of online learning and capitalized on the internet's ability to quickly grow student enrollment. For example, by 2010, Liberty University had a residential student body of almost 12,000 students but had over 45,000 students pursuing degrees online.[45] By 2013, Liberty crossed the 100,000 total enrolled student count and their combined enrollment has since continued to be over six figures.[46] Even before the COVID-19 lockdowns of 2020 and 2021, all of higher education began to view online education as a necessary part of reaching and serving students, and Southern Seminary was no exception.

SBTS has remained appreciative of the benefits found only through in-person learning in which students meet in a physical classroom. However, despite the premium value Southern has placed on a residential student body, SBTS's enrollment has still benefitted from the online education. According to statistics provided by the registrar's office, the first time that Southern Seminary formally utilized the world wide web as a medium for theological education was during the 2001–2 academic year.[47] During that school term, SBTS had an online enrollment of 127 master's level students.[48] Moving forward to the 2019–20 academic year, Southern's online enrollment at the master's level had grown to 2,744 students.[49] Southern Seminary may not have accumulated 100,000 online students like Liberty University, but the impact to the institution is arguably as great—ever since the 2019–20 academic year, Southern has had more online students than residential learners.[50]

Sometimes in the rush to utilize online education in order to swell enrollment numbers and generate revenue, school administrators have been eager (and still are) to apply this lucrative path to all academic disciplines

---

43. Jones et al., *Teaching the World*, 10.
44. Jones et al., *Teaching the World*, 10.
45. Randlett, "Training Worship Leaders," 89.
46. Randlett, "Training Worship Leaders," 89–90.
47. SBTS, "Enrollment History."
48. SBTS, "Enrollment History."
49. SBTS, "Enrollment History."
50. SBTS, "Enrollment History."

and degree offerings.[51] However, due to smaller, specialized student bodies requiring the musical skill-building disciplines involved in practice and performance, music and worship degrees have generally been outliers when compared to other disciplines when viewed on the basis of cost and benefit.[52]

One of the advantages institutions seek when implementing online instruction is the lower cost of instruction per student. Due to their inherently hands-on and active nature, music and worship courses generally require in-person instruction and smaller class sizes. These conditions drive up an institution's cost per student. For example, if the entire student body is required to take lecture-styled courses, students can be consolidated into the largest lecture classrooms or in online forums. These types of class configurations (whether online or in person) may likely accommodate over 100 students per one instructor. This logistical arrangement provides the seminary with a relatively low cost per student in both personnel and facility costs. Music and worship courses have little chance of taking advantage of this type of arrangement. For example, classes in the DBW at Southern Seminary routinely average fewer than twenty students per instructor.[53] The Special Task Force Report of 2009 demonstrated how this issue alone causes worship students to incur higher instructional costs than students in other degree tracks—sometimes much higher.[54]

Regarding Changes in Faculty

Another change that occurred between 1980 and 2019 involved the number and composition of the faculty. In 1980, at the end of Forrest Heeren's tenure as dean of the SCM, the faculty resembled what may have been found within any top-tier conservatory or school of music. In addition to professors teaching basic courses in music theory, sight-singing, conducting, hymnology, and piano, every applied area was also represented by a faculty specialist within their field, i.e., brass instruments, choral conducting, musicology, composition, instrumental conducting, etc. This disciplinary norm for schools of music was driven by NASM accreditation requirements as

---

51. Jones et al., *Teaching the World*, 11.
52. Greenway, teleconference interview by author, September 6, 2021.
53. SBTS Office of Registrar, "Boyce Music and Worship Enrollment Stats."
54. SBTS, "Special Task Force," 32–33.

Conclusion

well as its use as a recruiting tool demonstrating to potential students what the SCM had to offer in the way of musical expertise and training.[55]

In 1980, in order to serve the large number of students, preparing them for the job competencies and culture of church music programs, the SCM operated with fourteen full-time faculty, four adjuncts, and twenty-four part-time instructors (mostly DMA students). The comparison of the 1980 faculty to the one of 2018–19 is numerically striking. In 2018–19,

---

55. The SCM faculty listed in the 1980–82 SBTS *Academic Catalog* was as follows: Ronald E. Boud (piano, composition, theory), Forrest Heeren (dean, voice, music education, ministry), G. Maurice Hinson (piano), Donald Paul Hustad (organ, philosophy of music ministry), Boyd M. Jones II (organ), J. Phillip Landgrave (ministry, composition, voice), Richard R. Lin (voice, conducting, ministry), Hugh T. McElrath (hymnology, voice), S. Milburn Price Jr. (incoming dean, church music repertoire, conducting), G. Douglas Smith (brass instruments, conducting, composition), Ronald A. Turner (voice, composition, theory), and Jay W. Wilkey (voice, vocal pedagogy, opera theatre, church music drama). There were also adjunct faculty: Martha C. Powell (music librarian), C. Michael Hawn (voice, music education, ministry), Eugene Sutherland (music ministry), and Paul A. Richardson (voice, musicology). Finally, the SCM employed twenty-four instructors, most of whom were doctoral students. These instructors handled many of the pre-graduate proficiency classes and many of the applied lessons. Some of these instructors deserve special notation notice: David Carle, whose DMA research served as the foundation work for chaps. 2 and 3 of this dissertation; Brenda Honeycutt, daughter of then seminary President Roy Honeycutt; James Rightmyer, future SCM faculty and influential Louisville-area church musician; Timothy Sharp, future Executive Director of the American Choral Directors Association and interviewee for this research project; and Sandra C. Turner, future faculty and wife of faculty Ronald Turner.

Thirty-eight years later, the DBW/Boyce music and worship faculty in 2018–19 were the following: Gregory B. Brewton (department chair, voice, ensemble director, worship ministry courses including biblical and theological foundations of worship, methodology, leading, and planning of worship, conducting, directing ensembles, and professional doctoral instruction and supervision), R. Scott Connell (worship ministry courses including biblical and theological foundations of worship, methodology, leading, and planning of worship, coordination of undergraduate music and worship students, directing ensembles, and voice) Joseph R. Crider (Director of the Institute of Biblical Worship, worship ministry courses including biblical and theological foundations of worship, methodology, leading, and planning of worship, professional and research doctoral instruction and supervision, leadership of chapel orchestra and Norton Hall band), Esther R. Crookshank (musicology, hymnology, ethnodoxology, research doctoral instruction and supervision), Charles T. Lewis Jr. (Director of Doxology vocal ensemble, music theory, written harmony, musical dictation, and aural skills). In order to provide necessary applied lessons in voice, piano, guitar, and other areas such as composition, the Department of Biblical Worship also employed several adjunct faculty and instructors: Derek Nelson (theory and composition), Jonny Barahona (music technology and worship band), David Owens (guitar and bass lab), Dr. Paul Davidson (voice, piano, and director for the Seminary School for the Arts), Dr. Marc Brown (voice, field ministry, worship band techniques), and Chandi Plummer (voice, vocal pedagogy, choir).

Southern Seminary's DBW (including Boyce College worship majors) was around one-third of the 1980 enrollment: 175 compared to around 550. Worship leader training in 2018–19 also functioned with far fewer faculty and instructors, five full-time faculty and six adjuncts. Another noteworthy comparison comes through the teacher-to-student ratios for both years. Both 1980 and 2019 had teacher-to-student ratios of around one teacher per thirteen students. Anecdotally, interviewees from both of these periods of worship leader training at SBTS understood the programs they experienced as healthy and growing.[56]

FACULTY DOWNSIZING ACROSS THE ACADEMY

Another broad understanding gained through observing the differences between 1980 and 2019, is that the downsizing of the full-time faculty from fourteen to five does not represent an outlier position among the landscape of higher education. Nationwide, the number of full-time professors has continued to shrink while the number of adjunct instructors grows.[57] The staffing trend of limited full-time faculty complimented by a large group of adjuncts is not uncommon but does have its critics. Detractors see this model as a threat to the academy for several reasons. First, adjuncts are not as likely to pursue creative or innovative ideas due to their perceived lack of job security.[58] Adjuncts also have less time to counsel students because they are frequently piecing their incomes together by simultaneously teaching for several institutions. In fact, a 2014 congressional report found 89 percent of adjunct faculty worked for at least two different schools, 27 percent taught at three schools, and 13 percent at four or more.[59]

Administrators may respond with sympathy to the plight of adjunct instructors but generally feel forced into their increasing reliance on part-time faculty due to budget pressures and shifting enrollment trajectories.[60] According to federal data in 2019, "part time teachers represented 40% of the total academic work force [in higher education], compared with 24%

---

56. Price, phone interview by author, August 9, 2021; Crider, phone interview by author, August 13, 2021; and Greenway, interview.
57. Douglas-Gabriel, "It Keeps You Nice and Disposable."
58. Douglas-Gabriel, "It Keeps You Nice and Disposable."
59. Douglas-Gabriel, "It Keeps You Nice and Disposable."
60. Douglas-Gabriel, "It Keeps You Nice and Disposable."

in 1975."[61] In addition to full-time faculty and adjunct faculty, a third category of faculty exists—contingent faculty. This designation includes part-time adjuncts, graduate student workers, and full-time instructors whose contracts are not on a tenure track.[62] According to federal data in 2019, contingent faculty "account for nearly three-quarters of instructional staff in higher education."[63] Although the smaller full-time faculty of the DBW has its challenges, their current staffing model has become statistically normal in the academy. Also noteworthy is that the faculty of the DBW have demonstrated that although each may have a greater workload than faculty of previous generations, enrollment growth and quality of education can be accomplished and sustained within the new model.[64]

ADDITIONAL CONCLUSIONS

Regarding Changing Job Competencies: 1980 versus 2019

By comparing Donald Roland Bearden's 1980 research with Kenneth Alan Boer's 2019 work, these two empirical studies provide a clear juxtaposition between the job competencies and worship leader training curricula of 1980 and 2019. Bearden's dissertation, "Competencies for a Minister of Music in a Southern Baptist Church: Implications for Curriculum Development," was written to "develop and validate musical and music-related competency statements which would describe the needed skills, behaviors, and knowledge for a minister of music in a Southern Baptist Church."[65] Bearden compiled information gathered from SBC music leaders and church music educators along with curriculum outlines from church music degree programs found in SBC colleges and universities.[66] Bearden then used his compiled data to construct 106 competency statements and randomly sent them to church music educators, ministers of music, and denominational leaders to rank the skills in order of importance.[67] He organized these competency statements into twelve topics: (1) philosophy and

---

61. Douglas-Gabriel, "It Keeps You Nice and Disposable."
62. Douglas-Gabriel, "It Keeps You Nice and Disposable."
63. Douglas-Gabriel, "It Keeps You Nice and Disposable."
64. SBTS, "Boyce Music and Worship Enrollment Stats."
65. Bearden, abstract, viii.
66. Bearden, abstract, viii.
67. Bearden, abstract, ix.

history; (2) hymnody; (3) worship planning; (4) musicianship; (5) personal musical performance; (6) vocal; (7) choral conducting; (8) choral planning; (9) children's music; (10) other music training; (11) instrumental music; and (12) church music administration.[68]

Bearden's study yielded five conclusions consisting of the following: (1) general competency statements for ministers of music in Southern Baptist churches; (2) areas of special importance such as philosophy of music related to the nature and purpose of the church; music education, worship leadership, and a program administration are the primary function; (3) a musical profile for a minister of music serving a Southern Baptist church; (4) an understanding of the differences of assessed importance between church music educators and denominational leaders/ministers of music for competency statements dealing with history and tradition of church music and traditional musical skills; and (5) several important non-music competency areas including communications and human relations, a concept of a spiritual ministry through music, general worship planning and leadership, and an educational and psychological background.[69]

Bearden's study also determined a need for church music curricula to feature (1) extensive supervised field experiences; (2) church music faculty with extensive full-time experience in churches; (3) contacts and opportunities for communication with students in other areas of ministry preparation; and (4) basic church music training in upper levels of undergraduate programs with graduate level studies in seminaries or graduate schools.[70]

Boer's dissertation, as previously mentioned, was written "to determine the characteristics described in worship leader job descriptions in the Southern Baptist Convention and examine the correspondence of these characteristics with worship leadership degree programs at Southern Baptist-affiliated colleges and universities."[71] Boer accomplished his task through completing a content analysis of worship leader job descriptions posted on the website of the SBC as well as course descriptions from worship leader degree programs at select SBC-affiliated institutions.[72] Boer employed a four-phase instrumentation. In his first phase he gathered his

---

68. Bearden, abstract, ix.
69. Bearden, abstract, ix–x.
70. Bearden, abstract, x.
71. Boer, "Comparative Content Analysis," 101.
72. Boer, "Comparative Content Analysis," 101.

Conclusion

information (as previously described).[73] Boer analyzed his data in phases two, three, and four.[74] In phase two, Boer analyzed job descriptions, in the third phase he searched course descriptions for the presence of characteristics identified in phase two.[75] In phase four, the results on phases two and three were compared with one another in a statistical analysis.[76]

Boer used precedent literature to create his job competency "characteristics list" which consisted of five categories.[77] Boer's categories included (1) Knowledge and Planning, which held characteristics like worship planning, philosophy and history of church music, hymnology, theology of worship, biblical and theological knowledge, and music history, literature, and repertory; (2) Personal Musicianship and Leadership, which incorporated characteristics such as corporate worship leadership, music theory and composition, vocal skills, keyboard skills, informal musicianship such as playing by ear, conducting, and guitar skills; (3) Administrative, Organizational Skill had no sub-characteristics; (4) Group Musicianship and Leadership included characteristics like choral conducting, leading instrumental ensembles, worship technology, leading a worship band, leading music with children and adolescents, leading vocalists and vocal teams, directing musical theatre or drama, and recruitment and musical development of volunteers; and (5) Relationships and Character that involved communication and people skills, leadership skills, personal devotional life, personal character, spiritual pastoral care for the congregation, discipleship and mentoring of volunteers, and relationship with the senior or lead pastor.[78]

When Boer compiled all of the job descriptions in aggregate, the characteristic or job competency with the most frequent KSAO (his acronym for Knowledge, Skills, Abilities, and Other Characteristics) was "lead corporate worship publicly," represented by 87.7 percent of all job descriptions.[79] The second, third, and fourth highest ranking KSAOs, representing 65.5 percent to 66.1 percent of the job descriptions respectively, were "people skills and teamwork with staff," "management and administrative skills,"

---

73. Boer, "Comparative Content Analysis," 104.
74. Boer, "Comparative Content Analysis," 104.
75. Boer, "Comparative Content Analysis," 105.
76. Boer, "Comparative Content Analysis," 105.
77. Boer, "Comparative Content Analysis," 126.
78. Boer, "Comparative Content Analysis," 126.
79. Boer, "Comparative Content Analysis," 136.

and "leadership skills."[80] The fifth through ninth positions for most desired job competencies in worship leaders were the following: "plan worship services"; "lead or oversee choir"; "lead vocalists"; "lead worship band"; and "oversee worship technology."[81]

Comparing Bearden's desired job competency findings from 1980 with those discovered by Boer in 2019 yield an interesting comparison. In 1980, the most necessary job competencies for worship leaders included a philosophy of music related to the nature and purpose of the church, developing and leading a music education program for all ages in the church, leading congregational worship, and administrating the musical programs of the church. In 2019, the list changes somewhat with leading corporate worship, people skills with staff, administration skills, leadership skills, planning worship services, leading musical groups, and overseeing technology. The following table displays the changing values held by churches concerning the competencies desired by churches for their music and worship leaders:

TABLE 2. PREFERRED WORSHIP LEADER COMPETENCIES IN 1980 AND 2019

Competency	Bearden, 1980	Boer, 2019
Philosophy of Worship	#1	—
Lead Ensembles and/or Music Education	#2	#8
Leading Corporate Worship	#3	#1
Administration	#4	#3
Personal Music Performance	#5	—
People Skills	#6	#2
Worship Planning	#7	#5
Overseeing Technology	—	#7
Leadership Skills	#8	#4

Between these two sample years, more contrasts than similarities exist. One noteworthy comparison between desired competencies from both 1980 and 2019 is that both display high values for leading corporate worship and for administrative ability. Apart from these similarities, most

80. Boer, "Comparative Content Analysis," 136.
81. Boer, "Comparative Content Analysis," 136.

Conclusion

comparisons yield noticeable differences. In 1980 the most desirable competency for a minister of music was for them to have a personal philosophy of worship.[82] In 2019, however, the desirability for the worship leader to hold a philosophy of worship fails to be mentioned in the study at all. In fact, Boer's most comparable characteristic, "Theology of Worship" only earned a place that was five spaces from the bottom of his list of competencies—just one place higher than "Oversee Handbell Ensemble."[83]

Another interesting contrast comes through the competency of "Personal Music Performance."[84] Anecdotally, congregations who worship with contemporary-styled music (as opposed to traditionally styled worship) place a premium on the personal musical performance of their worship leader. These two studies appear to contradict that anecdotal understanding. In Bearden's 1980 research, churches (largely traditional in worship style) valued the personal performance of their worship leaders to the extent that it rated fifth highest in desirability.[85] In Boer's 2019 study, personal performance as an instrumentalist and as a vocalist rated only 22nd and 26th place respectively.[86]

An omission from the 1980 study that ranked highly in 2019 involved the overseeing of worship technology. Beyond the absence of that competency, which did not exist in 1980 for obvious reasons, most skills were present in both studies.

One significant contrast between the desired competencies of 1980 and 2019 appears in Boer's 2019 use of an entire category called "Relationships and Character."[87] These qualities generally entail skills that do not generally correspond to music and worship coursework but are qualities that nonetheless can become significant within the dynamics of a church staff and congregation. Boer found that within job descriptions for full-time worship leaders, these "internal/personal characteristics" amounted to nearly half of the total qualities mentioned.[88] In the 1980 study, these

---

82. Bearden, abstract, ix–x.
83. Boer, "Comparative Content Analysis," 128.
84. Bearden, abstract, ix–x.
85. Bearden, abstract, ix–x.
86. Boer, "Comparative Content Analysis," 127–28.
87. Boer, "Comparative Content Analysis," 126.
88. Boer, "Comparative Content Analysis," 132.

qualities were only represented by the general area of "People Skills," and rated only sixth highest in Bearden's findings.[89]

One final contrast between these two studies implicitly points to a major difference between the desired worship leaders' qualities in 1980 and 2019. Bearden's study involved examining both undergraduate and graduate programs of study in church music, focusing mostly on the graduate level. Additionally, Bearden compiled his competency list from those already working in the field, with most if not all holding formal education in music and church music.[90] Boer's study focused almost exclusively on undergraduate worship leadership curricula. Boer makes the point that in his research of worship leader job postings he frequently encountered wording like, "A college degree is required or you better be really good!"[91] Boer surmises that "churches may prefer that candidates have received formal education, but skills and underlying character may prove to be ultimately more important to them."[92] Possibly exemplifying an impact from CGM and Contemporary Worship, Boer's study appears to demonstrate that by 2019, the standard educational background for SBC worship leaders may have shifted from a graduate degree to an undergraduate degree.

Bearden's and Boer's empirical studies of worship competencies from 1980 and 2019 provide a clear view of the target sought by the worship leader training curricula of Southern Seminary during those same years. When observed side by side, the competency differences between the years of 1980 and 2019 appear significant. However, the differences appear less drastic when examined in light of the significant paradigm shifts that had occurred between those years including the changes in evangelical worship culture (the effects of CGM and contemporary worship), denominational transitions in the SBC, and SBTS's administration change (and its impact on constituencies). Those responsible for worship leader training at Southern Seminary faced a significant task in trying to continue their mission of training worship leaders for SBC churches. In their struggle, their best tool for remaining relevant to their constituent churches was found in adapting their curriculum to fit new job competencies. Some former graduates and constituents of the SCM may view the curriculum changes between 1980 and 2019 in negative ways. However, a more reasonable perspective might

---

89. Bearden, abstract, ix–x.
90. Bearden, abstract, ix–x.
91. Boer, "Comparative Content Analysis," 162.
92. Boer, "Comparative Content Analysis," 162.

CONCLUSION

be to view the curriculum changes in light of doing what is necessary in order to fulfill the mission to train worship leaders for the churches of the SBC.

COMPARING CURRICULA: 1980 AND 2019

Throughout its history, the curricula for worship leader training at Southern Seminary has been in constant transition. Some of the curriculum's most significant and qualitative changes occurred with the coming of Joseph Crider and Charles Lewis in 2010. In comparison, during dean Forrest Heeren's administration, fewer changes were made. As opposed to Crider and Lewis's attempts to catch up with modern job competencies, the curriculum of Heeren's era was largely seen as a means of satisfying the accreditation entities of NASM and SACS and producing the highest quality musicians possible.[93]

The changes in curriculum between the 1980 master of church music and the 2019 master of arts in worship leadership also represent the culture changes impacting worship in SBC churches during that period and the natural shifts in job competencies accompanying those changes. These culture and competency changes can be observed when directly comparing the proficiency/placement requirements and program curriculums for the most popular degrees in each year. Concerning the entrance requirements for the master of church music the 1980–1982, the SBTS catalog states:

> The placement examination given in August and January will determine the placement of the student in certain of the courses to be taken for the M.C.M. degree. The purpose of the examinations is to determine the deficiencies from undergraduate work, to aid in the designing of a course of study, and to evaluate the level of applied study at which the student enters. If a student comes to seminary without any preparation in a certain area, he may choose not to take the placement examination in that area, but rather enroll automatically in its respective pre-graduate course.
>
> Students who prepare carefully and pass a majority of tested areas will find that the transition into graduate study is greatly facilitated. In contrast, students who are ill-prepared often find that deficiency courses take a disproportionate part of the first year's study, and often necessitate a lengthening of residence.

---

93. Price, interview.

A placement (pre-graduate) examination grade of C to C+ is required in the areas of Written Harmony, Sight Singing, Ear Training, Keyboard Harmony, Counterpoint, Orchestration, form and Analysis, Music History through the Baroque, Music History after the Baroque, and Conducting. This grade of C to C+ will waive pre-graduate requirements except in the areas of Written Harmony, Sight Singing, Ear Training, Keyboard Harmony, Music History through the Baroque, and Music History after the Baroque. In these six subjects, a grade of between 75–85 will require the student to take elective graduate credit as follows:

> Sight Singing—take 5101 (2 hours)
> Ear Training—take 5102 (2 hours)
> Keyboard Harmony—take 5752 (1 hour)
> Music History through the Baroque—take 5201 through 5203 (1 hour)
> Later Music History—take 5204 through 5206 (1 hour)

In these above six areas a grade of B waives all pre-graduate requirements.[94]

The printed curriculum for Master of Church Music in 1980–82 is as follows:[95]

Church Music Core (26 hours)
    Music Courses (14 hours)

Composition /Arranging 5151, 5152, 5153, 5154 (select one)	2
Ministry 4100, 4116, 4118 (select two)	4
Ministry 4104, 4108, 4112 (select two)	4
Conducting 5260	2
Instrumental Music 5860, 5856, 5857, or 5080–5099	1
Literature-Applied Skills 5570, 5661, 5762, 4114	1
Field Education 5051 and 5052	0
Recital Attendance (four semesters)	0
Ensemble Participation (four semesters)	0
Theology and Religious Education (12 hours)	
Old Testament 2020	3
New Testament 2220	3

---

94. SBTS, *Academic Catalog (1980–82)*, 132–33.
95. SBTS, *Academic Catalog (1980–82)*, 136.

Conclusion

    Formation for Christian Ministry 4001   2

    Religious Education 4008, 4170, 4180, 4200, 4210, 4220,   2
4230, 4570, 4576, 4580, 4586, 4600, 4610, 4620, or 4630 (select one)

    Applied Area (12 hours)

        a. Concentration   6–9

        b. Related applied   3–5

Vocal Majors: Two hours graduate credit in Ensemble or one hour credit may be taken in Vocal Pedagogy (5580)

Piano Majors: One hour credit in Piano Pedagogy (5780) and one hour in a) Graduate Class Organ (5650) or b) Organ Pedagogy (5680) or c) Organ Service Playing (5661).

Organ Majors: One hour credit in Organ (5680) and Piano Pedagogy (5780)

Instrumental Majors: Two hours graduate credit in Instrumental Ensembles

        c. Minor(s)   1–2

        d. Laboratory, Ensembles   (4)

MCM Degree Second Major Options

Within the M.C.M. degree, there are fifty-five hours of credit. The *first* [italics theirs] major (core curriculum) consists of fourteen (14) hours of church music course and twelve (12) hours of theology and religious education courses. This twenty-six hours of instruction constitutes the very heart of the unique qualities of a church music degree within a theological seminary community.

In addition to the first major of church music, the student elects a *second* [italics theirs] or auxiliary major. This second major is usually determined while enrolled in Music Bibliography 5460 or within the student's second semester of graduate study. Certain conditions for enrolling in each of the second major areas are discussed in the course 5460. Talent and interest determined during the student's early study at the seminar will be the major factor in securing necessary faculty approval.

The second major will provide the graduate church music major with the opportunity to continue skills which may have been discovered in the undergraduate college degree course of study, Such a second major should strengthen the church music ministry major of each student.

> There are eight second, or auxiliary majors, all approved by the National Association of Schools of Music, consisting of Performance, Pedagogy, Composition, Conducting, Theory, Music Education, Musicology, and Ministry. The Ministry major provides for broader service in the church, such as Music and Youth or Music and Elementary Education, etc.
>
> All of the eight second majors require a written and/or oral comprehensive examination to be administered by their individual major advisors usually during the last semester of study.[96]

Rather than provide the repetitive and page consuming list for all second majors, I will provide the example of the curriculum of one second major option, the Conducting second major:

Conducting [Second Major]

Church Music Core	26 hours
Conducting	12 hours
Performance	12 hours
Electives	5 hours

Total 55 hours

*2 additional hours in Church Music Core

[97]

Concerning the entrance requirement for the master of arts in worship leadership in 2019–20, the SBTS catalog states the following:

> While no examinations or auditions are required for acceptance into music and worship degree programs offered by the Billy Graham School, new students entering worship leadership or church music degree programs must take the diagnostic placement examinations and auditions prior to their first semester of study.
>
> Students entering the Master of Divinity in Worship Leadership or the Master of Arts in Worship Leadership will have placement tests in music theory, ear training, sight singing, and conducting. Worship Leadership student are not required to have a 25-minute recital in college.
>
> If a student comes to the seminary without any preparation in a certain area (such as music theory or conducting), he/she may choose not to take the placement examination in that area

---

96. SBTS, *Academic Catalog (1980-82)*, 136–37.
97. SBTS, *Academic Catalog (1980-82)*, 137.

Conclusion

but rather to enroll automatically in the respective pre-graduate course.

Upon evaluation of the placement examination, the student may be required to take one or more of the following pre-graduate courses:

>Introduction to Conducting
>Music Theory I
>Aural Skills I
>Music Theory II
>Aural Skills II
>One or two semesters of pre-graduate applied studies
>Two semesters of pre-graduate minor applied studies

Worship Leadership students will be given a proficiency exam in piano or guitar. Students may choose which instrument they would like to pursue for their accompaniment proficiency. Students showing deficiencies in this skill will enroll in coursework to prepare them for the proficiency exam. Students who are taking piano for their concentration will need to pass the voice proficiency.[98]

The printed curriculum for master of arts in worship leadership in 2019–20 is as follows:[99]

Remedial/Pre-requisite Courses

31980	Written Communication (if required)		(2)

Master of Arts Core Studies (36 hours)

20200	Introduction to the Old Testament I	3
20220	Introduction to the Old Testament II	3
22100	Biblical Hermeneutics	3
22200	Introduction to the New Testament I	3
22220	Introduction to the New Testament II	3
26200	Southern Baptist Heritage and Mission	3
27060	Systematic Theology I	3
27070	Systematic Theology II	3
27080	Systematic Theology III	3
32100	Personal Evangelism	3
40150	Personal Spiritual Disciplines	3

---

98. SBTS, *Academic Catalog (2019–20)*, 103.
99. SBTS, *Academic Catalog (2019–20)*, 125.

45260	Discipline and Family Ministry	3
Worship Leadership Concentration (28 hours)		
40200	The Worshiping Church	3
40605	Psalms, Hymns, and Spiritual Songs	2
40610	Discipling Worship Ministry I	2
40615	Discipling Worship Ministry II	2
40620	Worship Leadership and Design	2
40625	Vocal Ensemble Leadership	2
40630	Worship Band Techniques	2
40635	Technology for Music and Worship Ministry	2
40670	Song Writing for Worship Leaders	2
40680	Worship Band Lab: Guitar or	1 ½
40681	Worship Band Lab: Keyboard or	
40682	Worship Band Lab: Bass Guitar or	
40683	Worship Band Lab: Drum	
40693	Worship Leadership Field Education Leadership	½
40688	Worship Choir Lab	½
40694	Worship Leadership Field Education: Current Trends	½
41016	Integrative Seminar in Church Music and Worship	2
55100	Private Study: Voice (2 semesters)	2
40675	Graduate Worship Project	2
	Ensembles (4 semesters)	0
Total Master of Arts in Worship Leadership Requirements		64
Written Communication (if required)		+2

One of the most significant differences between 1980 and 2019 as demonstrated by these two degrees comes through their entrance and proficiency requirements. While placement examinations were required for musical skills in both eras, the number of examinations required in 1980 was far greater than in 2019.

The 2019 catalog also stated that there were no examinations or auditions required for gaining entrance into the DBW.[100] In 1980, students who failed to demonstrate proper musical proficiency were given enrollment privileges in order to take undergraduate-level music courses for remediation until such time they could re-take and hopefully pass their entrance

---

100. SBTS, *Academic Catalog (2019–20)*, 103.

Conclusion

examinations and auditions.[101] For some entering church music students, fulfilling the entrance requirements for the MCM degree through completing undergraduate remediation courses prior to program entrance could take a year or more to compete, similar to leveling courses undertaken by a potential PhD student seeking to gain entrance to their desired program of study. In 2019, this sort of pre-admittance barrier did not exist for worship leadership students. By 2019, all musical remediation could be comfortably accommodated into the course schedule of students after their formal admittance to the program.[102]

Another difference between these two curricula is in their number of required hours in each degree. In 1980, the MCM degree required 55 hours of coursework.[103] However, when considering the mandatory requirements involved in addition to the listed course work, such as undergraduate courses and musical proficiencies, this degree often required one or two additional years for a student to complete. Anecdotally, my own experience involved coming to the SCM after completing a bachelor's degree in music from an accredited music school. However, due to the SCM's high proficiency requirements, my 55-hour MCM degree turned into a 91-hour transcript. The master of arts in worship leadership of 2019, on the other hand, involved 64 hours of coursework, but with far fewer additional proficiency requirements.[104]

The flexibility and complexity of these two degrees also deserves comparison. The MCM degree of 1980 had many variables for how a student might individualize their program. The eight options for second majors, or auxiliary majors included performance, pedagogy, composition, conducting, theory, music education, musicology, and ministry; these options provided for broader learning but could also add unwanted complexity and serve to prolong the graduation date for many students. The master of arts in worship leadership of 2019 on the other hand, clearly marked out the courses needed to complete the degree and also presented the expected course load for students during each semester of their time at Southern.[105] This simple, straightforward approach may deny students of some degree personalization found in 1980, but assists in setting accurate expectations

---

101. SBTS, *Academic Catalog (1980–82)*, 132–33.
102. SBTS, *Academic Catalog (2019–20)*, 103.
103. SBTS, *Academic Catalog (1980–82)*, 136–37.
104. SBTS, *Academic Catalog (2019–20)*, 103.
105. SBTS, *Academic Catalog (2019–20)*, 103.

for the student's time and financial commitment required to complete the degree. In this way, the degree of 2019 bears similarity to the original degrees offered in the early growing years of the SCM.[106]

FINAL OBSERVATIONS

After researching the story of worship leader training at Southern Seminary from its beginning to 2019, focusing on changes occurring after 1980, two observable patterns have surfaced that bear recognition. The first of these two major patterns acknowledges the understanding that each new administration held concerning their role in worship leader training and its relation to their opinion of their predecessor's performance. Without exception, from John Broadus teaching hymnology in 1859; to Prof Johnson instructing pastors on how to lead "Music" in 1920; to Donald and Frances Winters mentoring students in choral conducting in 1944; to Forrest Heeren establishing a culture of musical excellence in 1952; to Milburn Price guiding students to think philosophically about music ministry in 1980; to Lloyd Mims establishing the Worshiping Church course for pastors and worship leaders to study worship methodology together in 1993; to Tom Bolton cultivating students' flexibility to handle a variety of musical styles in 2000; to Joe Crider discipling worship leaders to become pastors who lead worship in 2010; all who taught and mentored worship leaders at Southern Seminary did so in view of God's holy and unswerving calling in their lives to prepare worship leaders to serve the churches of the SBC so that God would be glorified and His people encouraged.

After President Fuller's trailblazing leadership and the Winters' foundational teaching during the first generation of leadership for the SCM, a common opinion appears to have been held by everyone who subsequently led Southern's worship leader training program. Every time a new leader established their administration, each held a respectful opinion of their predecessor, but each also expressed a suspicion that their predecessor had been more concerned with developing excellent performers than with producing capable leaders for local churches. In this understanding, every new leader (Heeren, Price, Mims, Bolton, and Crider) each believed that the most significant part of their own calling was to be one of making worship leader training at Southern more relevant and practical for leading music and worship in local churches. Though this generationally consistent

---

106. Carle, "History of School of Church Music of SBTS," 50.

CONCLUSION

opinion cannot be characterized as being critical of past administrations, it does demonstrate how each leader in every period of worship leader training at Southern Seminary remained true to the original institutional mandate to train musicians and worship leaders for service in the churches of the SBC.

The story of worship leader training at Southern Seminary has ups and downs relating to enrollment numbers. The SCM began in 1944 with an opening class of twenty students and from that point demonstrated consistent growth until the mid-1980s when enrollment began to wane. The enrollment dropped to its lowest in 2009, when significant administrative changes were made to rejuvenate the program to relevance and aim towards a healthy student enrollment. Through its life span, worship leader training always relied on visionary husbandry of their non-musical administrative leaders. Despite support that the worship leader training program has enjoyed from every stewarding president and dean, the periods of greatest enrollment growth and stability have been enjoyed under the leadership of certain administrators who appear to have had a personal love of and value for the mission of worship leader training.

In 1944, President Ellis Fuller believed in worship leader training so much that he started the SCM himself, serving as its director during his entire presidency and doing everything he could to provide financial support, educational validation, and friendship to its faculty. President Duke McCall shed the presidential precedent of leading the SCM, but in calling Heeren as dean, ensured the school would continue to grow and become a vital part of Southern Seminary. Later, during the most challenging days of McCall's presidency, Heeren's unswerving support of McCall helped the president weather the storm that accompanied his dismissal of thirteen theology faculty. McCall recognized Heeren's loyalty and was in turn loyal to support Heeren. This comradery helped to establish success and enrollment growth for worship leader training that remains unparalleled in the seminary's history.

Finally, after the SCM was stripped of its status as a free-standing school and successively shuffled to the oversight of two different schools (school of church ministry and the BGS), Dean Adam Greenway provided nurturing oversight of what was then a fragile revitalization with Joseph Crider and the department of biblical worship. Greenway's gracious oversight helped to ensure new growth and vitality for worship leader training at Southern that lasted throughout his deanship. Though every generation of worship leadership training encountered their own challenges, periods representing the greatest growth and stability always came when the non-music administration placed significant value in the mission of preparing worship leaders for the churches of the SBC.

RECOMMENDATIONS FOR APPLICATION AND FUTURE RESEARCH

The story of worship leader training at Southern Seminary, particularly from 1980 to 2019, demonstrates a continued willingness to follow God's call to provide worship leaders for the constituent churches of the SBC. By following the enrollment data from its heights in the late 1970s and early 1980s, to its plummet in the 2000s, and its subsequent moderate rebound in the 2010s, readers may become easily enticed to reduce the goal of the SCM and DBW to nothing more than producing positive enrollment statistics. Taking this path would be an unfortunate mistake.

During his interview for this project, Kentucky Baptist state music and worship consultant, Jason Stewart, shared a troubling condition persisting in the churches of the Kentucky Baptist Convention (KBC). According to Stewart and statistics held by the KBC, around 400 KBC churches worship every week without a single person to lead worship through singing or playing an instrument.[107] Considering such statistics, the case made to the SBC in the 1920s and 1930s concerning the sad and low state of worship in SBC churches might still be made today. One hundred years ago, the realization of poor worship conditions in SBC churches prompted a nation-wide effort to improve worship leader training. This effort was largely successful, ultimately contributing to the worship department of the Sunday school board of the SBC, national and state SBC conferences and camps focusing on music and worship training, and development of music and worship training programs in SBC colleges and seminaries, including Southern Seminary. The work and notoriety of this push for better worship training in the SBC provided the foundation for the "Camelot years" that Southern and other seminaries experienced during the 1970s and 1980s. What might a similar effort look like today? What forms might it take? Among the people of the SBC, is there a collective will to again take up the banner of training worship leaders to help the hundreds of churches bereft of music and worship leadership? Can the SBC unify around the cause of

---

107. Stewart, interview.

Conclusion

worship or will the negative impacts of the CGM keep churches divided due to differences in musical style preference? Only time will tell.

This study might also generate fresh research on the part of another scholar. The story of worship leader training at Southern Seminary, particularly between 1980 and 2019, anecdotally mirrors the stories of multiple churches struggling with the worship culture and musical style paradigm shift lingering in many congregations. Additionally, there are still many music and worship departments in colleges, universities, and seminaries which may be struggling to find their new identity while maintaining musical accreditation standards and enrollment numbers. Worship leader training at Southern Seminary survived, but not without concerted prayer, hard work, and supportive administration. Other schools and churches might take courage from Southern Seminary's story.

Because this is the first study to delve into a comprehensive study of the worship leadership curricula at Southern Seminary, this study may also inspire future researchers to advance the understanding of Southern's worship leadership program in different ways. Some potential extensions may include the following:

1. Extend the study beyond 2019. In 2019, many of the faculty and leadership that helped to turn around the enrollment decline in worship leader programs departed with Adam Greenway when he assumed the presidency of SWBTS in Fort Worth, Texas. In 2020, the COVID-19 pandemic had significant impacts on Southern Seminary and the rest of the world. These two events accelerated curricular, program, and educational delivery method changes at Southern Seminary as well as in the broader community of higher education. How has worship leader training programs at SBTS faired since?

2. An empirical study to determine if the reoriented worship degrees that began in the early 2010s are accomplishing their goal of preparing student to serve in SBC churches in a more relevant way than was perceived in the declining years leading to the program shift. This might also include more recent changes occurring after the COVID-19 pandemic.

3. Other similar studies could be undertaken of other Christian colleges, universities, and seminaries.

4. More concentrated studies might take place to focus on certain time periods or particular individuals covered during the 160-year period involved in this study.

CONCLUSION

This chapter traced the development of the degree programs in church music and worship offered at SBTS during the period circa 1980 through 2019, with particular attention to the master of church music and master of arts in worship leadership. The end goal was to document from primary sources the changes in key degree programs of the SCM and department of biblical worship at SBTS from 1980 to 2019 in the context of cultural mega shifts and shifts in educational philosophy that precipitated those changes.

More broadly, this study provides an overview of the complete history of worship leader training at SBTS. John A. Broadus, one of the four original faculty, taught hymnology to the seminary's pastoral students. In 1859, Southern Seminary's founders recognized the pastoral importance of leading the congregation's voices in songs of worship to the triune God. The story of Southern's training of worship leaders for service in Southern Baptist churches continued through the seminary's post-Civil War transition to Louisville, Kentucky, in 1877, its move from downtown to Lexington Road in 1926, and the birth of the SCM in 1944, under the leadership of President Ellis A. Fuller. Employing a case study-based research model founded on a framework borrowed from Teresa Volk, this study followed established patterns in music education historical research.[108] By gathering information myself from interviews rather than relying on research instruments such as questionnaires, I followed paths rooted in case study qualitative research as identified by John Creswell.[109]

Within the larger history of worship leader training at Southern Seminary, a beautiful period of growth occurred in the 1970s and early 1980s due to synchronization between the predominant worship culture found in SBC churches, the needed job competencies for worship leaders in those churches, the curriculum used to train students in those competencies, and the clear support of seminary administrative leadership. As culture within American evangelicalism changed, methods and values from the church growth movement came to prominence along with the widespread use of

---

108. Volk, "Looking Back in Time," 49–59.
109. Creswell, *Research Design*, 185.

Conclusion

contemporary worship. During the same time period, a significant theological shift in the SBC brought with it a leadership change at Southern Seminary that altered established constituencies upon which the SCM's flourishing had relied. Under the combined forces of change from without and within, the SCM entered a prolonged period of slow decline and diminished enrollment. This decline in enrollment precipitated a momentous administrative reorganization whereby the SCM came under the authority of first the school of church ministries (2009) and then the Billy Graham school for missions, evangelism, and ministry (2013). In addition to the administrative changes, a compelling revitalization of the worship leader curriculum took place in 2009, bringing Southern's worship leader training program into better harmony with prevailing worship culture and the job competencies required for worship leaders in SBC churches. These changes slowly but consistently helped to turn the enrollment declines of the 1990s and 2000s into a period of modest but steady growth in the 2010s as Southern Seminary continued educating and training worship leaders for the churches of the SBC.

This study concluded by offering ideas framing the story of Southern's worship leader training into the larger story of worship in American evangelicalism and the worship life of congregations in the SBC. This study also purposed to reassure and provide encouragement to the thousands of graduates and supporters of the Southern Seminary community, along with those graduates from the aforementioned "glory days" of the SCM, who may have felt discouraged or marginalized by the changes that have occurred.

The story of worship leader training at Southern Seminary is one that mirrors the ministry life of every person who understands God's missional calling to fulfill the Great Commandment and the Great Commission. For both individuals and institutions, following God's call is never easy, but remains the true path for those who desire to one day hear Christ's words, "Well done, good and faithful servant. Enter into the joy of your master" (Matt 25:23).

APPENDIX 1

Chronological Timeline of Faculty and Degree Offerings

WITHIN THE SCM AND DBW

1859	Broadus teaches a unit on hymns and hymn writers within his Homiletics course. This practice continues.
1860	Broadus further developed the Hymnology content with the publication, *Syllabus as To Hymnology*. (Second edition in 1892)
1870	Broadus' book, *A Treatise on the Preparation and Delivery of Sermons* including a chapter on "Conduct of Public Worship."
1892	Edwin Charles Dargan begins assisting Broadus in homiletics.
1895	John Albert Broadus dies on March 16th
1900–01	The last year Broadus' Hymnology class was taught to all seminarians
1913	"Music" courses re-appear in the course schedule on Wednesday afternoons. These classes were taught to all seminarians adjunctively by seminary students or graduate students until 1920.
1920–21	At the request of President E.Y. Mullins, R. Inman Johnson begins teaching "Music and Elocution" to pastoral students.

Appendix 1

1926–27	The mandatory extra-curricular choir rehearsals appear in the official schedule of classes, meeting Thursday afternoons at 2 pm. This continues until the formation of the School of Church Music in 1944.
1937–43	The Committee on Church Music works by appointment of the Sunday School Board of the Southern Baptist Convention. This committee works to improve the state of music and worship in Southern Baptist Churches. Members included Southern Seminary supporter, Mr. E. A. Converse Jr. and SBTS Professor of Music and Voice Culture, Professor R. Inman Johnson.
1944	Frances Winters (served 1944–52) Claude Almand (served 1944–53) Inman Johnson (served 1938–65) W. Lawrence Cook (Not listed in full-time faculty archive)
1946	Donald Winters (served 1946–52) Helen Walker (Not listed in full-time faculty archive)
1947	Degree added: <u>Master of Sacred Music</u> Audrey N. Nossaman (served 1947–54) Donald Wheeler Packard (served 1947–57) Frank Kenneth Pool (served 1947–54)
1949	Hugh T. McElrath (served 1949–92)
1951	Duke K. McCall elected President of Southern Seminary
1952	Forrest Heeren appointed Director (later Dean) of the SCM (served 1952–81)
1953	Walter Odell Dahlin (served 1953–57) Farrold Stephens (served 1953–57)
1954	Paul Rogers Jenkins (54–56) James Henry Wood (54–58)
1955	Degree discontinued: <u>Bachelor of Sacred Music</u>
1956–57	Degree added: <u>Doctor of Sacred Music</u> Faculty grows to 10 full-time faculty: William C. Bushnell (served 1957–65) Ray Pylant Ferguson (served 1957–58) Russell A. Hammar (served 1957–60)

CHRONOLOGICAL TIMELINE OF FACULTY AND DEGREE OFFERINGS

	Grady Maurice Hinson (served 1957–95)
	Mabel Warkentin Sample (served 1956–63)
1958	John Norman Sims (served 1958–67)
1961	Archie P. Kliewer (served 1961–66)
1963	Jay Weldon Wilkey (served 1963–90)
1965	James W. Good (served 1965–78)
	Phillip J. Landgrave (served 1965–2000)
1966	Donald Paul Hustad (served 1966–86)
1967	Richard R. Lin (served 1967–83)
1969	Martha Powell (Music Librarian) (served 1969–2015)
1970	Cooke Hall built to house the SCM
1975	Charles Michael Hawn (served 1975–77)
	Gordon Douglas Smith (served 1975–2010)
1976	Ronald Boud (served 1976–95)
1977	Ronald Alan Turner (served 1977–2010)
1978	Boyd Marion Jones (served 1978–98)
1979	Carl Gerbrandt (served 1979–83)
1981	Forrest Heeren retires as Dean of the SCM
	Elizabeth Ann (Betty) Bedsole (served 1981–95)
	Shelby Milburn Price (served 1981–93)
1983	Milburn Price appointed Dean of the SCM
	SCM enjoys several years of highest enrollment (between 600–800 students); this lasts for much of the 1980s.
	Lloyd Lee Mims (served 1983–2000)
	Paul Akers Richardson (served 1983–95)
1984	Degree added: <u>Master of Divinity (emphasis in Church Music)</u>
	Ragan Courtney (served 1984–89)
	Mozelle Clark Sherman (served 1984–2000)
1985	Cooke Hall enlarged with the completion of the Cooke Hall Annex, which linked Cooke Hall with the rear of Alumni Chapel (organ practice rooms, IRH, faculty studios, elevator)

Appendix 1

	John H. Dickson (served 1985–2000)
1991	Rebecca Sue Straney Russell (served 1991–95)
1992	Mary Alice Seals (served 1992–96)
1993	Milburn Price retires; becomes Dean of the School of Fine Arts at Samford University. R. Albert Mohler elected President of Southern Seminary. Lloyd Mims appointed Dean of the SCM.
1994	Esther Rothenbusch Crookshank (serving 1994–) Sandra Fralin (served 1994–2012) Sandra Chucalo Turner (served 1994–2010)
1995	The Billy Graham School of Missions, Evangelism, and Church Growth is born. Maurice Hinson "retires" but continues teaching until his death in 2015. David Louis Gregory (Music Librarian) (served 1995–2009)
1996	SCM renamed School of Church Music and Worship Degrees Offered (1996–98) (from CMW Catalog) Master of Church Music First major in Church Music with second major in Theory, Composition, Music Education, Musicology, Conducting, Applied Performance, Applied Pedagogy, or Church Music Drama. Master of Divinity (with emphasis in Church Music) Doctor of Music Ministry Doctor of Musical Arts (emphasis in Applied Performance or Research/Performance) 9 full-time faculty, 3 senior professors, and 1 resident artist Thomas W. Bolton (served 1996–2012)
1999	Boyce Bible College becomes Boyce College Begins offering Bachelor of Science degree in Biblical Studies: Worship and Music Studies. Begins offering Bachelor of Science degree Biblical Studies: Worship and Biblical Studies.
2000	Professor Stam launches the Institute for Christian Worship Philip Landgrave "retires" but continues as Senior Professor until 2016

Chronological Timeline Of Faculty And Degree Offerings

	Mozelle Sherman "retires" but continues as Senior Professor until 2016
	Degree added: <u>Master of Arts in Worship</u> (2000–2001 CMW Catalog)
	Degree added: <u>Master of Music: with emphasis in Church Music</u>
	Degree added: <u>Master of Divinity: with emphasis in Worship</u>
	Carl "Chip" Stam (served 2000–2011)
2001	Lloyd Mims resigns; becomes the Dean of the School of Music and Fine Arts at Palm Beach Atlantic University.
	Tom Bolton appointed Dean of the School of Church Music and Worship
	Michael Lancaster (served 2001–9)
2002	Gregory Bacon Brewton (served 2002–21)
2004	Nathan Platt (served 2004–10)
2007	Degree Added: <u>Bachelor of Science in Biblical Studies: Music Ministry major</u>
2009	SCMW becomes the Department of Biblical Worship within the School of Church Ministries
	Tom Bolton retires as the last Dean of the School of Church Music and Worship; continues as Professor of Church Music
	In transition to becoming the Department of Biblical Worship, the faculty downsizes from 11 to 4 full-time professors: mostly through attrition.
	Michael Lancaster resigns
2010	Degrees added: <u>options of Worship Leadership minors in MDiv and MA degrees</u>
	Degree added: <u>Master of Arts in Worship Leadership and Church Ministry</u>
	Diploma added: <u>Diploma in Worship Leadership</u>
	Richard Scott Connell (served 2010–18)
2011–12	Beloved Professor and founder of the Institute for Christian Worship, Chip Stam, passes away after a long battle with cancer.
	Degree added: <u>Doctor of Educational Ministry (Christian Worship)</u>

Appendix 1

	Degree added: <u>Doctor of Ministry (Christian Worship)</u>
	Degree added: <u>Doctor of Philosophy (Christian Worship)</u>
	Joseph Crider (served 2011–19)
	Charles Thomas Lewis (served 2011–19)
2012	Tom Bolton retires
2013	Adam Greenway appointed Dean of the BGS
2014	Degree added: <u>Master of Arts in Worship Leadership: Professional Track</u>
	Institute for Biblical Worship re-launched with new name and expanded vision under the leadership of Joseph Crider.
2015	Degree added: <u>Advanced Master of Divinity (Worship Leadership)</u>
	DBW and Boyce Music and Worship degrees granted 10-year approval from NASM.
2018	R. Scott Connell departs to become Worship Pastor at FBC Jacksonville, Florida
2019	Adam Greenway departs to accept the Presidency of Southwestern Baptist Theological Seminary; several SBTS faculty follow, including Joseph Crider and Charles Lewis.
	R. Scott Connell returns as non-residential faculty (serving 2019-)
	Matthew D. Westerholm (serving 2019-)
	Matthew C. Boswell (serving 2019–25)
	Kha D. Do (serving 2019-)

APPENDIX 2

FACULTY LISTING

TABLE A1. FACULTY AND LIBRARIANS FOR SCHOOL OF CHURCH MUSIC/DEPARTMENT OF BIBLICAL WORSHIP

Faculty Name	Lifespan	Years of Service	Extended Term of Service	Abstract of Principles	Terminal Degree/SBTS Title/Other Ministry Roles/ Other Miscellaneous Roles
Almand, Claude	1915–57	1944–53			MM (LSU, 1938) PhD (Eastman School of Music, 1940)/ Conducting, Theory, and Composition/During his time at SBTS, Almand also taught at the University of Louisville. In 1953, Almand left SBTS and UofL to become the Dean of the School of Music at Stetson University/the Almand Chair of Composition remains an endowed faculty position at Stetson University.
Barrow (later Robinson), Rose Marie		1965–68			MCM (SBTS, 1966)/Barrow (Robinson) served as the first Music Librarian.
Bedsole, Elizabeth Ann (Betty)	1943–	1981–95		Aug. 30, 1988	EdD (University of Illinois; Music Education)/Professor of Church Music/Music Education Specialist/Children's Choir Coordinator, St. Matthews Baptist

Appendix 2

Faculty Name	Lifespan	Years of Service	Extended Term of Service	Abstract of Principles	Terminal Degree/SBTS Title/Other Ministry Roles/ Other Miscellaneous Roles
Bolton, Thomas W.	1946-	1996–2012		Aug. 24, 1999	PhD (University of North Texas; Musicology/Voice) Dean School Church Music & Worship; Professor of Church Music in the School of Church Ministries/Minister of Music in several significant churches including FBC Little Rock, Arkansas.
Boswell, Matthew C.	1979-	2019–2025			PhD (Christian Worship and Biblical Spirituality, SBTS, 2019)/Assistant Professor of Church Music and Worship/ Pastor of Trails Church in Prosper, TX/ Founder of Doxology and Theology
Boud, Ronald	1941-	1976–95		Sept. 1, 1981	DMA (Organ performance and pedagogy, SBTS, 1971)/ Professor of Organ/Active in Music Evangelism through Moody Bible Institute/protégé of Donald Hustad
Brewton, Gregory Bacon	1956–2021	2002–21		Aug. 21, 2007	DMM (Church Music and Ministry, SBTS, 2001) Church Music & Worship, Assoc. Dean Worship Leadership; associate dean school of church ministries; Coordinator of music studies, Boyce College
Bushnell, William C.	1921–2010	1957–65		Jan. 1964	EdD (Music, Teachers College of Columbia University, 1961) Professor of Church Music

Faculty Name	Lifespan	Years of Service	Extended Term of Service	Abstract of Principles	Terminal Degree/SBTS Title/Other Ministry Roles/ Other Miscellaneous Roles
Connell, R. Scott	1969-	2011–18		August 31, 2017	PhD (Christian Worship and Biblical Spirituality, SBTS, 2015)/Music & Worship leadership (Boyce); Listed as Instructor 2011–2015, Assistant Professor 2015; Elected to faculty in spring 2017/ Worship Pastor, Christian School Principal, Program Coordinator for Boyce College Music and Worship
Courtney, Ragan	1941-	1984–89		—	BA (Louisiana College), Graduate (The Neighborhood Playhouse School of Theatre, New York City) Professor of Christian Drama
Crider, Joseph	1962-	2011–19		Aug. 25, 2015	DA (University of Northern Colorado, 1990)/Mildred and Ernest Hogan Professor of Church Music and Worship/Worship Pastor in many churches/Director of the Institute for Biblical Worship
Crookshank, Esther Rothenbusch	1958-	1994-		Aug. 25, 1998	PhD (Musicology, University of Michigan, 1991)/Ollie Hale Chiles professor of church music; Research professor in hymnology, musicology, and ethnodoxology/ Director of the Academy of Sacred Music at SBTS; Associate Dean, SCMW 2008
Dahlin, Walter Odell	1921–2014	1953–57		—	EdD (Teachers College, Columbia University, 1951) Taught music history, instrumental music, and conducting

Appendix 2

Faculty Name	Lifespan	Years of Service	Extended Term of Service	Abstract of Principles	Terminal Degree/SBTS Title/Other Ministry Roles/ Other Miscellaneous Roles
Dickson, John H.	1953-	1985–2000		Aug. 29, 1989	DMA (University of Texas at Austin, 1985)/Professor of Church music. Choral conducting: Oratorio Chorus, Seminary choir
Do, Kha	1990-	2019-			PhD (Christian Worship and Biblical Counseling, SBTS in progress), MDiv (Worship Leadership, SBTS, 2018)/ Assistant Professor of Music and Worship for Boyce College/Coordinator of Worship program at Boyce College.
Ferguson, Ray Pylant	1932–2002	1957–58		—	BM (Oklahoma Baptist University) MM (Syracuse University) Assistant professor of church music in organ/ Fulbright grant to study music in Germany with Helmut Walcha 1954–57/Left SBTS to become professor of organ at Oberlin Conservatory in Cleveland
Fralin, Sandra	1943–2017	1994–2009		—	DMA (SBTS, 2000)/Instructor/Adjunct Professor in Church Music 1994–2009/ Taught Orchestration and Music Theory/Music Library Staff/Her doctoral dissertation about the Louisville Orchestra was used as the basis for a film, *Music Makes a City* (2010).

Faculty Listing

Faculty Name	Lifespan	Years of Service	Extended Term of Service	Abstract of Principles	Terminal Degree/SBTS Title/Other Ministry Roles/ Other Miscellaneous Roles
Gerbrandt, Carl	1940–2013	1979–83		—	DMA (Peabody Conservatory of Music at Johns Hopkins University, 1974) Taught Church music, directed choirs, opera producer, applied voice *Laid the groundwork for the Church Music Drama program developed by Mozelle Clark Sherman
Good, James W.	1934–	1965–78		Sept.11, 1969	DCM (SBTS, 1967) Taught organ, piano, music theory
Gregory, David Louis	1957–	1995–2009		—	DMA (SBTS, 1994)/Adjunct Professor of Church Music, Hymnology/Music Librarian of SBTS from 1995–2009/ After leaving SBTS, Gregory has served as the University Librarian at Morehead State University
Hammar, Russell A.	1920–90	1957–60		—	EdD (Teachers College, Columbia University, 1952) Professor of Church music
Hawn, Charles Michael	1948–	1975–77		—	DMA (SBTS, 1975)/Assistant Professor of Church Music/Vocal instructor, countertenor/Became a Distinguished Professor in church music and ethnodoxology while teaching at Southern Methodist University

Appendix 2

Faculty Name	Lifespan	Years of Service	Extended Term of Service	Abstract of Principles	Terminal Degree/SBTS Title/Other Ministry Roles/ Other Miscellaneous Roles
Heeren, Forrest H.	1915–98	1952–81	1981–1986	Jan. 1964	EdD (Teachers College, Columbia University, 1952)/Dean, School of Church Music/Voice, conducting, vocal pedagogy, choir director/Former Head of Vocal Department at SWBTS and North Texas State University/Sang in the NBC symphonic choir under Toscanini
Hinson, Grady Maurice	1930–2015	1957–95	1995–2015	Jan. 1964	DMA (Piano and Piano Pedagogy, University of Michigan, 1959)/Professor of Music/Taught piano at SBTS for 57 years/Author of several seminal texts in piano repertoire including *Guide to the Pianist's Repertoire* (4 editions)
Hustad, Donald Paul	1918–2013	1966–86		Sept. 11, 1969	DMus (Organ, Choral Conducting, Service Playing, Northwestern University, 1963)/V.V. Cooke Professor of Organ/Former Director of Music at the Moody Bible Institute and full-time Organist with the Billy Graham Evangelistic Association, Contributor and advisor to Hope Publishing company/Author of one of the first seminal texts in philosophy and theology of church music, *Jubilate* (1981)
Jenkins, Paul Rogers	1929–2015	1954–56		—	M.M. (University of Michigan, 1952) Organ

Faculty Listing

Faculty Name	Lifespan	Years of Service	Extended Term of Service	Abstract of Principles	Terminal Degree/SBTS Title/Other Ministry Roles/ Other Miscellaneous Roles
Johnson, R. Inman	1895– 1991	1938–65		#29	ThM (SBTS, 1920) Honorary Doctor of Divinity (University of Richmond)/Professor of music and public speaking; Instructor of elocution and music in catalogs from 1921–22/Elected to the Full Faculty in 1939/Associate Professor of Music and Voice Culture in 1938–1939/Professor of Music and Speech in 1955 directory
Jones, Boyd Marion	1953–	1978–98		Aug. 30, 1988	DMA (Organ, Yale University School of Music, 1984) Professor of Organ and harpsichord/Winner of several national and international organ performance competitions/Recording artist for several domestic and international projects
Kliewer, P. Archie	1922– 2013	1961–66		—	Finished Coursework for DMA (University of Illinois) Gave a faculty recital in 1965, no dissertation on OCLC/Professor of voice at SBTS and at Belmont University
Lancaster, Michael	1954–	2001–9		—	DMA (Choral Conducting, University of Southern California, 1988) Associate Professor of Church music/Conducting professor, Director Seminary Choir, Associate Dean for the School of Church Music

Appendix 2

Faculty Name	Lifespan	Years of Service	Extended Term of Service	Abstract of Principles	Terminal Degree/SBTS Title/Other Ministry Roles/ Other Miscellaneous Roles
Landgrave, J. Phillip	1935–2021	1965–2000	2000–2016	Sept. 12, 1968	DSM (Church Music and Voice, SBTS, 1965) DMA (Church Music and Voice, SBTS, 1970) Professor of Church Music, voice, composition, ministry, and conducted Seminary Vocal Ensemble
Lewis, Charles Thomas, Jr. "Chuck"	1963–	2011–19		August 31, 2017	PhD (Christian Worship and Biblical Spirituality, SBTS, 2015) Elected to faculty spring 2017/Professor Church Music & Worship/ Taught theory, musical dictation, aural skills, and Director of Doxology/Worship Pastor in several churches
Lin, Richard R.	1925–2015		1967–83	Feb. 2, 1971	DMA (Voice and Choral Conducting, University of Missouri Kansas City, 1964). Professor of Church Music/Taught conducting, voice, and choral literature/ Conducted and led the SBTS Oratorio Chorus to city prominence as a choral ensemble, performing frequently with the Louisville Orchestra/Also taught at Oklahoma Baptist University and Golden Gate Baptist Theological Seminary

Faculty Listing

Faculty Name	Lifespan	Years of Service	Extended Term of Service	Abstract of Principles	Terminal Degree/SBTS Title/Other Ministry Roles/Other Miscellaneous Roles
McElrath, Hugh Thomas	1921–2008	1949–92		Sept. 1959	PhD (Musicology, Eastman School of Music at the University of Rochester, 1967) Professor of Church Music/Taught Voice, Church Music, and Hymnology/Member of the inaugural class of BSM students in the School of Church Music in 1944/Taught at Southern for 50 years ('48-'98)/President of SBC Church Music Conference/Theology and Doctrine Committee for the 1991 Baptist Hymnal
Mims, Lloyd Lee	1950-	1983–2000		Aug. 29, 1989	DMA (Voice, Conducting, SBTS, 1984) Dean School of Church Music/Taught Voice, developed and taught the Worshiping Church course for pastors and worship leaders/Builder and Conductor of the Seminary Orchestra/Minister of Music in several churches/Dean Emeritus of the School of Fine Arts at Palm Beach Atlantic University
Nossaman, Audrey N.	1923-	1947–54		—	BM (Westminster Choir College, 1947) Taught voice and conducting/She left SBTS in 1954 to study in Milan, Italy on a Fulbright Grant
Packard, Donald Wheeler	1914–89	1947–57		—	PhD (Eastman School of Music, University of Rochester, 1952) Taught music theory and composition/After SBTS he served as Music Department Chair at Kentucky Southern College

Appendix 2

Faculty Name	Lifespan	Years of Service	Extended Term of Service	Abstract of Principles	Terminal Degree/SBTS Title/Other Ministry Roles/Other Miscellaneous Roles
Platt, Nathan	1969-	2004-10		—	DMA (Voice and Conducting, SBTS, 2004), Professor Music & Worship/Program Coordinator for Boyce College Music and Worship Degrees/Director of Aletheia vocal ensemble/Upon the passing of Chip Stam, Platt assumed most of his teaching responsibilities until the new faculty hires of 2010
Pool, Frank Kenneth	1925-80	1947-54		—	BA (Furman University) MM (University of Michigan, 1946) Taught organ and keyboard repertoire
Powell, Martha	1936-	1969-2015	2015-	—	M.M. (Eastman School of Music, University of Rochester) M.L.S. (Rutgers University, 1969) Music Librarian (1969-1995), Dir. Library Technical Services (Cataloging) (1995-2014); Volunteered in retirement (2015--)
Price, Shelby Milburn, Jr.	1938-	1981-93		Oct. 20, 1981	DMA (Choral Conducting, Voice, University of Southern California, 1967) Dean, School of Church Music/Co-author of several books dealing with topics in church music and worship including, *The Dialogue of Worship* (1998) and *A Survey of Christian Hymnody* (1999)/Retired Dean of the School of Performing Arts at Samford University/Former National President of the American Choral Directors Association

Faculty Listing

Faculty Name	Lifespan	Years of Service	Extended Term of Service	Abstract of Principles	Terminal Degree/SBTS Title/Other Ministry Roles/Other Miscellaneous Roles
Richardson, Paul Akers	1951–	1983–95		Aug. 30, 1988	DMA (Musicology and Voice, SBTS, 1979)/Professor of Church Music/Taught voice, diction and hymnology/Handled much of the material submitted for accreditation reports to agencies such as NASM and SACS/Taught at Samford University from 1995 -20/Co-author with Harry Eskew on *Singing Baptists: Studies in Baptist Hymnody in America* (1994)
Russell, Rebecca Sue Straney	1956–	1991–95		—	DMus (Voice, Opera, Indiana University, 1999) Professor of Church Music/Taught Applied Voice
Sample, Mabel Warkentin	1926–2008	1956–63		March 1, 1962	MSM (SBTS, 1954. Taught choral methods, piano and music theory, school of church music (married name was Sample; was Warkentin)
Seals, Mary Alice	1955–	1992–96		—	DMM (Music and Ministry, SBTS, 1991) Assistant to the Dean/Taught Supervised Ministry Experience classes for Church Music students/Minister of Music at FBC Raleigh, NC for 20 years
Sherman, Mozelle Clark	1932–	1984–2000	2000–2016	Sept. 1, 1987	PhD (Communications, University of Wisconsin Madison, 1971) Professor of Church Music/Founding Director Church Music Drama program/Taught voice, acting for singing/Director of many diverse musical theatre productions over her carrier spanning over 50 years.

Appendix 2

Faculty Name	Lifespan	Years of Service	Extended Term of Service	Abstract of Principles	Terminal Degree/SBTS Title/Other Ministry Roles/ Other Miscellaneous Roles
Sims, John Norman	1928–2004	1958–67		Sept. 10, 1964	DSM (Union Theological Seminary, 1960) Professor of Church Music
Smith, Gordon Douglas "Doug"	1939–	1975–2010		Aug. 26, 1980	A.Mus. D. (University of Michigan, 1969) Mildred and Ernest Hogan Professor of Church Music/Taught Conducting, Applied Brass Instruments, and directed Seminary Winds/Associate Dean School of Church Ministries 2009/10
Stam, Carl "Chip"	1953–2011	2000–2011		Aug. 25, 2009	M.M (Choral Conducting, University of North Carolina Chapel Hill, 1978) Professor of Church Music and Worship/Conductor of SBTS Oratorio Chorus/First professor to specialize in teaching courses specifically in worship studies/Founding Director of the Institute for Christian Worship/Author of weekly Worship Quote of the Week/Worship pastor for several churches including Clifton Baptist/Director of the Kentucky Baptist Men's Chorale
Stephens, Farrold	1919–2003	1953–57		—	MA (Columbia University, 1953) Additional Vocal Study (Juilliard School of Music, The Music Academy of the West, and San Francisco Theological Seminary) Resident artist and Instructor of Voice

Faculty Listing

Faculty Name	Lifespan	Years of Service	Extended Term of Service	Abstract of Principles	Terminal Degree/SBTS Title/Other Ministry Roles/ Other Miscellaneous Roles
Turner, Ronald Alan	1946-	1977–2010		Aug. 28, 1984	DMA (Voice and Choral Conducting, SBTS, 1976) Carolyn King Ragan professor of Church Music/Taught Music Theory, Aural Skills, and Voice/Directed the SBTS Men's Chorale
Turner, Sandra Chucalo	1948-	1994–2010		Aug. 28, 2001	DMA (Piano, SBTS, 1987) Professor of Church Music/ Taught Piano, Organ, Group Piano, and Keyboard Harmony
Westerholm, Matthew David	1975-	2019-		August 27, 2024	PhD (Christian Worship, SBTS, 2016) Associate Professor of church music and worship/Teaches classes in worship theology, methodology, and leadership, supervises Norton Hall worship band/Director of Institute for Biblical Worship/Since 2021, serves as Department Chair for Biblical Worship
Wilkey, Jay Weldon	1934–2017	1963–90		Sept. 1966	PhD (Vocal Pedagogy, Indiana University, 1965) Voice and Music Education
Winters, Donald	1910–89	1946–52		—	BM (Westminster Choir College, 1939) MM (Westminster Choir College, 1941) Honorary Doctorate (Blue Mountain College, 1970) Conducting, repertoire, organ, voice/Founding faculty, School of Church Music

Appendix 2

Faculty Name	Lifespan	Years of Service	Extended Term of Service	Abstract of Principles	Terminal Degree/SBTS Title/Other Ministry Roles/ Other Miscellaneous Roles
Winters, Frances Weaver	1908–93	1944–52		—	BM (Westminster Choir College, 1941) Honorary Doctorate of Humane Letters (William Caray, 1977) Choral methods, hymnology, worship/Founding faculty, School of Church Music
Wood, James Henry	1921–2003	1954–58		—	M.A. (University of Iowa, 1947) SMD (Union Theological Seminary) Voice, vocal literature

APPENDIX 3

INTERVIEW PARTICIPANTS

TABLE A2. INTERVIEW PARTICIPANTS

Name	Years of Service/ Residence	Terminal Degree/SBTS Title/Other Ministry Roles/Other Miscellaneous Roles
Bolton, Thomas W.	1996–2012	PhD (University of North Texas; Musicology/Voice) Dean School Church Music & Worship; Professor of Church Music in the School of Church Ministries/Minister of Music in several significant churches including FBC Little Rock, Arkansas.
Crawley, Douglas	1992–2001	DMA (Vocal performance and Ministry, SBTS, 1997) Doctoral Student and Adjunct Faculty/Performed voice recitals, leading roles in several Church Music Drama productions, taught classes in Instrumental Conducting, Theory, Pedagogy, Supervise Ministry, Worshiping Church, Applied Voice, and choral ensemble direction/Has served as Worship pastor in several high-profile SBC Churches/Has since served as Associate Dean of Worship Studies at Liberty University
Crider, Joseph R	2011–2019	DA (University of Northern Colorado, 1990)/Mildred and Ernest Hogan Professor of Church Music and Worship/ While at SBTS, Crider taught courses in the theology of worship, methodology, planning, and biblical foundations along with supervising professional and research doctoral students in worship/Crider served as Director of the Institute for Biblical Worship /Crider has also served as worship pastor in many leading SBC churches/Since 2019, he has served as the Dean of the School of Church Music at Southwestern Baptist Theological Seminary in Fort Worth, Texas

Appendix 3

Name	Years of Service/ Residence	Terminal Degree/SBTS Title/Other Ministry Roles/Other Miscellaneous Roles
Dickson, John H	1985–2000	DMA (University of Texas at Austin, 1985)/Professor of Church Music/Associate Dean for Doctoral Studies/Taught Choral conducting, Directed Oratorio Chorus and Seminary choir
Greenway, Adam W	2013–2019 (as BGS Dean)	PhD (Evangelism and Apologetics, SBTS, 2007)/Dean of the Billy Graham School of Missions, Evangelism, and Ministry 2013–2019/Since 2019, the President of Southwestern Baptist Theological Seminary in Fort Worth, Texas
Landgrave, Gloria (Wife of deceased Church Music Professor Philip Landgrave)	Dr. Philip Landgrave taught at SBTS from 1965–2000	DSM (Church Music and Voice, SBTS, 1965) DMA (Church Music and Voice, SBTS, 1970) Professor of Church Music, voice, composition, ministry, and conducted Seminary Vocal Ensemble/Took ensembles and other collections of worship students on mission trips both domestically and internationally/Served as Minister of Music in several churches.
Mims, Lloyd Lee	1983–2000	DMA (Voice, Conducting, SBTS, 1984) Dean School of Church Music/Taught Voice, developed and taught the Worshiping Church course for pastors and worship leaders/Builder and Conductor of the Seminary Orchestra/Minister of Music in several churches/Dean Emeritus of the School of Fine Arts at Palm Beach Atlantic University
Price, Shelby Milburn, Jr.	1981–1993	DMA (Choral Conducting, Voice, University of Southern California, 1967) Dean, School of Church Music/Co-author of several books dealing with topics in church music and worship including, *The Dialogue of Worship* (1998) and *A Survey of Christian Hymnody* (1999)/Retired Dean of the School of Performing Arts at Samford University/Former National President of the American Choral Directors Association
Seals, Mary Alice	1992–1996	DMM (Music and Ministry, SBTS, 1991) Assistant to the Dean/Taught Supervised Ministry Experience classes for Church Music students/Minister of Music at FBC Raleigh, NC for 20 years
Sharp, Timothy	1979–1982	DMA (Choral Conducting, SBTS 1982) While working on his doctorate, Sharp served as an instructor, teaching variety of courses including choral conducting/After graduating from Southern, Sharp served as the Director of Choral Activities at Belmont University in Nashville, TN from 1997–2000/ Dean of Fine Arts at Rhodes College in Memphis, TN from 2000–2008/ Executive Director of the American Choral Directors Association from 2008–2020

Interview Participants

Name	Years of Service/ Residence	Terminal Degree/SBTS Title/Other Ministry Roles/Other Miscellaneous Roles
Smith, Gordon Douglas	1975–2010	DMus (University of Michigan, 1969) Mildred and Ernest Hogan Professor of Church Music/Taught Conducting, Applied Brass Instruments, and directed Seminary Winds/ Associate Dean School of Church Ministries 2009/10
Stewart, Jason (Bubba)	1994–1998	MDiv/Church Music (SBTS, 1998) Steward served in worship ministry in local churches from 1990–2004. In 2004 Stewart became the Worship Consultant for the Kentucky Baptist Convention, first part time and then in 2013 in a full-time capacity. As a seminary student, Stewart was a church music student and the personal driver for President, R. Albert Mohler. As KBC Worship Consultant, Stewart has an unparalleled knowledge and understanding of the state of the worship ministries in Kentucky churches.
Swain, Matthew and Angela C	1998–2010	MM (Angela) (SBTS, 2007), coursework toward DMA (SBTS, 2010); MCM (Matthew) (SBTS, 2000), DMM and coursework towards DMA (SBTS, 2010)/These two SCMW graduates studied and served at SBTS during Tom Bolton's administration and Chip Stam's faculty years. They have served local churches and since 2014 have served as Music and Worship faculty at Midwestern Baptist Theological Seminary in Kansas City, Missouri

APPENDIX 4

ENROLLMENT TRENDS

Table A3. Total enrollment trends in worship leadership degrees (1988–89 through 2018–19)

Academic Year	Boyce College	Seminary	Total Enrollment
*1988–89	-	539	539
*1989–90	-	475	475
*1990–91	-	405	405
*1991–92	-	357	357
*1992–93	-	329	329
*1993–94	-	309	309
*1994–95	-	307	307
*1995–96	-	221	221
*1996–97	-	219	219
*1997–98	-	221	221
*1998–99	-	139	139
*1999–00	-	207	207
*2000–01	-	223	223
*2001–02	-	235	235
*2002–03	-	219	219
*2003–04	-	214	214
*2004–05	-	221	221
*2005–06	-	251	251
*2006–07	-	259	259

Enrollment Trends

*2007–08	-	235	235
*2008–09	-	167	167
+2009–10	34	79	113
+2010–11	28	73	101
+2011–12	25	53	78
+2012–13	43	49	92
+2013–14	53	50	103
+2014–15	67	81	148
+2015–16	81	83	164
+2016–17	80	92	172
+2017–18	69	88	157
+2018–19	69	96	165

Note: Undergraduate enrollment not included 1988–89 through 2008–9; doctoral enrollment not included 2009–10 through 2018–10.

Appendix 4

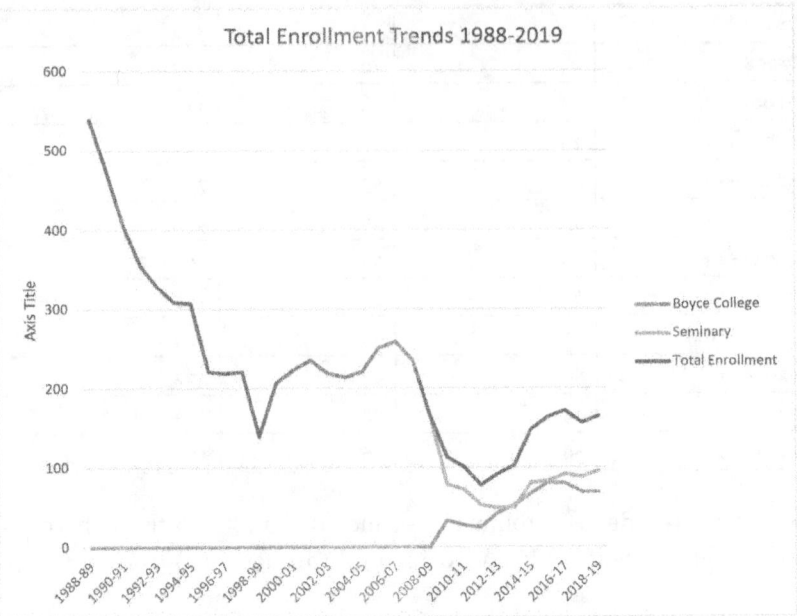

Figure A1. Music and worship enrollment trends 1988–2019

Note: Conflicting data exists for Church Music and Worship enrollment during the 1998–99 academic year. According to the SBTS Office of Academic Records, total enrollment for Church Music and Worship students was 139; however, according to independent data reported in the 1998–99 SCMW Annual Report to the Board of Trustees, the total enrollment was on 88 students. Though no explanation exists for this discrepancy, the difference is noted.

www.ingramcontent.com/pod-product-compliance
Lightning Source LLC
Chambersburg PA
CBHW062019220426
43662CB00010B/1396